Child Abuse
a reader and sourcebook

A

'Child Abuse' Course Team

The Open University
Vida Carver (Joint Course Team Chairman)
Susan Hurley (Northern Region)
Penny Liddiard

Newcastle upon Tyne Polytechnic
Constance M. Lee (Joint Course Team Chairman)
Richard Fothergill
Bill Roberts

External Assessors
Beryl Day
Margery Taylor

Child Abuse
a reader and sourcebook

edited by Constance M. Lee

The Open University Press
Milton Keynes · New York

The Open University Press
12 Cofferidge Close, Stony Stratford
Milton Keynes, MK11 1BY, England

Open University Educational Media Inc.
110 East 59th Street
New York, NY 10022, U.S.A.

First published 1978

Designed by the Educational Development Unit
of Newcastle upon Tyne Polytechnic

ISBN 0 335 00230 7

Foreword

Early detection of child abuse demands an observant eye, a level head and an open mind. This adds up to good judgment, knowledge and a capacity to co-operate with other professional and lay people. In spite of all the newly aroused public concern, action in this field is peculiarly difficult for at least three reasons. First because it is far from easy to detect and judge accurately the significance of what goes on in the home; secondly because we are reluctant to believe that parents could intentionally injure their own children; and thirdly because formal intervention in the relations between parents and children is a most delicate matter involving cultural attitudes and value judgments. For all these reasons and because of deep-seated belief in the importance of the blood tie children may suffer severely before they are discovered and action taken. But, conversely, zeal to rescue children from their wicked parents can also do much damage.

Battering parents are very different kinds of people: they include the immature, the aggressive, the withdrawn, the lonely and the desperate, some of whom need support and help themselves. Battered children also differ greatly, from the persistently crying or unthriving baby to the school child who is the scapegoat of the family. And 'battering' can include emotional deprivation as well as physical injury. In any event detection, however difficult, is only the first stage. It is then essential that through review committees and other means there should be well-planned and good interdisciplinary and interagency decisions about action that will prevent further injury to the child and if possible help the parents, even though the child is temporarily or permanently removed.

This Reader is particularly valuable because it brings together in a readily accessible form some of the best current knowledge on a very complex subject, knowledge which has so far been scattered about in British and American books and journals and thus not easily within the reach of busy professional people. It should be of considerable value both for personal reading and reference and for group discussions. It is also a contribution to the next stage when we must try collectively to discover more about how to protect children at risk and how to help and heal damaged children, who may otherwise suffer lifelong scars, most of all in their personal development and thus in their capacity to nurture their own children.

July 1977   Eileen Younghusband

Contents

Part Seven Appendices

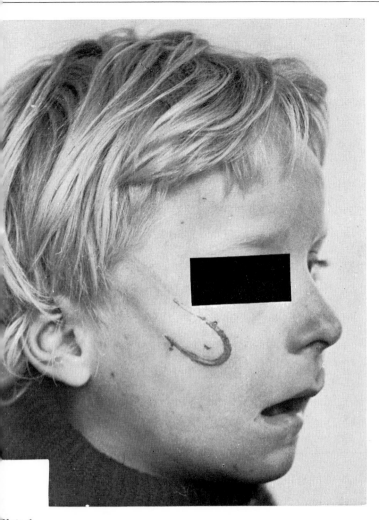

Plate 1.
The mark on the cheek has been caused by a blow with a strap. The sudden pressure of force to the skin creates increased pressure which ruptures the blood vessels around the edge of the object, producing the outline of its shape.

Plate 2.
Facial bruising caused by squeezing between thumb and fingers. The diffuse bruising on the left side of the jaw is the result of the coalescing of individual finger bruises, often caused by attempts to stop a child crying by pulling the cheeks forward. This child also has two bruises on the right side of the jaw, made by the thumb. Squeezing and pulling of the face by a left handed person produces a pattern of bruises reversed from that shown in the picture.

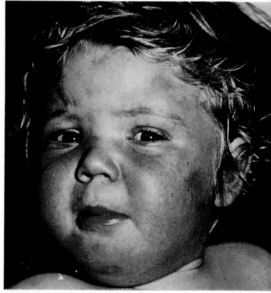

Plate 2

Plate 4.
Finger tip bruising above the right eye and in the centre of the right cheek. Two older finger tip bruises are present on the right upper arm. The right eye shows bruising of both lids. Such bruises, often on the face, are the commonest, most easily visible and the most easily recognizable sign in many early cases of non-accidental injury. This child also shows 'Frozen Awareness'. Both he and the child in picture 3 lay on their sides, curled up in the foetal position and cried when approached by any adult.

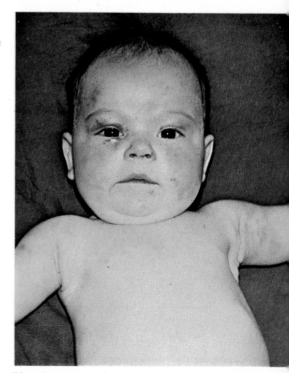

Plate 4

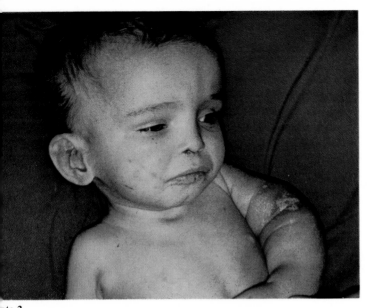

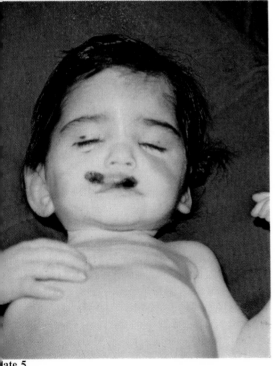

Plate 3.
This child's expression illustrates 'Frozen Awareness' or 'Frozen Watchfulness', phrases which describe the apprehensive expression and demeanour of some children who have been subjected to violence over a long period. This child was severely neglected, had an extensive napkin rash and fractures of the lower end of the left humerus and right ulna.

Plate 5.
Cigarette burns of the upper lip. The effects of the cigarette burns vary with duration and pressure of application. Applied lightly and for a short time, the lesion is a round red area about 6 mm in diameter. With greater pressure or duration a round lesion about 2 cm in diameter is produced.

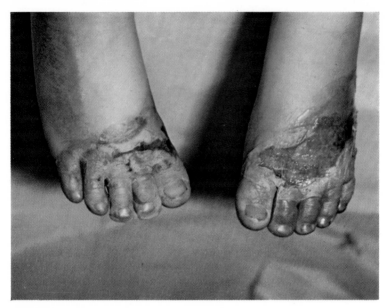

Plate 6. Scalds of both feet. The sharp edge around the upper limits of the scalds suggest that this child was deliberately lowered into hot water, though accidental scalds may also show a regular outline.

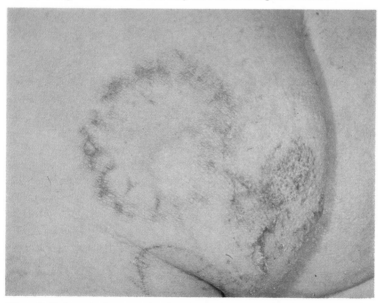

Plate 7. Enlarged photograph of teeth marks on the left buttock of a two-year-old boy. The child had had part of one testicle removed by a very severe bite. Casts of the parents' teeth impressions enabled a dental surgeon to identify positively that the bites on the buttocks were made by the child's mother.

Introduction

This book of readings has been compiled as one part of a course on child abuse prepared jointly by the Open University and the Newcastle upon Tyne Polytechnic. Although the selection of papers has been made with particular reference to the linked study text *Child Abuse: a study text*, edited by Vida Carver and published simultaneously with this volume, the material has been arranged to make it suitable for a much wider group of readers. Concern for abused children and their parents is increasing and with it the number of studies, reports and articles on various aspects of a complex problem, but there are still comparatively few collections of papers available. Complex problems involve many professional workers, the approach has therefore been multidisciplinary.

The wide range of abuse to which children are subjected has also been considered, emotional deprivation and failure to thrive as well as physical injury. Consequently the readings have been selected on a number of criteria, their relevance to the range of professional workers and others likely to be involved with child abuse, the complexity of the subject itself and the personal choice of the writers of the course. A source book which is closely related to a course of limited length inevitably puts constraints upon the compilers. In striving to meet all these criteria some aspects of the subject have had to be treated less fully than would have been wished and some omitted altogether although where this has happened, references for further reading have been included.

The aim has been to assist professional workers, nurses, midwives and health visitors; doctors, therapists and social workers; teachers, lawyers, the police and others, as well as those who teach the professional and social skills necessary in preventing and treating child abuse.

Newcastle
July 1977

Constance M. Lee

Editor's acknowledgements

For their assistance in obtaining a variety of reading material, thanks to the library staff of the Newcastle upon Tyne Polytechnic and the Open University, particularly Audrey Cook, Sheila Dale, Anne Ramsey and Ian Winkworth.

Special thanks also to staff of the Children's Division of the Department of Health and Social Security.

Particular thanks to Wynne Brindle, Wendy Doggett and Gerry Bearman of the Copyrights Department of the Open University; to Sue Dale, who designed the book, and Diane Cox, who copy-edited it.

Finally the contribution made by the administrative and secretarial staff of both institutions is gratefully acknowledged, in particular thanks to Lesley Brazier, Patricia Bruce, Stella Fisher, Valerie Hall; and for photo-copying facilities to Diana Platt and the staff of the Community and Social Studies Faculty Office, Newcastle upon Tyne Polytechnic.

CML

Part One Normal child rearing

The emphasis on early detection of suspected child abuse has highlighted the need to recognize deviation from normal in physical and emotional development. Detecting the abnormal places the professional worker with a non-medical background in some difficulty, unless the worker has had experience in caring for children. For this reason it was decided to include in the 'Child Abuse' course brief reference to the normal child. The appendix contains weight and developmental testing charts as well as references for further study.

Gross failures in parent–child relationships have focused attention on normal bonding between parent and child. A brief extract of a study in bonding has been included in this section, as well as aspects of child development and the parental role.

1 Parent-infant bonding

John Kennell, Diana Voos and Marshall Klaus

The early affectional bond

... Early in life the infant develops an attachment to one individual, most often the mother. Throughout his lifetime the strength and character of this attachment will influence the quality of all future bonds to other individuals. An attachment can be defined as an affectional bond between two individuals that endures through time and space and serves to join them emotionally. Significant attachments are such unique relationships that it is not unusual for an individual to have fewer than ten throughout his lifetime. It is useful to differentiate human attachments according to the individuals involved so that we may focus on the specific characteristics and functions of one relationship before we return to a consideration of the whole family.

Perhaps the strongest of these affectional ties in the human is that of the mother to her child. Why are mothers willing to make the sacrifices necessary to care for an infant day after day? How do they develop such a powerful bond to these tiny infants who at first sleep for hours on end and only awaken to cry, eat, burp, soil, and fall asleep again? What is the process by which this relationship develops?

Although the development of the attachment of an infant to his mother has been widely investigated in the past three decades, beginning with the publications of Bowlby 1958 and Spitz 1945, the tie in the opposite direction, from a mother to her infant, has only recently been the focus of study. More recent still has been the interest in the father and his relationship to his newborn child. Nonetheless, studies and observations from a variety of sources now make it possible to fit together a tentative model of how affectional bonds between the human mother and her infant develop. It is also possible to identify factors that may alter or distort this process either temporarily or permanently. . . .

KENNELL, J., VOOS, D. and KLAUS, M. (1976) 'Parent–infant bonding', in Helfer, R. E. and Kempe, C. H. (eds.) *Child Abuse and Neglect*, Cambridge (Mass.), Ballinger, pp. 25–53.

Pregnancy and post partum period

Early pregnancy

For most women, pregnancy is a time of change and of strong emotions which are sometimes positive, other times negative, and frequently ambivalent. During pregnancy, a woman experiences the physical and emotional changes within herself as well as the growth of the fetus in her uterus. How she feels about these changes will vary widely according to whether the pregnancy was planned, whether she is married, whether she is living with the father, whether she has other children, whether she is working or wants to work, her memories of her childhood, and how she feels about her parents.

Prenatal interviews with women during their first pregnancy have uncovered anxiety which has often seemed to be of pathological proportions. Brazelton has clarified the importance of the psychological changes and turmoil that occur during pregnancy for the subsequent development of attachment to the new infant. He considers the turbulent, emotional changes during pregnancy as 'readying the circuits for new attachments.' He believes 'that the emotional turmoil of pregnancy and the neonatal period can be seen as a positive force for the mother's adjustment for the possibility of providing a more individualized environment for the infant.' (Brazelton 1963.) Some of the steps important in attachment are:

1. Planning the pregnancy
2. Confirming the pregnancy
3. Accepting the pregnancy
4. Fetal movement
5. Accepting the fetus as an indivudual
6. Birth
7. Seeing the baby
8. Touching the baby
9. Caretaking

Caplan (1960) considers pregnancy to be a developmental crisis involving two particular adaptive tasks for the mother. The first is the identification of the fetus as an 'integral part of herself' and the second is awareness of the fetus as a separate individual. The second stage is usually initiated with the sensation of fetal movement (quickening), which is a remarkably powerful event. During the period following quickening, the woman must begin to change her concept of the fetus from a part of herself to a living baby who will soon be a separate individual. Bibring et al. (1961) believe that this realization prepares the woman for delivery and physical separation from her child. This preparedness lays the foundation for a relationship to the child.

After quickening, a woman will usually begin to have fantasies about what the baby will be like, attributing personality characteristics to the infant and developing a sense of attachment and value toward him or her. She will develop a mental image of the neonate as being a particular sex, having a certain color of hair, eyes, and shape of nose. After sensing fetal movement further acceptance of the pregnancy and marked changes in attitude toward the fetus may be observed. Unplanned, and originally unwanted infants may seem more acceptable. There will usually be some outward evidence of the mother's preparation for the infant, such as the purchase of clothes or a crib, the selection of a name, and the rearrangement of space to accommodate a baby. . . .

After the first trimester, behaviors suggesting rejection of the pregnancy include the mother's preoccupation with her physical appearance, with negative self-perception, excessive emotional withdrawal or mood swings, excessive physical complaints, absence of any response to quickening, or lack of any preparatory behavior during the last trimester. Brazelton (1963) suggests that prospective fathers go through an upheaval similar to that of the mothers. In our lonely nuclear family structure in the United States, the young father is often the only available support for his wife. There rarely are other supportive figures nearby, such as family physicians, ministers, close friends or neighbors, who can help the expectant parents.

To enable us to understand the complex events that occur during the perinatal period, we will direct our attention primarily to the mother-infant dyad. However, it is essential for us to emphasize that the father, the other siblings, and the extended family are of vital importance to this dyad. . . .

Delivery

To better understand the attitude and behavior of mothers as well as mother-infant interaction in the first hours and days of life, it is helpful to consider the effects of various delivery procedures and anesthetic interventions. The information available about this period suggests that mothers who remain relaxed during labor, and who cooperate and have good rapport with those caring for them, are more apt to be pleased with their infants at first sight (Newton and Newton 1962). The effects of anesthesia, cesarean section, and amnesic drugs on attachment and mothering behavior have not been studied systematically.

Throughout the United States prospective parents have shown an increased interest in the quality of their childbirth experience. There have been strong objections to the impersonal and medically oriented delivery in the hospital, where the woman loses all control over the events of her labor and delivery and where her husband may have only a limited role to play. The enthusiastic increase in prepared childbirth has led to discussions about how best to achieve a childbirth experience that is safe and will accommodate the wishes of the prospective parents. . . .

Early post partum period – maternal-sensitive period

There is evidence that mothers have difficulty forming an attachment when they are separated from their babies during the first hours after delivery. Minor problems (such as slight hyperbilirubinemia, mild respiratory distress, and poor feeding) resulting in separation during this period may disturb and distort maternal affectional ties. This disturbance of mothering may last for a year or throughout childhood, even though the infant's problems were completely resolved prior to discharge.

In the first of several carefully controlled investigations involving primiparous mothers with normal full term infants, an 'early and extended contact' group of fourteen mothers were given the routine contact with their babies and were also given their nude babies in bed for one hour in the first two hours after delivery and for five extra hours on each of the next three days of life. The control group of fourteen mothers received the care that is routine in most United States hospitals: a glimpse of the baby at birth, a brief contact for identification at six to eight hours, and then visits of 20–30 minutes for feedings every four hours. The groups were matched as to age and marital and socio-economic status of the mothers, and were not significantly different in the sex and weight of the infants.

To determine if the additional mother-infant contact early in life resulted in altered maternal behavior, the mothers returned to the hospital 28–32 days after delivery for three separate observations: (1) a standardized interview, (2) an observation of the mother's performance during a physical examination of her infant, and (3) a filmed study of the mother feeding her infant. There were significant differences between the two groups in all three observations. The mothers in the early and extended contact group tended to pick up the infant when it cried and to stay at home with the infant during the first month. If they did go out, the mothers in this group tended to think about their babies more often and usually returned earlier than expected.

During the physical examination, the extended contact mothers would stand and watch their infants and show more soothing behavior when their babies cried. . . . Figure [1] shows the fondling and 'en face' scores for both groups of mothers during a ten-minute, one frame per second filmed feeding analyzed for 25 behaviors. Although the amount of time the mothers in each group spent looking at their babies was not significantly different, the extended contact mothers showed significantly more 'en face' and fondling. Therefore, by all three measures, differences between the two groups of mothers were apparent at one month. These methods were de-

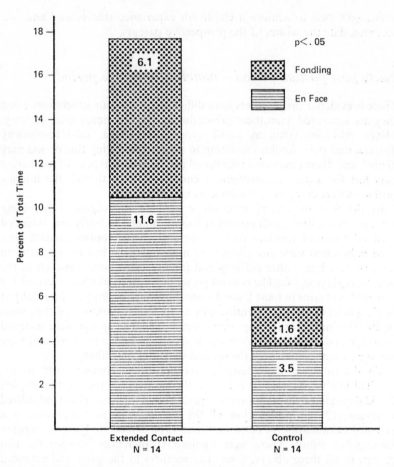

Figure 1. Filmed feeding analysis at one month, showing the percentage of 'en face' and fondling times in mothers given extended contact with their infants and in the control group.

signed to discover differences in attachment between the two groups, and not to evaluate good or bad mothering.

At one year, the two groups of mothers again showed significant differences (Kennell et al. 1974), with the extended contact mothers spending a greater percentage of time near the table assisting the physician while he examined their babies and soothing them when they cried. At two years, five mothers were selected at random from each group, and the linguistic behaviors of the two groups of mothers while speaking to their children were compared. The extended contact mothers asked twice as many questions, and used more words per proposition, fewer content words, more adjectives, and fewer commands than did the controls (Ringler et al. 1975).

In an interesting and significant observation of fathers, Lind (1973) noted that paternal caregiving in the first three months of life was markedly increased when the father was asked to undress his infant twice and to establish eye-to-eye contact with him for one hour during the first three days of life. This evidence provides strong support for the existence of a sensitive period in the first minutes and hours after birth that is important for parent-infant attachment. Four of five other recent studies in Brazil and Guatemala, where the amount of contact between a mother and her normal, full term neonate was varied, also support this concept.

Studies of the effects of rooming-in at the hospital also indicated the importance of the early postnatal period. When rooming-in was instituted a number of years ago, an increase in breast feeding and a reduction in anxious phone calls was found (McBryde 1951). In Sweden, mothers randomly assigned to rooming-in arrangements were more confident, felt more competent in caregiving, and thought they would need less help in caring for their infants at home than nonrooming-in mothers. They also appeared to be more sensitive to the crying of their own infants than were mothers who did not have the rooming-in experience (Lind 1973). This suggests that close continual contact after birth may be important in encouraging more relaxed maternal behavior.

Species specific behavior and early reciprocal interaction

After delivery the mother exhibits a characteristic pattern of behavior with her newborn infant. Filmed observations show that a mother presented with her undressed, full term infant begins touching the infant's extremities with her fingertips and in less than ten minutes proceeds to encompassing, massaging palm contact on the infant's trunk.

A strong interest in eye-to-eye contact has been expressed by mothers of both full term and premature infants. When the words of mothers who had been presented with their infants in privacy were taped, 70 per cent of the statements referred to the eyes. The mothers said, 'Open up your eyes so I will know that you are there'; 'Let me see your eyes'; and 'Show me your eyes so that I'll know that you love me.' Robson (1967) has suggested that eye-to-eye contact appears to elicit maternal caregiving responses. Mothers are extremely interested in looking 'en face' at their infants. 'En face' is defined as the position in which the mother keeps her face aligned so that her eyes are in the same vertical plane of rotation as those of her

9

infant. Complementing the mother's interest in the infant's eyes is the early functional development of the infant's visual pathways.

One midwife (Raven Lang) who has made observations of home deliveries has observed that the infant quiets down when given to the mother. Almost always the mother touches the baby's skin with her fingertips starting with the face. It is always a gentle stroking motion. This occurs before the initial nursing and before delivery of the placenta. Then the baby is usually put to the breast. The infant does not suck at first, but continually licks the mother's nipple (Lang 1972), which is a powerful stimulus for prolactin secretion.

Recently, a virtual explosion of information about the states and abilities of newborn infants has contributed to our understanding of why the period immediately after birth is so important for the parent. Early observations of the competence of newborn infants indicate six separate states of consciousness in the infant, which range from deep sleep to screaming. Desmond et al. (1966) observed that the infant is in state 4 for a period lasting from 45 to 60 minutes immediately following delivery. In this state the infant's eyes are wide open and he is alert, active, and able to follow during the first hour of life (Brazelton 1963). After this hour, the infant goes into a deep sleep for three to four hours. From the discoveries of the infant's early responsiveness to his environment we have realized why this period is particularly significant for the mother and baby. Each partner of this dyad is intimately involved with each other in an array of mutually rewarding interactions on a number of sensory levels. Their behaviors complement each other and serve to bind them together.

The infant elicits behavior from the mother that in turn is satisfying to him. And the mother brings out behaviors in the infant that in turn are rewarding to her. For example, the infant's hard crying is likely to bring the mother near and trigger her to pick him up. When she picks him up, he is likely to quiet, open his eyes, and follow. Looking at the process in the opposite direction, when the mother touches the infant's cheek, he is likely to turn his head, bringing him into contact with her nipple, which he will suck. His sucking in turn is pleasurable to both of them. The mother speaks to the baby in a high-pitched voice and infants respond more to a high-pitched voice than to lower tones. The baby has been shown to have the amazing ability to move in rhythm to words spoken to him in languages as diverse as English and Chinese.

The consistency of the mother's care during the first few days reestablishes the infant's biorhythmicity which is disturbed by the shock of delivery. The mother's milk gives the baby antibodies and cells that may provide important immunologic benefits. The baby's sucking stimulates oxytocin release which contracts the mother's uterus and leads to the expulsion of the placenta. When the infant licks the mother's nipple and areola, or nurses, the secretion of prolactin is stimulated, which increases milk production. During their early contact the mother may provide the infant with respiratory and gastrointestinal flora that protect the baby from the invasion of other organisms such as hospital strains of staphylococci. The mother also provides warmth for the infant through bodily contact. These are only several of the interactions that may occur during the first contact between mother and newborn. Each behavior tends to trigger a number of others. However, the interactions should not be likened to a chain reaction where each link leads to only one other link in the series. Rather the effects are similar to the multitude of ever-widening rings caused by a pebble dropped into a pool. In a sense, there exists a failsafe system that is overdetermined to insure the continued proximity of mother and child.

There is an ideal opportunity for the beginning of strong attachment of the mother and father to the infant when the father is present during labor and delivery. If the mother and father have a private interlude together with the undressed baby in the first hour after birth, there is an opportunity to touch and interact with the baby. The evidence that is available at the present time suggests that the interaction of the parents with their infant, when started in the first hour, will continue in the following days and lead to increased attentiveness and interest. . . .

Evidence that contact during this early period is not always essential for mother-infant bonding, and the establishment of satisfactory family bonds, is provided by the number of children who are well cared for and protected by their parents and the many intact families where the early attachment was minimal but later bonds between family members appear to be adequate. On the other hand, when there are disturbances of parent-to-infant bonds and father-mother bonds, the question may be asked, 'Would the outcome have been different if parent-infant contact had occurred shortly after birth and under optimal circumstances?' Should we have particular concern about family units being formed now and in the next decades because almost every prospective parent in the present generation was separated from his or her parents in the early postpartum period?

It is not generally appreciated that in many European countries, mothers and healthy newborn babies are never separated and remain together in the hospital following delivery. In hospitals in the United States, the mother and baby usually only have interrupted contact during the post partum period in the hospital. The contact and interaction of a mother and her baby during this period (the first few days following the initial 12–24 hours), may be of great significance for the further development of the attachment bonds. Short episodes of contact may provide the only opportunity for starting an attachment in many American hospitals where separation after birth and feedings every four hours are the rule.

In the twentieth century the predominant tendency of fathers to avoid caretaking involvement with their infants has been considered a cultural, sex role phenomenon. However, the emerging studies of father-infant interaction, such as those of Lind and Parke (1974) suggest that fathers can become bonded to their babies in the early period following delivery and will then be much more involved with their care. If the father does not have an attachment to the infant and if the mother's bonds are tenuous because she has not had early and continuous contact, then the vicissitudes of life may strain the mother-infant attachment, resulting in moderate or severe consequences similar to the child abuse described by Margaret Lynch. If the infant has a neonatal illness or a series of illnesses in the first year, or if the mother herself is ill, the bonds may not be strong enough to assure the safety and well-being of the infant. . . .

After delivery, the father, mother, and baby should have a period alone. This is usually possible only if the infant is normal and the mother is well. She should be given the baby undressed in bed and allowed to examine him completely. A heat panel easily maintains or, if need be, increases the body temperature of the infant. Several mothers have told us of the unforgettable experience of holding their nude baby against their own bare chest and nursing. We recommend skin-to-skin contact. The father sits or stands at the side of the bed by the infant. This allows the parents and infant to become acquainted. Because the eyes are so important for both the parents and baby, we withhold the application of silver nitrate to the eyes until after this rendezvous.

The mother, father, and infant should be together for about 30 to 45 minutes. If the mother has had medication she and the baby often fall into a deep sleep after 10 or 15 minutes. In Guatemalan hospitals, where drugs and anesthesia are used more sparingly, mothers were usually awake after 45 minutes of privacy with their infants. The mother and father never forget this significant and stimulating shared experience. This should be a private session, with no interruptions. Affectional bonds are further consolidated in the succeeding four to five days through continued close association of baby and mother, particularly when she cares for him. Contact with the father and other children during the period of hospitalization is encouraged. . . .

The affectional bonds a mother and father establish with their infant during the first days of life are crucial for his future welfare. When the bonds are solidly established, parents are motivated to learn about their baby's individual requirements and to adapt to meet his needs; they are willing to change diapers thousands of times, to respond to the baby's cries in the night, and to provide stimulation appropriate in intensity, timing, and quality. Fully developed specificities keep parents from striking their baby who has cried for hours night after night—even when they are exhausted and alone.

Studies of mother-to-infant and father-to-infant attachment have begun to define the characteristics of the bonds of attachment. Thus far, there have been no empirical investigations of the interrelationship of attachment bonds among the individuals who make up a family. However, information from the literature and observations of many deliveries suggest that the time of delivery may be optimal for beginning new or enhancing existing attachments.

When several people attend a birth, as in the home deliveries in the Santa Cruz area described by Raven Lang, they have reported feeling a particularly strong attachment to the infant which persists throughout succeeding years. Does this special attachment provide important evolutionary mechanism to substitute caretakers for the infant during the time when maternal mortality at childbirth was commonplace? Conversely, mothers develop remarkably strong attachments to those people who attend her during delivery. It is not unusual for a mother to greet a pediatrician or obstetrician who happened to be in the delivery room only briefly, with great enthusiasm and affection, even though the physician may not remember the woman or delivery. She responds as if there were particularly strong attachment valences free to latch onto anyone nearby.

This phenomenon should be considered carefully. The father present at the delivery is essential so that the mother's attachment will be to him and the baby rather than to hospital personnel. The evidence that dysfunction of the family and the weakness of familial bonds are related to the practice of separating mother and baby after birth and excluding the husband from the labor, delivery, and postdelivery experiences is becoming most convincing. Only further research will help clarify these observations.

References

BIBRING, G. L., DWYER, T. F., HUNTINGTON, D. S. and VALENSTEIN, A. F. (1961) 'A Study of the Psychological Processes in Pregnancy and of the Earliest Mother-Child Relationship. I. Some Propositions and Comments', *The Psychoanalytic Study of the Child*, **16**, 9–27.

BOWLBY, J. (1958) 'The Nature of the Child's Tie to His Mother', *International Journal of Psychoanalysis*, **39**, 350–373.

BRAZELTON, T. B. (1963) 'The Early Mother-Infant Adjustment', *Pediatrics*, **32**, 931–938.

BRAZELTON, T. B., SCHOOL, M. and RABEY, J. (1966) 'Visual Responses in the Newborn', *Pediatrics*, **37**, 284–290.

CAPLAN, G. (1960) *Emotional Implications of Pregnancy and Influences on Family Relationships in the Healthy Child* Cambridge, Mass., Harvard University Press.

DESMOND, M. M., RUDOLPH, A. J. and PHITAKSPHRAIWAN, P. (1966) 'The Transitional Care Nursery: A Mechanism of a Preventative Medicine', *Pediatric Clinics of North America*, **13**, 651–668.

GREENBERG, M., ROSENBERG, I. and LIND, J. (1973) 'First Mothers Rooming-In with Their Newborns: Its Impact Upon the Mother', *American Journal of Orthopsychiatry*, **43**, 783–788.

KENNEL, J. H., JERAULD, R., WOLFE, H., CHESLER, D., KREGER, N. C., MCALPINE, W., STEFFA, M. and KLAUS, M. H. (1974) 'Maternal Behavior One Year after Early and Extended Post-Partum Contact', *Developmental Medicine and Child Neurology*, **16**, 172–179.

LANG, R. (1972) *Birth Book* Ben Lomond, California, Genesis Press.

LIND, J. (1973) Personal communication.

MCBRIDE, A. (1951) 'Compulsory Rooming-In in the Ward and Private Service at Duke Hospital', *J.A.M.A.*, **45(a)**, 625.

NEWTON, N. and NEWTON, M. (1962) 'Mothers' Reactions to Their Newborn Babies', *J.A.M.A.*, **181**, 206–211.

PARKE, R. (1974) 'Family Interaction in the Newborn Period: Some Findings, Some Observations, and Some Unresolved Issues' in Riegal, K. and Meacham, J. (eds.) *Proceedings of the International Society of Behavior Development*.

RINGLER, N. M., KENNEL, J. H., JARVELLA, R., NAVOJOSKY, B. J. and KLAUS, M. H. (1975) 'Mother-to-Child Speech at 2 Years – Effect of Early Postnatal Contact', *Behavioral Pediatrics*, **86**, 141–144.

ROBSON, K. (1967) 'The Role of Eye-to-Eye Contact in Maternal-Infant Attachment', *Journal of Child Psychology and Psychiatry*, **8**, 13–25.

SPITZ, R. A. (1945) 'Hospitalism: An Inquiry into the Genesis of Psychiatric Conditions in Early Childhood', *The Psychoanalytic Study of the Child* **I**, 53–74.

2 Growth and crises of the healthy personality
E. H. Erikson

I shall try to describe those elements of a really healthy personality which
. . . are most noticeably absent or defective in neurotic patients and which
are most obviously present in the kind of man that educational and
cultural systems seem to be striving, each in its own way, to create, to
support, and to maintain.

I shall present human growth from the point of view of the conflicts,
inner and outer, which the healthy personality weathers emerging and re-
emerging with an increased sense of inner unity, with an increase of good
judgement, and an increase in the capacity to do well, according to the
standards of those who are significant to him. . . .

On health and growth

. . . How does a healthy personality grow or, as it were, accrue from the
successive stages of increasing capacity to master life's outer and inner
dangers—with some vital enthusiasm to spare?

Whenever we try to understand growth, it is well to remember the
epigenetic principle which is derived from the growth of organism *in utero*.
Somewhat generalized, this principle states that anything that grows has a
ground plan, and that out of this ground plan the *parts* arise, each part
having its *time* of special ascendancy, until all parts have arisen to form a
functioning whole. At birth the baby leaves the chemical exchange of the
womb for the social exchange system of his society, where his gradually
increasing capacities meet the opportunities and limitations of his culture.
How the maturing organism continues to unfold, not by developing new
organs, but by a prescribed sequence of locomotor, sensory and social
capacities, is described in the child-development literature.

In the presentation of stages in the development of the personality, we
employ an *epigenetic diagram*. . . . An epigenetic diagram looks like this
(see Diagram A).

The double-lined squares signify both a sequence of stages (I to III) and
a gradual development of component parts; in other words the diagram

ERIKSON, E. H. (1967) 'Growth and crises of the healthy personality', in Lazarus,
R. S. and Opton, E. M., Jr., (eds.) *Personality, Selected Readings*, Harmondsworth,
Penguin, pp. 167–96.

Diagram A

	Component 1	Component 2	Component 3
Stage I	I_1	I_2	I_3
Stage II	II_1	II_2	II_3
Stage III	III_1	III_2	III_3

Diagram B

First Stage (about first year)	Basic Trust	Earlier form of Autonomy	Earlier form of Initiative
Second Stage (about second and third years)	Later form of Basic Trust	Autonomy	Earlier form of Initiative
Third Stage (about fourth and fifth years)	Later form of Basic Trust	Later form of Autonomy	Initiative

formalizes a *progression through time of a differentiation of parts.* This indicates (1) that each item of the healthy personality to be discussed is *systematically related to all others* and that they all depend on the *proper development in the proper sequence of each item;* and (2) that each item *exists in some form before 'its' decisive and critical time* normally arrives.

If I say, for example, that a *sense of basic trust* is the first component of mental health to develop in life, a *sense of autonomous will* the second, and a *sense of initiative* the third, the purpose of the diagram may become clearer (see Diagram B).

This diagrammatic statement, in turn, is meant to express a number of fundamental relations that exist among the three components, as well as a few fundamental facts for each.

Each comes to its ascendance, meets its crisis, and finds its lasting solution . . . *toward the end of the stages* mentioned. All of them exist in the beginning in some form. . . . A baby may show something like 'autonomy' from the beginning, for example, in the particular way in which he angrily tries to wriggle his hand free when tightly held. However, under normal conditions, it is not until the second year that he begins to experience the whole *critical alternative between being an autonomous creature and being a dependent one;* and it is not until then that he is ready for a *decisive encounter* with his environment, an environment which, in turn, feels called upon to convey to him its *particular ideas and concepts of autonomy and coercion* in ways decisively contributing to the character, the efficiency, and the health of his personality in his culture.

It is this *encounter*, together with the resulting crisis, which is to be described for each stage. Each stage becomes a *crisis* because incipient growth and awareness in a significant part function goes together with a shift in instinctual energy and yet causes specific vulnerability in that part. One of the most difficult questions to decide, therefore, is whether or not a child at a given stage is weak or strong. Perhaps it would be best to say that he is always vulnerable in some respects and completely oblivious and insensitive in others, but that at the same time he is unbelievably persistent in the same respects in which he is vulnerable. It must be added that the smallest baby's weakness gives him power; out of his very dependence and weakness he makes signs to which his environment ... is peculiarly sensitive. A baby's presence exerts a consistent and persistent domination over the outer and inner lives of every member of a household. Because these members must reorient themselves to accommodate his presence, they must also grow as individuals and as a group. It is as true to say that babies control and bring up their families as it is to say the converse. A family can bring up a baby only by being brought up by him. His growth consists of a series of challenges to them to serve his newly developing potentialities for social interaction.

Each successive step, then, is a potential crisis because of a radical *change in perspective*. There is, at the beginning of life, the most radical change of all: from intrauterine to extrauterine life. But in postnatal existence, too, such radical adjustments of perspective as lying relaxed, sitting firmly, and running fast must all be accomplished in their own good time. With them, the interpersonal perspective, too, changes rapidly and often radically, as is testified by the proximity in time of such opposites as 'not letting mother out of sight' and 'wanting to be independent'. . . .

Basic trust *versus* basic mistrust

I

For the first component of a healthy personality I nominate a sense of *basic trust*, which I think is an attitude toward oneself and the world derived from the experiences of the first year of life. By 'trust' I mean what is commonly implied in reasonable trustfulness as far as others are concerned and a sample sense of trustworthiness as far as oneself is concerned. When I say 'basic', I mean that neither this component nor any of those that follow are, either in childhood or in adulthood, especially conscious. In fact, all of these criteria, when developed in childhood and when integrated in adulthood, blend into the total personality. Their crises in childhood, however, and their impairment in adulthood are clearly circumscribed. . . .

Let us see what justifies our placing the crisis and the ascendancy of this [basic trust] at the beginning of life.

As the newborn infant is separated from his symbiosis with the mother's body, his inborn and more or less coordinated ability to take in by mouth meets the mother's more or less coordinated ability and intention to feed him and to welcome him. At this point he lives through, and loves with, his mouth; and the mother lives through, and loves with, her breasts.

For the mother this is a late and complicated accomplishment, highly dependent on her development as a woman; on her unconscious attitude toward the child; on the way she has lived through pregnancy and delivery; on her and her community's attitude toward the act of nursing—and on the response of the newborn. To him the mouth is the focus of a general first approach to life—the *incorporative* approach. In psychoanalysis this stage is usually referred to as the 'oral' stage. Yet it is clear that, in addition to the overwhelming need for food, a baby is, or soon becomes, receptive in many other respects. As he is willing and able to suck on appropriate objects and to swallow whatever appropriate fluids they emit, he is soon also willing and able to 'take in' with his eyes whatever enters his visual field. His tactual senses, too, seem to 'take in' what feels good. In this sense, then, one could speak of an '*incorporative stage*', one in which he is, relatively speaking, receptive to what he is being offered. Yet many babies are sensitive and vulnerable, too. In order to ensure that their first experience in this world may not only keep them alive but also help them to coordinate their sensitive breathing and their metabolic and circulatory rhythms, we must see to it that we deliver to their senses stimuli as well as food in the proper intensity and at the right time; otherwise their willingness to accept may change abruptly into diffuse defense—or into lethargy.

. . . It is . . . in his earliest encounters that the human infant meets up with the basic modalities of his culture. The simplest and the earliest modality is '*to get*', not in the sense of '*go and get*' but in that of receiving and accepting what is given; and this sounds easier than it is. For the groping and unstable newborn's organism learns this modality only as he learns to regulate his readiness to get with the methods of a mother who, in turn, will permit him to coordinate his means of getting as she develops and coordinates her means of giving. The mutuality of relaxation thus developed is of prime importance for the first experience of friendly otherness. . . .

Where this *mutual regulation* fails, the situation falls apart into a variety of attempts to control by duress rather than by reciprocity. The baby will try to get by random activity what he cannot get by central suction; he will activate himself into exhaustion or he will find his thumb and damn the world. The mother's reaction may be to try to control matters by nervously changing hours, formulas, and procedures. One cannot be sure what this does to a baby; but it certainly is our clinical impression that in some sensitive individuals (or in individuals whose early frustration was never compensated for) such a situation can be a model for a radical disturbance in their relationship to the 'world', to 'people', and especially to loved or otherwise significant people. . . .

During the 'second oral' stage the ability and the pleasure in a more active and more directed incorporative approach ripen. The teeth develop and with them the pleasure in biting *on* hard things, in biting *through* things, and in biting *off* things. This *active-incorporative* mode characterizes a variety of other activities (as did the first incorporative mode). The eyes, first part of a passive system of accepting impressions as they come along, have now learned to focus, to isolate, to 'grasp' objects from the vaguer background and to follow them. The organs of hearing similarly have learned to discern significant sounds, to localize them, and to guide an appropriate change in position (lifting and turning the head, lifting and turning the upper body). The arms have learned to reach out determinedly and the hands to grasp firmly. . . .

The *crisis* of the oral stage (during the second part of the first year) is difficult to assess and more difficult to verify. It seems to consist of the coincidence in time of three developments: (1) a physiological one: the general tension associated with a more violent drive to incorporate, appropriate, and observe more actively (a tension to which is added the discomfort of 'teething' and other changes in the oral machinery); (2) a psychological one: the infant's increasing awareness of himself as a distinct person; and (3) an environmental one: the mother's apparent turning away from the baby toward pursuits which she had given up during late pregnancy and postnatal care. . . .

Where breast feeding lasts into the biting stage (and, generally speaking, this has been the rule) it is now necessary to learn how to continue sucking without biting, so that the mother may not withdraw the nipple in pain or anger. Our clinical work indicates that this point in the individual's early history provides him with some sense of basic loss, leaving the general impression that once upon a time one's unity with a maternal matrix was destroyed. Weaning, therefore, should not mean sudden loss of the breast and loss of the mother's reassuring presence too, unless, of course, other women can be depended upon to sound and feel much like the mother. A drastic loss of accustomed mother love without proper substitution at this time can lead (under otherwise aggravating conditions) to acute infantile depression (Spitz, 1945) or to a mild but chronic state of mourning which may give a depressive undertone to the whole remainder of life. . . .

It is against the combination of these impressions of having been deprived, of having been divided, and of having been abandoned, all of which leave a residue of basic mistrust, that basic trust must be established and maintained. . . .

The psychiatrists, obstetricians, pediatricians, and anthropologists, to whom I feel closest, today would agree that the *firm establishment of enduring patterns for the balance of basic trust over basic mistrust* is the first task of the budding personality and therefore first of all a task for maternal care. But it must be said that the *amount of trust* derived from earliest infantile experience does not seem to depend on absolute *quantities of food or demonstrations of love* but rather on the *quality* of the maternal relationship. Mothers create a sense of trust in their children by that kind of administration which in its quality combines sensitive care of the baby's individual needs and a firm sense of personal trustworthiness within the trusted framework of their community's life style. . . .

Autonomy *versus* shame and doubt

I

. . . The over-all significance of this stage lies in the maturation of the muscle system, the consequent ability . . . to coordinate a number of highly conflicting action patterns such as 'holding on' and 'letting go', and the enormous value with which the still highly dependent child begins to endow his autonomous will.

Psychoanalysis has enriched our vocabulary with the word 'anality' to designate the particular pleasurableness and willfulness which often attach to the eliminative organs at this stage. . . . Bowel and bladder training has become the most obviously disturbing item of child training in wide circles of our society.

What, then, makes the anal problem potentially important and difficult?

The anal zone lends itself more than any other to the expression of stubborn insistence on conflicting impulses because, for one thing, it is the model zone for two contradictory modes which must become alternating; namely, *retention* and *elimination*. Furthermore, the sphincters are only part of the muscle system with its general ambiguity of rigidity and relaxation, of flexion and extension. This whole stage, then, becomes a battle for *autonomy*. For as he gets ready to stand on his feet more firmly, the infant delineates his world as 'I' and 'you', 'me' and 'mine'. Every mother knows how astonishingly pliable a child may be at this stage, if and when he has made the decision that he *wants* to do what he is supposed to do. It is impossible, however, to find a reliable formula for making him want to do just that. Every mother knows how lovingly a child at this stage will snuggle and how ruthlessly he will suddenly try to push the adult away. At the same time the child is apt both to hoard things and to discard them, to cling to possessions and to throw them out of the windows of houses and vehicles. All of these seemingly contradictory tendencies, then, we include under the formula of the retentive-eliminative modes. The matter of mutual regulation between adult and child now faces its severest test. If outer control by too rigid or too early training insists on robbing the child of his attempt *gradually* to control his bowels and other functions willingly and by his free choice, he will again be faced with a double rebellion and a double defeat. Powerless in his own body (sometimes afraid of his bowels) and powerless outside, he will again be forced to seek satisfaction and control either by regression or by fake progression. In other words, he will return to an earlier, oral control, that is, by sucking his thumb and becoming whiny and demanding; or he will become hostile and willful, often using his feces (and, later, dirty words) as ammunition; or he will pretend an autonomy and an ability to do without anybody to lean on which he has by no means really gained.

This stage, therefore, becomes decisive for the ratio between love and hate, for that between cooperation and willfulness, and for that between the freedom of self-expression and its suppression. From a sense of *self-control without loss of self-esteem* comes a lasting sense of autonomy and pride; from a sense of muscular and anal impotence, of loss of self-control, and of parental overcontrol comes a lasting sense of doubt and shame.

To develop autonomy, a firmly developed and a convincingly continued stage of early trust is necessary. The infant must come to feel that basic faith in himself and in the world (which is the lasting treasure saved from the conflicts of the oral stage) will not be jeopardized by this sudden violent wish to have a choice, to appropriate demandingly, and to eliminate stubbornly. *Firmness* must protect him against the potential anarchy of his as yet untrained sense of discrimination, his inability to hold on and to let go with circumspection. Yet his environment must back him up in his wish to 'stand on his own feet' lest he be overcome by that sense of having exposed himself prematurely and foolishly which we call shame, or that secondary mistrust, that 'double-take', which we call doubt.

Shame is an infantile emotion insufficiently studied. Shame supposes that one is completely exposed and conscious of being looked at—in a word, self-conscious. One is visible and not ready to be visible; that is why we dream of shame as a situation in which we are stared at in a condition of incomplete dress, in night attire, 'with one's pants down'. Shame is early expressed in an impulse to bury one's face, or to sink, right then and there, into the ground. . . .

Too much shaming does not result in a sense of propriety but in a secret determination to try to get away with things when unseen, if, indeed, it does not result in deliberate *shamelessness*. . . . Many a small child, when shamed beyond endurance, may be in a mood (although not in possession of either the courage or the words) to express defiance in similar terms. . . .

21

There is a limit to a child's and an adult's individual endurance in the face of demands which force him to consider himself, his body, his needs, and his wishes as evil and dirty, and to believe in the infallibility of those who pass such judgment. Occasionally he may be apt to turn things around, to become secretly oblivious to the opinion of others, and to consider as evil only the fact that they exist: his chance will come when they are gone, or when he can leave them. . . .

Denied the gradual and well-guided experience of the autonomy of free choice, or weakened by an initial loss of trust, the sensitive child may turn against himself all his urge to discriminate and to manipulate. He will *overmanipulate himself*, he will develop a *precocious conscience*. Instead of taking possession of things in order to test them by repetitive play, he will become obsessed by his own repetitiveness; he will want to have everything 'just so', and only in a given sequence and tempo. By such infantile obsessiveness, by dawdling, for example, or by becoming a stickler for certain rituals, the child then learns to gain power over his parents and nurses in areas where he could not find large-scale mutual regulation with them. Such hollow victory, then, is the infantile model for a compulsion neurosis. . . .

II

[To return from considerations of the abnormal to practical advice.] . . . Be firm and tolerant with the child at this stage, and he will be firm and tolerant with himself. He will feel pride in being an autonomous person; he will grant autonomy to others; and now and again he will even let himself get away with something.

Why, then, if we know how, do we not tell parents in detail what to do to develop this intrinsic, this genuine autonomy? The answer is: because when it comes to human values, nobody knows how to fabricate or manage the fabrication of the genuine article. My own field, psychoanalysis, having studied particularly the excessive increase of guilt feelings beyond any normal rhyme or reason, and the consequent excessive estrangement of the child from his own body, attempted at least to formulate what should *not* be done to children. These formulations, however, often aroused superstitious inhibitions in those who were inclined to make anxious rules out of vague warnings. Actually, we are learning only gradually what exactly *not* to do with *what kind* of children at *what age*. . . . At around eight months the child seems to be somehow more aware, as it were, of his *separateness;* this prepares him for the impending sense of autonomy. At the same time he becomes more cognizant of his mother's features and presence and of the strangeness of others. Sudden or prolonged separation from his mother at that time apparently can cause a sensitive child to experience an aggravation of the experience of division and abandonment, arousing violent anxiety and withdrawal. Again, in the first quarter of the second year, if everything has gone well, the infant just begins to become aware of the autonomy discussed in this chapter. The introduction of bowel training at this time may cause him to resist with all his strength and determination, because he seems to feel that his budding will is being 'broken'. To avoid this feeling is certainly more important than to insist on his being trained just then because there is a time for the stubborn ascendancy of autonomy and there is a time for the partial sacrifice of secure autonomy, but obviously the time for a meaningful sacrifice is *after* one has acquired and reinforced a core of autonomy and has also acquired more insight. . . .

The sense of autonomy which arises, or should arise, in the second stage of childhood, is fostered by a handling of the small individual which expresses a sense of rightful dignity and lawful independence on the part of the parents and which gives him the confident expectation that the kind of autonomy fostered in childhood will not be frustrated later. This, in turn, necessitates a relationship of parent to parent, of parent to employer, and of parent to government which reaffirms the parent's essential dignity within the hierarchy of social positions. It is important to dwell on this point because much of the shame and doubt, much of the indignity and uncertainty which is aroused in children is a consequence of the parents' frustrations in marriage, in work, and in citizenship. Thus, the sense of autonomy in the child . . . must be backed up by the preservation in economic and political life of a high sense of autonomy and of self-reliance. . . .

Initiative *versus* guilt

I

Having found a firm solution of this problem of autonomy, the child of four and five is faced with the next step—and with the next crisis. Being firmly convinced that he *is* a person, the child must now find out *what kind* of a person he is going to be. And here he hitches his wagon to nothing less than a star: he wants to be like his parents, who to him appear very powerful and very beautiful, although quite unreasonably dangerous. He 'identifies with them', he plays with the idea of how it would be to be them. Three strong developments help at this stage, yet also serve to bring the child closer to his crisis: (1) he learns to *move around* more freely and more violently and therefore establishes a wider and, so it seems to him, an unlimited radius of goals; (2) his sense of *language* becomes perfected to the point where he understands and can ask about many things just enough to misunderstand them thoroughly; and (3) both language and locomotion permit him to expand his *imagination* over so many things that he cannot avoid frightening himself with what he himself has dreamed and thought up. Nevertheless, out of all this he must emerge with a sense of *unbroken initiative* as a basis for a high and yet realistic sense of ambition and independence. . . .

To look back: the first way-station was prone relaxation. The trust based on the experience that the basic mechanisms of breathing, digesting, sleeping, and so forth have a consistent and familiar relation to the foods and comforts offered gives zest to the developing ability to raise oneself to a sitting and then to a standing position. The second way-station (accomplished only toward the end of the second year) is that of being able to sit not only securely but, as it were, untiringly, a feat which permits the muscle system gradually to be used for finer discrimination and for more autonomous ways of selecting and discarding, of piling things up—and of throwing them away with a bang.

The third way-station finds the child able to move independently and vigorously. He is ready to visualize himself as being as big as the perambulating grownups. He begins to make comparisons and is apt to develop untiring curiosity about differences in sizes in general, and sexual differences in particular. He tries to comprehend possible future roles, or at any rate to understand what roles are worth imitating. More immediately, he can now associate with those of his own age. Under the guidance of older children or special women guardians, he gradually enters into the infantile politics of nursery school, street corner, and barnyard. His learning now is eminently intrusive and vigorous: it leads away from his own limitations and into future possibilities.

The *intrusive mode*, dominating much of the behavior of this stage, characterizes a variety of configurationally 'similar' activities and fantasies. These include the intrusion into other bodies by physical attack; the intrusion into other people's ears and minds by aggressive talking; the intrusion into space by vigorous locomotion; the intrusion into the unknown by consuming curiosity. . . .

This leads to the ascendancy of that human specialty which Freud called the 'latency' period, that is, the long delay separating infantile sexuality (which in animals is followed by maturity) and physical sexual maturation. . . .

While the struggle for autonomy at its worst concentrated on keeping rivals out, and was therefore more an expression of *jealous rage* most often directed against encroachments by *younger* siblings, initiative brings with it *anticipatory rivalry* with those who were there first and who may therefore occupy . . . the field toward which one's initiative is directed. Jealousy and rivalry, those often embittered and yet essentially futile attempts at demarcating a sphere of unquestioned privilege, now come to a climax in a final contest for a favored position with one of the parents; the inevitable and necessary failure leads to guilt and anxiety. The child indulges in fantasies of being a giant and a tiger, but in his dreams he runs in terror for dear life. . . .

All of this may seem strange to readers who have only seen the sunnier side of childhood and have not recognized the potential powerhouse of destructive drives which can be aroused and temporarily buried at this stage, only to contribute later to the inner arsenal of a destructiveness so ready to be used when opportunity provokes it. By using the words 'potential', 'provoke' and 'opportunity', I mean to emphasize that there is little in these inner developments which cannot be harnessed to constructive and peaceful initiative if only we learn to understand the conflicts and anxieties of childhood and the importance of childhood for mankind. But if we should choose to overlook or belittle the phenomena of childhood . . . we shall forever overlook one of the eternal sources of human anxiety and strife.

II

It is at this stage of initiative that the great governor of initiative, namely *conscience*, becomes firmly established. Only as a dependent does man develop conscience, that dependence on himself which makes him, in turn, dependable; and only when thoroughly dependable with regard to a number of fundamental values can he become independent and teach and develop tradition. . . .

Reference

SPITZ, R. A. (1945) 'Hospitalism: An Inquiry into the Genesis of Psychiatric Conditions in Early Childhood', *The Psychoanalytic Study of the Child*, **1**, 53–74.

3 The needs of children

Mia Kellmer Pringle

A willingness to devote adequate resources to the care of children is the hallmark of a civilised society as well as an investment in our future. Some argue that we do not know enough to provide positive care and creative education for all children; others object that child rearing is essentially a personal, private matter; while yet others retort that we cannot afford to spend more. So A. E. Housman's despairing appeal 'When will I be dead and rid of the wrong my father did?' continues to be a reproach to our affluent society.

Granted that more needs to be found out about how best to promote children's all-round development, surely enough is known already to take action. If even half of what we now know were accepted with feeling and applied with understanding by all who have the care of children, then the revolution brought about in children's physical health in the past forty years might well be matched by a similar change in their psychological well-being. By strengthening their emotional resilience and increasing their capacity for learning, they would be better prepared to adapt to a rapidly changing world.

In what follows, I shall summarise my views on the needs of children; indicate some changes which are required in the climate of opinion about children's rights and parental responsibilities; and, finally, raise some questions to which answers must be sought.

The needs of children

There are four basic emotional needs which have to be met from the very beginning of life to enable a child to grow from helpless infancy to mature adulthood. These are: the need for love and security; for new experiences; for praise and recognition; and for responsibility. Their relative importance changes, of course, during the different stages of growth as do the ways in which they are met.

PRINGLE, M. K. (1974) *The Needs of Children*, London, Hutchinson, pp. 148–54.

The need for love and security

Probably this is the most important because it provides the basis for all later relationships, not only within the family, but with friends, colleagues and eventually one's own family. On it depend the healthy development of the personality, the ability to care and respond to affection and, in time, to becoming a loving, caring parent. This need is met by the child experiencing from birth onwards a continuous, reliable, loving relationship – first, with his mother, then father and then an ever-widening circle of adults and contemporaries. The security of a familiar place and a known routine make for continuity and predictability in a world in which the child has to come to terms with so much that is new and changing. Also a stable family life provides him with a sense of personal continuity, of having a past as well as a future, and of a coherent and enduring identity.

The need for new experiences

Only if this need is adequately met throughout childhood and adolescence will a child's intelligence develop satisfactorily. Just as the body requires food for physical development and just as an appropriate balanced diet is essential for normal growth, so new experiences are needed for the mind. The most vital ingredients of this diet in early childhood are play and language. Through them, the child explores the world and learns to cope with it. This is as true for the objective outside world of reality as it is for the subjective internal world of thoughts and feelings.

New experiences facilitate the learning of one of the most important lessons of early life: learning how to learn; and learning that mastery brings joy and a sense of achievement. Educability depends not only on inborn capacity, but as much – if not more – on environmental opportunity and encouragement. The emotional and cultural climate of the home, as well as parental involvement and aspirations, can foster, limit or impair mental growth.

Play meets the need for new experiences in two major ways: it enables the child to learn about the world; and it provides a means of coping with and resolving conflicting emotions by allowing fantasy to over-ride reality and logic.

Probably the single and in the long run most crucial factor which promotes intellectual growth is the quality of the child's language environment: not merely how much he is talked to, but how relevant, distinctive and rich the conversation is. Language helps in learning to reason and to think, and also in making relationships.

Going to school is itself a major new experience which opens up a larger and more impersonal world. The child's progress will come to be powerfully affected by his teacher's attitudes, values and beliefs. Wide interests, enthusiasm for things of the mind and receptiveness to new ideas – all these are infectious. Teachers are in a powerful position to preserve, to awaken or to rekindle the curiosity and joy in learning about new things, shown by almost all young children.

The need for praise and recognition

To grow from a helpless infant into a self-reliant, self-accepting adult requires an immense amount of emotional, social and intellectual learning. It is accomplished by the child's modelling himself on the adults who are caring for him. The most effective incentives to bring this about – which require a continuous effort, sustained throughout the years of growing up – are praise and recognition. Eventually, a job well done becomes its own reward but that is a very mature stage; and even the most mature adult responds, and indeed blossoms, when given occasionally some praise or other forms of recognition.

Because growing up is inevitably beset by difficulties, conflicts and setbacks, a strong incentive is needed. This is provided by the pleasure shown at success and the praise given to achievement by the adults who love the child and whom he in turn loves and wants to please. Encouragement and reasonable demands act as a spur to perseverance. The level of expectation is optimal when success is possible but not without effort. It cannot be the same for all children nor for all time. Rather, it must be geared to the individual child's capabilities at a given point in time and to the particular stage of his growth.

Teachers play a vital role too in meeting the need for praise and recognition; if for no other reason than because every child spends about half his waking life in school for at least eleven years. This provides an unrivalled opportunity to establish a favourable attitude to learning and also, where necessary, to improve or even rebuild the foundation for a child's self-esteem and hence his attitude to effort and achievement. To succeed in this task, a teacher must act on the assumption that every pupil has as yet unrealised potential for development which an appropriate 'diet' can call out, rather than accept past failures as indicating immutably limited learning ability.

The need for responsibility

This need is met by allowing the child to gain personal independence, at first through learning to look after himself in matters of his everyday care, such as feeding, dressing and washing himself. It is met too by his having possessions, however small and inexpensive, over which he is allowed to exercise absolute ownership. As he gets older, responsibility has to be extended to more important areas, ultimately allowing him freedom over his own actions. Eventually, in full maturity, he should be able to accept responsibility for others.

Granting increasing independence does not mean withholding one's views, tastes and choices, or the reasons for them; nor does it mean opting out from participating and guiding the lives of children; nor, indeed, condoning everything they do. On the contrary, children need a framework of guidance and of limits. They are helped by knowing what is expected or permitted, what the rules are, together with the reasons for them, and whether these are in their interests or in the interests of others.

How can responsibility be given to the immature and to the irresponsible? There is no way out of the dilemma that unless it is granted, the child cannot learn to exercise it. Like every other skill, it needs to be practised under adult guidance which should gradually diminish. Training adolescents for responsibility is a particularly complex task. It requires a delicate balance between giving information and advice on the one hand and, on the other, leaving the making of decisions and coping with their consequences to the young person while yet being prepared to step in and help if things go badly wrong.

Schools have a vital contribution to make in this area. Those which emphasise cooperation rather than competition, which neither stream nor use corporal punishment have a lower incidence of bullying, violence and delinquency without any lowering of academic standards.

Failure to meet children's needs

If one of the basic needs remains unmet, or is inadequately met, then development may become stunted or distorted. The consequences can be disastrous (and costly) later on, both for the individual and for society. Symptoms of maladjustment are, like pain, danger signals, indicating intolerable tension between the personality and the environment. The range of possible symptoms is wide but basically they fall into two broad categories: fight or flight, attack or withdrawal. Aggressiveness calls forth much stronger adult reactions whereas the timid, over-conforming child tends to be overlooked; yet both types of behaviour are equally significant calls for help, indicating that emotional, social or intellectual needs are not being adequately met.

Prisons, mental hospitals, borstals and schools for the maladjusted, contain a high proportion of individuals who in childhood were unloved and rejected. Their number is high too among the chronically unemployable and among able misfits. Anger, hate, lack of concern for others and an inability to make mutually satisfactory relationships are common reactions to having been unloved and rejected.

A child growing up in a discordant home is also liable to become emotionally disturbed or anti-social. A quarrelling, inadequate or disturbed parent makes a poor adult model. Parental hostility has a particularly harmful effect on a child's later development, especially on his ability to give, as an adult, unselfish loving care to his own children. Thus parental hostility perpetuates itself from one generation to another in what is literally an extremely vicious circle.

If the need for new experiences is not adequately met throughout childhood and adolescence, then intellectual ability will remain stunted. Also, the more unstimulating, uneventful and dull life is, the more readily frustration, apathy, or restlessness set in. This is shown clearly by the contrast between the eagerness, alertness and vitality of normal toddlers whose life is filled with new experiences and challenges; and the aimlessness and boredom of adolescents with nothing to do and nowhere to go.

The urban environment is hostile to the young: there is little freedom or safety to explore or experiment, particularly without adult supervision. In seeking – legitimately – for the excitement of new experiences, where few are to be found or attainable, the forbidden, risky or dangerous are liable to acquire an aura of daring and excitement. What may start as a lark, giving vent to high spirits and the desire for adventure, can then all too easily turn into vandalism and mindless destruction.

Unfortunately, praise and recognition are almost invariably given for achievement rather than effort. In consequence, this need is most readily and often satisfied in the case of intelligent, healthy, adjusted and attractive children. In contrast, the intellectually slow, culturally disadvantaged, emotionally neglected or maladjusted get far less, if any, praise and recognition. Yet their need is immeasurably greater. Whatever small successes they achieve inevitably demand far more effort and perseverance; yet they receive less reward because they achieve less.

In school, praising for achievement instead of effort has very harmful effects on the slower learner as well as on the child with emotional or physical handicaps: he has no chance of shining and always finds himself near the bottom of his class. Such constant failure inevitably damages self-esteem and motivation. The teacher who believes that what matters most is the effort a child makes, and who praises whenever there is improvement however slow and limited, provides an appropriate incentive for all pupils, whatever their abilities. For better or for worse, the encouragement and expectations of parents and teachers have a most powerful influence on a child's progress.

There is controversy between those who demand equal educational opportunity for all; those who advocate that special attention ought to be devoted to the abler child; and those who argue that positive discrimination must be exercised in favour of the less able and under-privileged. The conflict between these viewpoints is, however, more apparent than real. It springs from the mistaken belief that all men are equal despite the enormous disparity in physical, intellectual and creative potential found in all walks of life. Equality of opportunity is the right of every child. To expect equal capacity to make use of this opportunity runs counter to common sense and experience.

Instead, we must act as if all children were equal and then respect, as well as accept and cater for, their differences. Within such a framework, it is legitimate both to provide a democracy of opportunity while at the same time to strive for excellence so as to ensure an aristocracy of achievement.

When the fourth basic emotional need, namely to exercise responsibility, is denied opportunities for fulfilment, then the child will fail to develop a sense of responsibility for himself, for others or for material objects. When such denial has gone hand in hand with a lack of training in self-control and in planning ahead, then such youngsters will tend to be impulsive, unwilling to wait and work for what they want, contemptuous of the rights of others – in short, irresponsible. A high proportion of the self-same young people will on leaving school find themselves in jobs which give them little, if any, responsibility. Work which fails to fulfil the need for involvement is likely to heighten the sense of alienation and rejection. Feeling that society has disowned them may well engender a feeling that they in turn owe nothing to society.

4 The nature of parent education
Orville G. Brim, Jr.

Educational programs for parents have existed in this country [USA] for as long as we have records. During the past three generations, from about 1880 on, there has been an uninterrupted expansion of these programs. At present many organizations, both public and private, commercial and nonprofit, at the national, state, and local levels are engaged in educating parents about child rearing. Parents are counseled by physicians, clergymen, teachers, and nurses. They participate in groups discussing child rearing which meet under the auspices of mental health, parent–teacher, and other associations; read books, pamphlets, magazines, or newspaper columns; view films, plays, and television programs; and listen to lectures and radio programs, all concerned with educating them in child care.

Here we analyze the basis for parent education and clarify the distinction between it and other related endeavors.

The social context

The development of the broad social movement to educate the American parent in child rearing has two fundamental causes. The first was the breakdown of cultural traditions in child-rearing practices, which in turn was a result of still other antecedent social changes. The latter include the change in the status of women in our society toward increased autonomy in both their family and nonfamily roles; the decline in frequency of intergenerational family relations, arising from the fact that now in our society most newly married couples establish residence apart from their parental homes; the increased contact through immigration and social mobility between members of different ethnic backgrounds and social classes who have contrasting cultural traditions of child care. All of these have contributed either to the isolation of the new parent from his own cultural traditions of child training, or to his exposure to different ways of rearing children which present a challenge to him.

The consequent breakdown in tradition forces the modern parent into

---

BRIM, ORVILLE G., JR. (1965) *Education for Child Rearing*, New York, The Free Press, pp. 17–28.

greater consciousness of his child-rearing practices and demands that he develop many aspects of his roles as a parent *de novo*, either from his own resources or with the assistance of persons outside his family group,whether they be neighbors, physicians, ministers, or professional parent educators. One surmises, therefore, that organized parent education programs were a response to this situation, developed to fill the need for guidance caused by the decline of traditional child-rearing practices.

However, it would be a mistake to conclude that parent education arose only in response to the needs of parents. The second fundamental cause of this social movement was the growing belief on the part of many persons that there existed better ways of rearing children than those prescribed by traditions. This belief was nurtured by the research on child development in both Europe and the United States, which began just after the turn of the century, and gave promise of providing a new body of scientific knowledge of the desirable ways to rear children.

Those holding this belief sought to teach to all parents the findings of child development research, so that they could consciously and deliberately select those child-rearing practices consonant with their own aims, and proved by science to be superior to their own cultural traditions. . . .

The development of parent education from this source served to challenge further the cultural traditions of parent role performance by presenting both theory and research data contradictory to long-held beliefs about child development. Thus, this second independent cause of the parent education movement made the first loom even larger as a contributing factor to the development of parent education. The result has been to create a national situation in which research on child development and parent–child relations continues to increase in volume, with an accompanying increase in the sensitivity to, and the demand for, the results of such research on the part of the American parent.

In this context one can view parent education as a movement aimed at altering the role performance of parents on a massive scale, endeavoring to move the modern parent away from his cultural traditions toward a greater conscious and rational role performance and also to supply, in response to parental demand, the guidance he seeks instead of following his own traditions. It is true that certain parent education programs may seek to substitute the beliefs of the parent educators themselves for the traditional beliefs of the parents. The parent faced with the crumbling of his traditional culture turns quite naturally to seek some new authority rather than accepting the burden of autonomy and conscious role determination. It has been the task of parent education to avoid meeting the demand placed upon it to serve as a new authority and instead to help the parent become more competent and independent in his role. . . .

D

A definition of parent education

Parent education can be defined as an activity using educational techniques in order to effect change in parent role performance. Nothing is implied about this activity being directed to a specific end such as physical health of the child; on the contrary, parent education is customarily employed in the pursuit of a variety of ends.

This definition leaves several points which require amplification. These concern (Allen 1948) the relation between education and other techniques of personal influence; (Auerbach 1953) the relation between educational efforts directed to influencing the role behavior of parents in contrast to role behavior in other situations; and (Brim 1957) the distinction between the ends of parent education and the ends of other programs of influence. We will consider these points in order.

Education and therapy

The distinction between education and therapy is difficult to make, and the problem has beset parent educators for a long time. Lindeman and Thurston in 1935 pointed out that 'parent educators are now searching for that new line of demarcation which reveals where education leaves off and psychotherapy begins.' We need simply add that twenty years later they are still searching. Nor is the confusion one-sided. Therapists also wrestle unsuccessfully with the problem, as seen in the various attempts to define therapy for the purposes of licensing or certification. In some instances the definitions presented of therapy are such as to have rendered illegal, except for licensed medical personnel, many activities commonly held to be educational (Sanford 1954). The distinction between education and therapy may be much like the legal distinction between sanity and insanity in that in any specific case it is very hard to apply. . . .

The working distinction which we will employ throughout this analysis is the following: educational techniques are those directed to the conscious (and near-conscious) aspects of the individual personality, and exposure to educational programs ideally should arouse only conscious beliefs and conscious motives. In contrast, therapeutic techniques are directed to unconscious motives, expectations, and attitudes, and the instrumental goal of therapy is to make the individual ready to profit from subsequent educational experiences. In this sense, therapy is a kind of interaction designed to dissipate the individual's defenses and to render him educable, that is, susceptible to change from various educational procedures.

Several points follow from this basic differentiation. The first is that education avoids pressing forward where the person is resistant, on the assumption that the resistance arises from strong defenses which in turn arise from unconscious motives. As Auerbach (1953) has pointed out, the distinction between a group educational experience and group therapy is that the former does not 'expose, explore and work through the pathology of its members.'

However, and secondly, there is no implication that education does not examine why a person feels as he does. To the extent that the 'why' is under conscious control it is suitable subject matter for the educational procedure. Only when the reasons are unconscious should education avoid examination of the causes of a person's feeling and behavior (Dybwad 1955).

Third, it follows that the changes resulting from education will comprise minor changes in the person's character, when compared to the major personality reorganization held to result from successful therapy. This is satisfactory, of course, in view of the assumption that most parents neither want nor need a major reorganization of their personality.

Fourth, note that both education and therapy can give information of a personal, specific kind. It is not satisfactory to attempt to differentiate education from therapy on the grounds that the former gives just general information, whereas the latter relates it specifically to the given individual in therapy. Indeed, the whole emphasis of modern educational theory, stemming from John Dewey and William H. Kilpatrick, is that education is most successful when the materials to be learned are related directly to the specific personal interests and experience of the student.

Fifth, distinctions have been offered on the basis of working with healthy aspects of the individual's personality in contrast to the pathologic aspects. For example, as Neubauer (1953) says, 'Therapy directs itself to the deviant aspects of personality, the symptoms or the character disturbance, with a view toward effecting change in individual pathology. Making use of specific technique consciously applied, it approaches conflicts in order to free the energies bound within them, thus making these energies available for healthy growth.

'Education is aimed at those faculties of the ego which are undisturbed by conflict. It is oriented toward the healthy factors of the personality and appeals to the ability to judge, to gain understanding, to learn to use one's experience for new and different [experiences and] situations, to plan, to make choices, to adapt to changing circumstance, to add new experiences.'

This distinction is useful if one also recognizes that individuals may have serious conflicts which arise from consciously and accurately recognized sources, and in this sense are potentially under conscious control. That is to say simply that some of the major conflicts experienced by persons would be solvable by educational techniques.

Sixth, we must recognize that both the educator and the therapist can establish an affective, warm, and personal relation with the pupil or

35

patient as the case might be. Indeed, one would suppose that such warmth would be every bit as conducive to the success of education as it is to that of therapy.

Finally, we note that the aim of therapy is the emotional health of the individual, and that this end is not restricted to any particular role. Although the specific problem leading the individual to the therapist usually arises in some specific role area such as in the family or in one's work, it is misleading to hold that therapeutic methods are directed to shifts in performance of any particular role, even though they may initially begin in a specific area. Therapeutic efforts are directed toward influencing the individual in a general way, that is, in terms of characteristics which customarily are not specifically related to any role.... Education contrasts with therapy in that while education is in fact general, much of it is specifically focused on some given role as in one's occupation, family, or community.

In sum, education is the attempt to influence a person by appeal to those motives and beliefs which are under conscious control, whereas therapy is an attempt to influence one by working with unconscious motives or beliefs which interfere with the individual's learning from educational techniques....

The parental role

Parenthood represents a particular status in our society, and associated with this, as with every social status, is a particular role which it is expected the parent will perform in interaction with the child. This status and role of the parent differ from others which the individual holds, for example, those of wife or husband or other adult statuses; and this provides a basis for a distinction between parent education and other educational efforts. The point has been made by others such as Lindeman (1932) and Kotinsky (1935) that parent education must be distinguished from other kinds of education in terms of the area of life to which it is directed.

First, in considering the relation between parent education and adult education one sees that parent education refers to efforts directed toward influencing a specific role, and adult education refers to educational efforts directed toward influencing *any adult* role, whether it be as community members, as American citizens, as parents, or whatever. Logically, therefore, parent education is a part of adult education, and the former educates persons in but one of their many adult roles. This point of view is not new, for it was recognized twenty or more years ago (Brunner 1935) that parent education was a subdivision of the growing adult education movement. In current discussions of adult education and in surveys of the extent of adult education (e.g. National Education Assoc. 1952) programs which are clearly and purely parent education in nature are often included. . . .

A second point in differentiation involves the relation between parent education and the broader activity of family life education. Family life education should, and customarily does, refer to those educational programs which are directed to influencing the performance of specific roles within the family context. Such roles include those of the child, the sib, the parent, and the husband and wife. Logically, therefore, parent education constitutes one-fourth of those activities designated as family life education (which, of course, in part belongs to adult education). Certainly there are distinctions between the education of . . . high school students as children, the education of individuals for their better performance of husband or wife roles as with marriage counseling, and the education of adults as parents. While it is true that the parental and marital roles are closely related, so that educational efforts which influence the performance of one frequently have their effects spill over into the other, the problem is primarily empirical and not definitional. We point out here only that it is possible and necessary, too, to distinguish between educational programs which have as their primary target change in parent role performance and other family life education programs which have as their primary target changes in performance as a husband or wife. It may well be that the future will see an increasingly close relation between the two types of family educational programs which more fully recognizes the integration of the parent and the spouse role.

At present, even though there are some separate organizations within the area of family life education for marriage counselors, for parent educators, and for others, the more broadly organized professional groups, such as the National Council on Family Relations, customarily include persons involved in both marriage and parent education programs. The programs of meetings of these organizations include materials on both parent education and marriage counseling.

A third distinction remains to be made, namely, between parental and preparental roles. Many educational programs try to influence the parent role performance, although they are in fact directed to individuals who are not yet parents. Such programs include formal courses in the field of 'human development,' which are given in colleges and universities, high schools, and even elementary schools (Brim 1957). Included also are the many classes for prospective mothers and fathers, and the individual counseling given by physicians and others during the pregnancy period.

Here we must make an arbitrary distinction in our definition. The term 'parent education' is assigned to those programs concerned with educational efforts directed to people already in the parent role, while the term 'preparental education' will be used to refer to those activities involving

37

individuals prior to their entrance in the parent role but designed to educate them for later role performance. . . .

The objectives of parent education

It is important to stress that the use of parent education is not limited to the pursuit of some single objective. We have said so far that parent education is an activity employing educational techniques and designed to influence parent role performance. But the influence upon the parent may serve many ends, and the fact is that parent education *has* been employed as a method of achieving various ends. In 1930 at the third White House Conference, considerable attention was given parent education, and it is noteworthy that in addition to the report (1932) of the Committee on the Family and Parent Education, many of the committees on other aspects of child welfare indicated that their recommendations for children could not be implemented without changing the parent, and that parent education should be used for this. Numerous publications (e.g., Kawin 1954, McGinnis 1953, National Congress 1930) attest to the variety of ends for which the education of parents has been used; for example, training for good citizenship, choosing a dentist, preventing blindness, improving diet, selecting clothing, procuring baby sitters, training in the use of money, teaching good manners, and so forth, as well as the major current emphasis on promoting the mental health of the child.

It is this variety of ends which permits a working distinction between the general concept of mental health education and that of parent education. First, we recognize that most parent education programs are primarily concerned with improving the mental health of the child. . . . It is important to point out that parent education is *not* used only for mental health ends. In contrast, 'mental health education' *is* directed to a single end, but seeks to achieve its objective through educating persons in *many* roles. Ginsberg (1955) and Gruenberg (1953) have noted that special educational activities in the service of mental health ends are directed at different groups of persons, including 'parents, children, teachers, doctors, pastors, lawyers, policemen, welfare workers, administrators, newsmen, and others.' (Gruenberg 1953).

In sum, we might say that parent education differs from mental health education in that the former focuses on a specific role but is directed to a variety of ends, whereas mental health education focuses on a specific end but is directed to changes in a variety of roles. But parent education and mental health education overlap to a significant degree in the effort to influence parent role performance for the purpose of mental health. Indeed, in such instances parent education and mental health education are virtually identical, and, therefore [any analysis of parent education],

. . must of necessity apply to an important segment of mental health education.

References

ALLEN, W. Y. and CAMPBELL, D. (1948) *The Creative Nursery Center: A Unified Service to Children and Parents*, New York, Family Service Assoc. of America.

AUERBACH, A. B. (1953) 'Parent Discussion Groups: Their Role in Parent Education' in *Parent Group Education and Leadership Training*, New York, Child Study Association of America, 1–8.

BRIM, O. G., JR. (1957) 'Recent Research on Effects of Education in Human Development' in Ojemann, R. H. (ed.) *Four Basic Aspects of Preventive Psychiatry*, Report of the First Institute on Preventive Psychiatry, Iowa City, State University of Iowa, ch. 4.

BRUNNER, E. DE S. (1935) 'Some Problems in Parent Education from the Standpoint of the General Field of Adult Education', *Parent Education*, **2**, 5–8.

DYBWAD, G. and GOLLER, G. (1955) 'Goals and Techniques of Parent Education' in *Casework Papers*, New York, Family Service Assoc. of America.

GINSBERG, S. W. (1955) 'The Mental Health Movement: Its Theoretical Assumptions' in Kotinsky, R. and Witmer, H. (eds.) *Community Programs for Mental Health*, Cambridge, Mass., Harvard University Press, 1–29.

GRUENBERG, E. M. (1953) 'The Prevention of Mental Disease', *Annals of the American Academy of Political and Social Science*, **286**, 158–166.

KAWIN, E. (1954) *Parenthood in a Free Nation*, Parent Education Project Chicago, University of Chicago Press.

KOTINSKY, R. (1935) 'Parent Education: An Attempt at Delimitation', *Parent Education*, **2**, 9–13.

LINDEMAN, E. C. (1932) 'A Philosophy for Parent Education' in *Parent Education: Types, Content and Method*. White House Conference on Child Health and Protection, Section III: Education and Training, Committee on the Family and Parent Education. New York, Century, 22–35.

LINDEMAN, E. C. and THURSTON, F. M. (1931) *Problems for Parent Educators*, New York, National Council of Parent Education.

MCGINNIS, E. and PFEIFFER, M. (1953) *Family Centered Education: Annotated Bibliography*. Washington, American Home Economics Association.

NATIONAL CONGRESS OF PARENTS AND TEACHERS (1930) *Parent Education: The First Yearbook*, Washington, The National Congress.

NATIONAL EDUCATION ASSOCIATION, DIVISION OF ADULT EDUCATION SERVICE (1952) *A Study of Urban Public School Adult Education Programs of the United States.* Washington, The Association.

NEUBAUER, P. B. (1953) 'The Technique of Parent Group Education: Some Basic Concepts', *Parent Group Education and Leadership Training*, New York, Child Study Association of America, 9–15.

SANFORD, F. H. (1954) 'Psychology, Psychiatry, and Legislation in New York', *American Psychologist*, **9**, 160–164.

WHITE HOUSE CONFERENCE ON CHILD HEALTH AND PROTECTION (1932) Section III: Education and Training, Committee on the Family and Parent Education, *Parent Education: Types, Content and Method.* New York, Century.

Part Two Predicting and predisposing factors

In this section Alfred White Franklin's short paper 'The nature of the task' draws attention to the complexity of the subject of child abuse. The factors which appear to contribute or predispose to abuse have been and are being studied. Catherine Peckham poses some of the problems in undertaking and interpreting epidemiological studies. David Gil's study summarizes information gathered following nearly 13,000 incidents of physical abuse in the USA and Margaret Lynch identifies factors and circumstances in dealing with abuse in individual families.

5 The nature of the task

Alfred White Franklin

'Child abuse', 'non-accidental injury to children', the 'battering of children' are some of the names that are given to one end product of family stress. So much effort is directed to providing an environment fit and safe for the nurture and education of children, of tomorrow's citizens, that society views with particular abhorrence those parents who turn against their children and do them harm. Positive harm reveals itself most clearly in physical injury, but the negative harm of deprivation, whether it be of love or food or any other necessity, shocks us too when we recognise it. These initial responses of abhorrence and shock are understandable but unhelpful. And because we feel this to be so, the last decade has seen serious attempts to look below the surface and to fathom how such things can be. The aim must be prevention. But successful prevention requires of us that we should recognise the many circumstances which in various combinations lead families into deprivation and abuse.

We have to begin somewhere. And because a critical period is reached with bodily damage, broken bones, bruises, brain haemorrhage, death itself, the obvious point of departure is medical. So it was John Caffey, a radiologist, and Henry Kempe, a paediatrician, who began to collect the information about these kinds of bodily damage, of end results which form a pattern that can be recognised. Clinical recognition is the prerequisite for medical study. When there is medical diagnosis there is always a differential diagnosis and this also requires the expertise of doctors.

But if diagnosis is to lead to treatment, it cannot be exclusively medical. To diagnose means to know through and through. What has to be known is not only that the clinical picture results from trauma rather than another pathological process in the child, but that these are parents who have traumatised their child within the family setting. The quality of the parents and the characteristics of the family setting must therefore be diagnosed, tasks which need both a psychiatric and a social approach.

To be parents to children requires rather more than the ability to reproduce. Perhaps good parenting can be taught, and if so, by example rather than by precept; perhaps it depends altogether on human character

---

WHITE FRANKLIN, A. (1975) 'The nature of the task', in White Franklin, A. (ed.) *Concerning Child Abuse*, Edinburgh, Churchill Livingstone, pp. 1–3.

and instincts; in either case life experiences and the material environment play no small modifying part. Parents must have been seriously damaged by life before they can stub out their lighted cigarettes upon their baby's skin. The analysis of such deviant behaviour demands both epidemiology and insight. Common antecedents begin to emerge. Some of them point to a crisis from which recovery is possible, others to irreparable personality damage, with obvious implications for management. Unfortunately in some cases in present circumstances neither complete protection nor lasting rehabilitation is attainable.

Meanwhile epidemiological studies of accidents have begun to reveal patterns which suggest that recognisable aetiological factors are present in accidents of all kinds: poisoning, falls, traffic accidents, burns and scalds. Studies are also in progress about violence and intrafamilial aggression and about the results of deprivation and ineffective mothering upon the development of the child. Paediatricians have come to recognise increasingly the harm done by emotional deprivation to the child's emotional adjustment and behaviour and more recent studies have shown in addition stunting of physical growth (in height and weight) and slowing of intellectual development. Nurturing failure, especially in the early years of life, is now seen to be responsible for much damage to growing and developing children.

If our aim is the prevention of all such damage, the scope of studies and observations must be wide, linking the subject of child abuse to accidents in general on the one hand and to family pathology on the other. And this is concerned not only with the intrinsic psychopathology of the family and of the individuals who compose it, but also with the socioeconomic stresses playing upon the family from the environment in which the members live and work. The mother may have a below average intelligence, the father or stepfather may be an aggressive psychopath, but defective housing, unemployment, and the hostility of neighbours may also form part of the aetiology, though deprivation and abuse are not confined to families in the lower social groups. Today 'non-accidental injury to children' is seen to take its place in the wide context of social disorders in which defective care within the family leads to developmental failure, injury, or death.

When all the enquiries are set in train, medical, psychological, epidemiological, social, about the individual family, there remains a serious problem for the community, for society has to concern itself with crime and punishment. Non-accidental physical injury to a child is still a form of criminal assault, and criminal assault is confronted by the law, by the law's officers and the law's administrators. At the critical period of injury, behaviour emerges from the twilight of fantasy and imagination into a harsh world of accusing fingers, even of an accusing conscience. These two people are the parents who have battered their child. How can amends be made, how can life in the community be lived so labelled? The protection of the injured child, the punishment of guilty parents, how are these to be reconciled with the rehabilitation of the family?

The tasks of the police, the magistrates' courts and the judges may not be simplified by a better understanding of the nature of child abuse. Indeed for a time decisions may become more difficult. Better understanding of the parents could induce a lenience, a sympathy for them with the sacrifice of the safety of the child. At present the protection of the child, the siblings and of children yet unborn must be regarded as paramount, and the prevention of any repetition of injury to a child as a crisis demanding urgent decisions. The decision to remove the child or all the children may have the worst possible effect upon the eventual rehabilitation of the family. So may the imposition of prison sentences, and yet society must protect itself from the dangers of the aggressive psychopath. A place of safety order may be the only way of protecting the child from death or permanent disability. Safe solutions demand the most thorough medical and social study of the whole family or household.

Some practical measures are [necessary], their success depends upon two prerequisites. Firstly, in every locality a working system must be devised to ensure protection for the children and all relevant help for the families. Secondly, all professional workers in the locality must use the system once their suspicions have been aroused. Mutual confidence must grow between the different services and each worker must respect the professional skill of his colleagues. The statutory responsibility for child protection by social services departments has to be reconciled with the clinical responsibility of the doctor and the legal obligations of the police. Consultation has everywhere to replace unilateral action. A system of area review committees and case conferences, proposed by the Department of Health and Social Security, [deserves] whole-hearted support. . . .

Three main areas of difficulty exist: the doctor's problems with confidentiality; the policeman's reputed preoccupation with convictions; and the obstacles which the social worker's personal involvement with a family may place in the way of her objective assessment of a situation.

The general practitioner is less often consulted by these families because they tend to go directly to hospital. Nevertheless, he should be familiar with the type of family in which abuse may occur, and if his suspicions are roused he would be well advised to channel his patient into the system either through his attached health visitor or directly to his local paediatric department for immediate consultation and possible admission for protection and diagnosis. Sometimes with older children the school teacher or the educational welfare officer may be the first person to become concerned. The school medical service may then be the channel of entry directly through the general practitioner, or in the future through the paediatrician with community responsibility. . . .

6   Problems in methodology
Catherine Peckham

... Epidemiological studies are important as they enable the distribution patterns of child abuse in the community to be appreciated, causative factors to be identified and indicators of risk, essential for preventive intervention, to be recognized.

At present, we know very little about the true incidence of child abuse. It is unlikely that the extent of this problem will ever be defined accurately since a large number—perhaps the bulk—of abused children will never come to official notice. Not only is the distinction between abuse and non-abuse imprecise but in a case where the child does not receive grave physical injury and where help is not sought, reporting will not occur. Investigations are only as good as the technique used in the identification of cases and the quality of case finding and identification are highly important when assessing the incidence of any condition.

Before attempting to assess the incidence of child abuse it is thus of particular importance to define what is meant by child abuse, since in the absence of any clear and accepted definition of the term there will be great variation in estimates made of the extent of the problem. Comparisons between different studies will only become possible when criteria for child abuse on which all can agree have been defined. For instance, the term 'child abuse' refers to a much larger area of child maltreatment than the term 'battered child syndrome', including the attitudes of parent or guardian as well as the child's injury. Thus broadening the concept of child abuse will increase the number of reported cases.

Even compulsory legalized reporting is dependent upon the general awareness of the problem by the medical profession and affected by individual reluctance or enthusiasm to co-operate. In a survey which was carried out in New York in 1968 the numbers of reported cases rose dramatically after an intensive programme of community education and newspaper publicity (Kempe and Helfer 1972). The method of case reporting is of fundamental importance in the assessment of incidence. Great care must be exercised in the interpretation of information relating one time period to another and between different geographical areas, especially between countries with differing standards of medical docu-

PECKHAM, C. (1974) 'The dimensions of child abuse', in Carter, J. (ed.) *The Maltreated Child*, London, Priory Press, pp. 21–3.

mentation. The number of cases reported may vary according to the reportable age, for example the young child is more vulnerable than the older child and the age distribution of the childhood population under consideration is therefore important. The nature of the conditions reported, the professional groups required to report and the agencies to which the reports are made may all influence the total number of cases reported. Equally there may be variation in identification and reporting of incidents among differing sections of the community. In countries with a large private medical sector standards of reporting may differ between the public and private sectors. These factors have not been fully taken into account in the past, although they are likely to affect the validity of comparisons.

In some reports the syndrome has been defined simply in terms of the physical injuries of the child, ignoring the motivation and behaviour of the attacking parent. A satisfactory definition should include both aspects, the outcome and the parent's motivation. Motivation is particularly important from two aspects: the adoption of preventive measures in children who have already experienced abuse and in the identification of groups of adults and children who are particularly at risk. Gil defined the physical abuse of children as 'the intentional non-accidental use of physical force, or intentional, non-accidental acts of omission, on the part of a parent or other caretaker interacting with a child in his care aimed at hurting, injuring or destroying that child.' (Gil 1970). There are difficulties in such definitions, including the problems of distinguishing between intentional and accidental behaviour, the way that chance can operate upon intentional acts and also the way that unconsciously intentional elements can influence accidental behaviour.

However, it is important to attempt to grade abused children in terms of severity of injury if this is to be an indicator of the impact of the problem on society. At the same time it is equally important to detect minor episodes of physical child abuse since these frequently are early warning signals with an associated high risk of subsequent severe injury.

The population from which cases are identified is a further important issue. As pointed out previously, when a narrow definition of child abuse is employed there is likely to be greater agreement in estimated incidence rates in different studies. Cases of children admitted to hospital fall into this narrow range and should not be confused with true incidence rates. The majority of studies have been based on hospital or agency information and are not necessarily representative of the population at large. Only studies on large sized populations or on a national scale can furnish more realistic details concerning the incidence of child abuse in the various subsections of the community. . . .

References

GIL, D. G. (1970) *Violence against Children*, Cambridge, Mass., Harvard University Press.

KEMPE, C. H. and HELFER, H. E. (eds.) (1972) *Helping the battered Child and his Family*, Philadelphia, Lippincott.

7 Violence against children
David G. Gil

This paper is based on the author's book *Violence Against Children—Physical Child Abuse in the United States*. Cambridge, Massachusetts: Harvard University Press, 1970 (A Commonwealth Fund Book). The series of nationwide studies [of physical child abuse] summarized here were conducted by the author between 1965 and 1969 with support from the Children's Bureau, US Department of Health, Education, and Welfare. Reports on these studies were published previously in *American Education, Child Welfare, Pediatrics,* and *Social Work Practice.*

Study design and definition of subject

... [The survey] gathered standardized information on every incident of child abuse reported through legal channels throughout the United States during 1967 and 1968, nearly 13,000 incidents. This broadly-based survey was supplemented by more comprehensive case studies of nearly 1400 incidents reported during 1967 in a representative sample of 39 cities and counties. Further data sources, especially concerning the cultural roots of child abuse, were interviews in October of 1965 with 1520 adults from across the country selected at random so as to be representative of the entire US adult population, and a six months survey during 1965 of daily and periodical newspapers and magazines published throughout the United States. . . .

[In an effort to minimise ambiguity the following definition was used:]

> Physical abuse of children is intentional, non-accidental use of physical force, or intentional, non-accidental acts of omission, on the part of a parent or other caretaker in interaction with a child in his care, aimed at hurting, injuring, or destroying that child.

GIL, D. G. (1973) 'Violence against children', in Dreitzel, H. P. (ed.) *Childhood and Socialisation*, New York, Macmillan Press, London, Collier Macmillan, pp. 114–32.

[During 1967 and 1968, 5993 and 6617 reports to child abuse registries fitted the above description. The following extracts have been selected (1) to demonstrate the characteristics of abused children, and (2) to illustrate the attitude of society to the use of physical force as a method of child discipline.]

The families of abused children

Nearly 30 per cent of the abused children lived in female-headed households. The child's own father lived in the home in 46 per cent of the cases and a stepfather in nearly 20 per cent. Over 2 per cent of the children lived in foster homes, and 0.3 per cent lived with adoptive parents. The child's own mother was not living in his home in over 12 per cent. Ten per cent of the mothers were single, nearly 20 per cent were separated, divorced, deserted, or widowed, and over two-thirds were living with a spouse. The homes of non-white children were less frequently intact than those of white children. The data on family structure suggest an association between physical abuse of children and deviance from normative family structure, which seems especially strong for non-white children.

The age distribution of parents of abused children does not support observations according to which parents tend to be extremely young.

The proportion of families with four or more children was nearly twice as high among the families of the reported abused children than among all families with children under 18 in the US population, and the proportion of small families was much larger in the US population. The proportion of larger families among non-white families in the study was significantly higher than among white families.

Educational and occupational levels of parents were markedly lower than of the general population. Non-white parents ranked lower on these items than white ones. Nearly half the fathers of the abused children were not employed throughout the year, and about 12 per cent were actually unemployed at the time of the abusive act. Unemployment rates were higher for non-white fathers. . . .

Compared to all families in the United States, the income of families of abused children was very low and that of families of non-white abused children even lower. At the time of the abusive incident over 37 per cent of the families were receiving public assistance. Altogether nearly 60 per cent of the families had received public assistance at some time preceding the abusive incident.

Data concerning the personal history of the parents of the reported abused children suggested a level of deviance in areas of psychosocial functioning which exceeds deviance levels in the general population.

The incidents and the circumstances surrounding them

In nearly 50 per cent of the incidents a mother or stepmother was the perpetrator and in about 40 per cent a father. However, since about 30 per cent of the homes were female-headed, the involvement rate of fathers was actually higher than that of mothers. Two-thirds of incidents in homes with fathers or stepfathers present were committed by fathers or stepfathers, while mothers or stepmothers were the perpetrators in less than half the incidents occurring in homes with mothers or stepmothers present. Over 70 per cent of the children were abused by a biological parent, nearly 14 per cent by a stepparent, less than one per cent by an adoptive parent, 2 per cent by a foster parent, about one per cent by a sibling, 4 per cent by other relatives, and nearly 7 per cent by an unrelated caretaker. Fifty-one per cent of the children were abused by a female perpetrator.

Perpetrators tended to have little education and a low socio-economic status. About 61 per cent of them were members of minority groups, 56.8 per cent had shown deviations in social and behavioral functioning during the year preceding the abuse incident and about 12.3 per cent had been physically ill during that year. Nearly 11 per cent showed deviations in intellectual functioning, 7.1 per cent had been in mental hospitals some time prior to the incident, 8.4 per cent before Juvenile Courts, and 7.9 per cent in foster care. Under 14 per cent had a criminal record. About 11 per cent had been victims of abuse during their childhood, and 52.5 per cent had been perpetrators of abuse prior to the current incident. . . .

A conceptual model of physical child abuse

Culturally sanctioned use of physical force in child rearing

One important conclusion of the nationwide surveys was that physical abuse of children as defined here is not a rare and unusual occurrence in our society, and that by itself it should therefore not be considered as sufficient evidence of 'deviance' of the perpetrator, the child, or the family. Physical abuse appears to be endemic in American society since our cultural norms of child rearing do not preclude the use of a certain measure of physical force toward children by adults caring for them. Rather, such use tends to be encouraged in subtle, and at times not so subtle, ways by 'professional experts' in child rearing, education, and medicine; by the press, radio and television; and by professional and popular publications. Furthermore, children are not infrequently subjected to physical abuse in the public domain in such settings as schools, child care facilities, foster homes, correctional and other children's institutions, and even in juvenile courts.

Strong support for considering child abuse as endemic in American society was provided by the public opinion survey, which revealed that nearly 60 per cent of adult Americans thought that 'almost anybody could at some time injure a child in his care.' That survey also indicated that several millions of children may be subjected every year to a wide range of physical abuse, though only several thousands suffer serious physical injury and a few hundred die as a consequence of abusive attacks. Against the background of public sanction of the use of violence against children, and the endemic scope of the prevalence of such cases, it should surprise no one that extreme incidents will occur from time to time in the course of 'normal' child rearing practices.

It should be noted that in most incidents of child abuse the caretakers involved are 'normal' individuals exercising their prerogative of disciplining a child whose behavior they find in need of correction. While some of these adults may often go farther than they intended because of anger and temporary loss of self-control, and/or because of chance events, their behavior does, nevertheless, not exceed the normative range of disciplining children as defined by the existing culture. Moreover, their acts are usually not in conflict with any law since parents, as well as teachers and other child care personnel, are in many American jurisdictions permitted to use a 'reasonable' amount of corporal punishment. For children are not protected by law against bodily attack in the same way as are adults and, consequently, do not enjoy 'equal protection under the law' as guaranteed by the XIVth Amendment to the US Constitution.

While, then, culturally sanctioned and patterned use of physical force in child rearing seems to constitute the basic causal dimension of all violence against children in American society, it does not explain many specific aspects of this phenomenon, especially its differential incidence rates among different population segments. Several additional causal dimensions need therefore be considered in interpreting the complex dynamics of physical child abuse.

Difference in child rearing patterns among social strata and ethnic groups

Different social and economic strata of society, and different ethnic and nationality groups tend to differ for various environmental and cultural reasons in their child rearing philosophies and practices, and consequently in the extent to which they approve of corporal punishment of children. These variations in child rearing styles among social and economic strata constitute a second set of causal dimensions of child abuse, and are reflected in significant variations in incidence rates among these strata and groups. Thus, for instance, incidence rates tend to be negatively correlated with education and income. Also, certain ethnic groups reveal characteristic incidence patterns. Some American Indian tribes will never use physical force in disciplining their children while the incidence rates of child abuse are relatively high among American blacks and Puerto Ricans.

Lest the higher incidence rates among black and Puerto Rican minority groups be misinterpreted, it should be remembered that as a result of centuries of discrimination, non-white ethnic minority status tends to be associated in American society with low educational achievement and low income. The incidence rates of child abuse among these minority groups are likely to reflect this fact, as much as their specific cultural patterns. Furthermore, exposure of these minority groups to various forms of external societal violence to which they could not respond in kind, is likely to have contributed over time to an increase in the level of frustration-generated violence directed against their own members. Relatively high rates of homicide among members of these minority groups seem to support this interpretation.

Higher reporting rates of physical child abuse, and especially of more serious incidents, among the poor and among non-white minority groups may reflect biased reporting procedures. It may be true that the poor and non-whites are more likely to be reported than middle class and white population groups for anything they do or fail to do. At the same time there may also be considerable under-reporting of reportable transgressions not only among middle class and white population groups but also among the poor and the non-white minorities. The net effect of reporting bias and of overall and specific under-reporting with respect to child abuse can, at this time, not be estimated.

It should not be overlooked, however, that life in poverty and in minority group ghettos tends to generate many stressful experiences which are likely to become precipitating factors of child abuse by weakening a caretaker's psychological mechanisms of self-control and contributing, thus, to the uninhibited discharge of his aggressive and destructive impulses toward physically powerless children. The poor and members of ethnic minority groups seem to be subject to many of the conditions and forces which may lead to abusive behavior toward children in other groups of the population and, in addition to this, they seem to be subject to the special environmental stresses and strains associated with socioeconomic deprivation and discrimination. This would suggest that the significantly higher reporting rates for poor and non-white segments of the population reflect a real underlying higher incidence rate among these groups.

It should also be noted that the poor and non-whites tend to have more children per family unit and less living space. They also tend to have fewer alternatives than other population groups for avoiding or dealing with aggressive impulses toward their children. The poor tend to discharge aggressive impulses more directly as they seem less inhibited in expressing feelings through action. These tendencies are apparently learned through lower class and ghetto socialization, which tends to differ in this respect from middle class socialization and mores. Middle class parents, apparently as a result of exposure to modern psychological theories of child rearing, tend to engage more than lower class parents in verbal interaction with their children, and to use psychological approaches in disciplining them. It may be noted, parenthetically, that verbal and psychological interaction with children may at times be as violent and abusive in its effects, or even more so, than the use of physical force in disciplining them. Life in middle class families tends to generate tensions and pressures characteristic of the dominant individualistic and competitive value orientations of American society, and these pressures may also precipitate violence against children. However, middle class families are spared the more devastating daily tensions and pressures of life in poverty. They also tend to have fewer children, more living space, and more options to relax, at times, without their children. All this would suggest a lower real incidence rate of physical child abuse among middle class families. . . .

[In this national survey an attempt was made to explore many contributing causal factors which could have precipitated child abuse. One major type of circumstance of abuse involved incidents developing out of disciplinary action taken by angry perpetrators.]

8 The critical path
Margaret A. Lynch

The abuse of a child is the result of a process with origins before that child's birth. A series of interrelated events, both medical and social, lead up to the final outburst.

The family's history can be set out in the form of a flow diagram or critical path, showing how a parent comes to abuse a child. In every case warnings are given before the actual abuse. By learning to read these warnings, it is possible to offer help before a disaster occurs.

The critical path illustrated [below] demonstrates how one child came to be abused by her mother. Cindy, a second child, was admitted to hospital at age 6 months, with severe failure to thrive and multiple minor bruises. Both parents came from unhappy backgrounds; the father, Robert, the youngest of five, grew up in poverty. His father was killed when he was 14. Thereafter he had to live up to his mother's unrealistic expectations. Mother, Linda, also from a large family was subject to rigid religious discipline. Robert and Linda were childhood sweethearts, but the romance ended when Robert, after failing in school, joined the forces to escape from his mother.

Linda was intelligent and held a responsible job, but her social life was a failure, with many unhappy affairs. She met Robert again when he was home on leave, married on impulse, and returned overseas with him. She was isolated and he felt trapped. They decided to have a child. The pregnancy was easy and their son John was born by planned Caesarean section because of mother's small stature. He was a happy responsive baby; both parents bonded to him immediately and were happy, but only for a short time. A row with their landlord led to a sudden move, and a planned holiday back home was disrupted because Robert was refused leave.

Linda returned home alone with her seven months old son. To her horror she realized she was pregnant. She was unable to return to her husband because of a threatened miscarriage; when she did return it was against medical advice. She spent months in hospital to avert premature labour. John spent this time in foster homes, his behaviour deteriorating. Even before delivery Linda warned about her ability to cope with a second

LYNCH, M. A. (1976) 'Child abuse: the critical path', *Journal of Maternal and Child Health*, July, pp. 25–9.

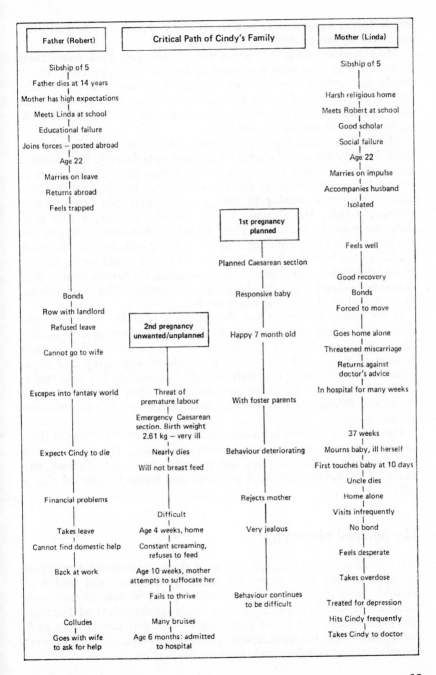

Father (Robert)	Critical Path of Cindy's Family	Mother (Linda)
Sibship of 5		Sibship of 5
Father dies at 14 years		Harsh religious home
Mother has high expectations		Meets Robert at school
Meets Linda at school		Good scholar
Educational failure		Social failure
Joins forces — posted abroad		Age 22
Age 22		Marries on impulse
Marries on leave		Accompanies husband
Returns abroad		Isolated
Feels trapped		
	1st pregnancy planned	
		Feels well
	Planned Caesarean section	
		Good recovery
Bonds	Responsive baby	Bonds
Row with landlord		Forced to move
Refused leave	**2nd pregnancy unwanted/unplanned**	
	Happy 7 month old	Goes home alone
Cannot go to wife		Threatened miscarriage
		Returns against doctor's advice
Escapes into fantasy world	Threat of premature labour	In hospital for many weeks
	Emergency Caesarean section. Birth weight 2.61 kg — very ill	With foster parents
		37 weeks
Expects Cindy to die	Nearly dies	Mourns baby, ill herself
	Will not breast feed	First touches baby at 10 days
		Uncle dies
Financial problems	Rejects mother	Home alone
	Difficult	Visits infrequently
Takes leave	Age 4 weeks, home	No bond
Cannot find domestic help	Constant screaming, refuses to feed	
		Feels desperate
Back at work	Age 10 weeks, mother attempts to suffocate her	
		Takes overdose
	Fails to thrive	Behaviour continues to be difficult
		Treated for depression
Colludes	Many bruises	Hits Cindy frequently
Goes with wife to ask for help	Age 6 months: admitted to hospital	Takes Cindy to doctor

child. Robert was unable to face reality and escaped into a fantasy world accumulating large debts.

The pregnancy ended at 37 weeks with an emergency Caesarean section. A healthy near term baby was expected, but Cindy was extremely ill and nearly died several times. Mother was unable to touch her for 10 days and breast feeding failed. The puerperium was stormy, Linda having the additional blow of her favourite uncle's death. She went home, feeling ill, leaving Cindy in the special care unit.

The parents visited Cindy infrequently and she was already a colicky difficult baby. She was discharged a stranger to her family. She screamed constantly and refused to feed. Robert took time off work, but when he returned they were unable to find domestic help. Linda became desperate and gave another warning by taking an overdose after attempting to suffocate Cindy. Her depression was treated in isolation with anti-depressants and tranquillisers. These helped to release her aggression and the assaults on Cindy continued. Robert actively colluded, unable to ask for help. They kept the child in the house so no one would see the bruises. Fortunately before any serious damage occurred, the parents went to their doctor and asked for Cindy to be admitted to hospital. This eventually led to successful therapy for the whole family.

In this family we can see how the parents' biography, social and emotional stresses and medical problems form the complex process leading up to the abuse of Cindy. The parents were more vulnerable than most because of their harsh backgrounds, emotional immaturity and social isolation. They began to rear their first child successfully but were unable to bond to their daughter—the unwanted, ill product of a difficult pregnancy and delivery. It was she who failed to thrive and was ultimately abused.

There never is a single cause for abuse. Before a child is battered there has been a build-up of stresses within the family. The parents' own biography frequently increases the potential for abuse (Pollock and Steele 1972). Subsequent social pressures and medical events all play a role.

The parents' biography

Many abusing parents themselves suffered abuse or emotional deprivation as children. They have grown up hostile to authority and unable to establish basic trust. Often they remain bonded in hate to their own parents. The women in particular have angry yet dependent relationships with their mothers. It is not surprising to find that people from such backgrounds meet and are accepted by only those with similar experiences; assortive mating therefore tends to occur.

Often they plan a pregnancy or marry in an effort to escape from a harsh and rigid home. Frequently they are both, in actual and in emotional age, too young for parenthood (Smith 1973, NSPCC 1975). In a recent series in Oxford (Lynch 1975) an area where less than 9 per cent of deliveries are to women under 20, 40 per cent of abusive mothers were under that age when they had their first child. Their own parents demanded much of them as children, so they in their turn have unrealistic expectations of a child's behaviour and development.

Social aspects

Abusing parents can come from any socio-economic group (Lynch 1975, Kempe 1971, Lynch 1976); certain characteristics however are shared. They are frequently isolated both physically and emotionally (Schneider 1972). They choose, wherever possible, to live in houses cut off from the rest of society; few have a telephone and when they do the number is ex-directory. Initial approaches from neighbours, social workers, health visitors and doctors are rejected. 'We keep ourselves to ourselves'.

They have few contacts outside their nuclear family. There is no one they trust; no one to call in a crisis. Even before they are driven to battering a child, such families have frequently accumulated a whole range of interlocking problems affecting every aspect of their lives; the marriage, housing, financial matters and employment (Lynch 1976).

In Oxford over half the mothers later referred for actual or threatened abuse had been seen by the social worker at the maternity hospital around the time the abused child was born (Lynch 1976). The diffuse nature of the mother's social problems at that time distinguished her from the majority of women seeking social work help. The problems these high-risk-women experienced with relationships in and outside the family also became very clear during the social work contact. Indeed many had evoked concern over their 'mothering' abilities even before they left the hospital.

Faced by a rising tide of emotional and social problems, many parents escape from reality into a fantasy world; a world that can become very difficult to break into.

Medical problems

A minority of children are abused by a psychotic parent (Kempe 1971). This is a particularly dangerous situation if the actual act of battering is part of the parent's delusional system. The majority of abusing parents have no formal psychiatric illness. If they have seen a psychiatrist they are likely to have been labelled personality disorder—untreatable. Until recently we were finding that up to 90 per cent of the mothers and many fathers had at some time been on tranquillisers or anti-depressants, usually benzodiazepines and tricyclics prescribed unwittingly for complaints of anxiety and depression. It is now recognized that these often useful drugs can, by removing inhibition, precipitate a battering episode (Grey 1976).

Any parent who is ill is more likely to have difficulties in relating to the child. Frequently we have found that mothers of abused children have minor health problems. Excessive tiredness, iron deficiency, anaemia, severe dental caries and headaches are all commonly found. Many have gynaecological problems and could benefit from contraceptive advice. Sometimes a parent may be seriously ill. Diagnoses of mothers treated at the Park Hospital for Children have included chronic renal disease, thyrotoxicosis, tuberculosis, multiple sclerosis and cerebral tumour.

Frequently one finds a history of marital and sexual difficulties which have exacerbated the parents' feeling of frustration. Sometimes it is the ill health of an unharmed sibling that aggravates the situation—an illness that is minor but extremely irritating such as eczema or mild wheezing. When a loved and accepted toddler's behaviour deteriorates following the birth of a new baby, the parents may well blame the new arrival, abusing him rather than the older sibling.

About 80 per cent of families with more than one child abuse only one. By comparing the biographies of battered children with those of their unharmed brothers and sisters we can see with clarity the very significant role ill health can play in the abused child's early life (Lynch 1973). As with Cindy, medical ill health, together with the inevitable separations, can lead to the bonding failure which so often precedes abuse.

The abused child is much more likely to have been the product of a difficult pregnancy and delivery. He may well have been premature or ill as a neonate, requiring intensive medical treatment in a special care unit. When compared with his unharmed siblings, he is more likely to have had other separations from the family in the first six months of life. Either he or his mother are more likely to have been sick in the first year. The effect that the long hospitalisation of a young mother can have on the relationship between her and her children is easily overlooked. Such a separation, especially in a family with no close extended family or friends, can be as traumatic as a separation which results from the admission of the child.

It is easy to understand how any of the early events described can interfere with the establishment of a healthy bond between parent and child. In the history of many abused children, as in Cindy's, we find not one, but a whole sequence of adverse medical events leading to the catastrophe of abuse.

Of course, many families are confronted with such problems and very few actually abuse their child. However for families with a high potential for abuse, such factors taken together with a knowledge of the family's biography can act as valuable warnings. An opportunity then exists for both doctor and family to recognize potential problems and to plan preventative action.

Also by being aware of the association between early ill health and subsequent abuse it is possible to identify groups of families who are likely to be more vulnerable than others. For example, over 40 per cent of abused children in our area were in the special care nursery because of prematurity or illness. Extra attention is now being paid to all parents with babies in the special care nursery (12 per cent of live births in 1975 required admission to the nursery). They are seen by an experienced social worker and given the opportunity to discuss practical and emotional problems. Only a very few are likely to abuse their child, but all can only be helped by this approach.

Any medical problem with the child, especially a continuing or recurrent one, can in vulnerable families contribute significantly to the process culminating in abuse. Particularly distressing and provoking is undiagnosed illness in a child. Examples seen in our service have included congenital blindness, chromosomal abnormalities, developmental delay due to cerebellar ataxia and haemophilia.

It is not only severe illness which can disrupt the parent–child relationship. Parents who abuse have high and unrealistic expectations of their child's behaviour and development (Schneider 1972). They are frequently demanding and rigid. Any child who steps outside the boundaries set by such parents is at risk of abuse; a child of the wrong sex, a messy feeder, a clumsy slow learner or a bed wetter. Some of these children will be constantly brought before the doctor with seemingly never ending complaints about their health or behaviour. With some knowledge of the child's family such visits can act as warnings of disturbed family relationships.

Prior to a severe assault many parents have given more explicit warning in the form of what we have termed open warning (Ounsted and Lynch 1976). They have taken their child to an accident room or doctor and displayed minor injuries. Often these injuries are diagnostic; bleeding from the mouth, bruising on the cheek or buttocks of a young baby. All too frequently the true significance of such injuries is ignored until after the child is injured again.

Conclusion

By understanding the process that leads to abuse it becomes possible to identify the factors and circumstances that increase the risk of battering. Only when all those concerned with the welfare of young families are prepared to take this holistic approach can effective prevention begin.

References

GREY, J. A. (1976) 'Drug effects on fear and frustration', in Iverson, L., Iverson, S. and Snyder, S. (eds.) *Handbook of Psychopharmacology*, New York, Plenum Press. In press.

KEMPE, C. H. (1971) Paediatric implications of the battered baby syndrome', *Archives of Disease in Childhood*, **46**, 28.

LYNCH, M. A. (1975) 'Ill health and child abuse', *Lancet*, **2**, 127.

LYNCH, M. A. et al. (1976) 'Early warning of child abuse in the maternity hospital', *Developmental Medicine and Child Neurology*. In press.

LYNCH, M. A. and OUNSTED, C. (1976) 'A place of safety', in Helfer, R. E. and Kempe, C. H. (eds.) *Child Abuse and Neglect. The Family and the Community*, Cambridge, Mass., Ballinger.

NSPCC (1975) *Registers of Suspected Non-accidental Injury*. A report on registers maintained in Leeds and Manchester by NSPCC Special Units.

OUNSTED, C. and LYNCH, M. A. (1976) 'Family pathology as seen in England', in Helfer, R. E. and Kempe, C. H. (eds.) *Child Abuse and Neglect. The Family and the Community*, Cambridge, Mass., Ballinger.

POLLOCK, C. and STEELE, B. (1972) A therapeutic approach to the parents, in Kempe C. H. and Helfer, R. E. (eds.) *Helping the Battered Child and his Family*, Philadelphia and Toronto, Lippincott.

SCHNEIDER, C. et al. (1972) 'Interviewing the parents', in Kempe, C. H. and Helfer, R. E. (eds.) *Helping the Battered Child and his Family*, Philadelphia and Toronto, Lippincott.

SMITH, S. M. et al. (1973) 'Parents of battered babies. A controlled study', *British Medical Journal*, **4**, 388.

Part Three Aspects of child abuse

The papers in this section deal with specific aspects of child abuse ranging from the medical diagnosis to the views of an abusing parent. Medical, paediatric and social perspectives are discussed as well as the predicament of the child. The importance of history-taking is emphasized by all the contributors and because in cases of suspected or known abuse this is a delicate matter, short articles on interviewing parents are included.

9 Clinical features of child abuse
David Hull

Bruising

Once a baby begins to toddle, he topples over often and bruises his legs and forehead frequently. However, bruising of the thorax, abdomen and around the mouth occurs far less frequently due to accident. Therefore, bruising in these areas in a child under the age of two or bruising anywhere in a baby who is not mobile is suspicious of non-accidental injury. Often, if a screaming baby is shaken rapidly by his parents then there may be finger-tip bruising in such a manner that it is not difficult to see how the baby has been held and squeezed. The finger and thumb marks may be seen along the back or across the chest or occasionally around the mouth (Figures 1, 2).

Bruises come and go quickly. A photograph will record the event but it is probably advisable to seek the parents' permission to do this and it won't be accepted in court unless the photographer is present to witness that he took the photograph of that child on that day. To exclude bleeding disorders, haematologists recommend a number of tests which might include a platelet count, partial thromboplastin test and prothrombin time. These investigations will exclude most known bleeding disorders.

Bony injuries

These are often the most characteristic finding in a 'battered baby'. Again, immobile babies rarely break their bones. Toddlers rarely sustain more than greenstick fractures. Snapping of the bone with marked displacement can be produced by rapid bending of the limb by an adult. However, the injuries are usually far more subtle and are related to the characteristics of the growing bone. At the end of each long bone is the growing plate, called the metaphysis, beyond which is the developing cartilage, or epiphysis (Figure 3). If the bone is pulled it gives at the weakest area, namely the metaphysis and produces on the radiograph the features of epiphyseal separation. These changes could be produced by

---

HULL, D. (1974) 'Medical diagnosis', in Carter, J. (ed.) *The Maltreated Child*, London, Priory Press, pp. 61–6.

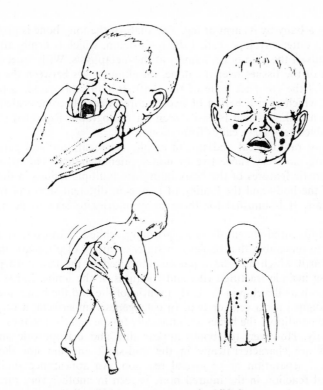

Figures 1 and 2. Finger tip bruising sometimes seen in child abuse.

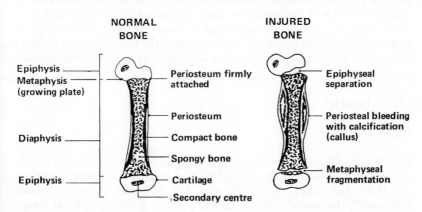

Figure 3. Diagrammatic representation of a normal bone and a bone injured by pulling and squeezing the growing limb.

63

swinging a baby by its arm or leg. The shaft of the long bone is protected by a thin outer envelope, called the periosteum, which is firmly attached at the ends of the long bone, namely at the metaphysis. With squeezing or rotation of the tissues over the bone, bleeding occurs between the periosteum and the compact bone of the shaft. Initially this causes a painful swelling which over a period of two or three weeks becomes calcified to produce a callus, which is easily seen on radiograph. Repeated injuries can produce very large callus formation.

The two radiological findings, of epiphyseal separation and periosteal thickening, are very suggestive of non-accidental injury. The other two characteristic features of the bony injury are multiple lesions in different parts of the body and the finding of lesions at different stages of healing and repair. It is unusual for these bony injuries to lead to permanent damage.

The differential diagnosis is surprisingly limited. However, it is important to remember that babies can suffer a variety of traumatic injuries during birth which may have passed unnoticed in the new-born period and these include fractured ribs and fractures of the limbs. Large callus formation may develop in the early months of life and the bones may not have realigned for a year or two. In osteogenesis imperfecta, a very rare inherited condition, the bones are unusually fragile and the fractures occur very easily. However, the bones appear thin and osteoporotic and the fractures are characteristically in the mid-shaft and are not those of epiphyseal separation or periosteal reaction. An appearance similar to periosteal reaction in the injured bone is seen in another very rare condition, infantile cortical hyperostosis. However, the radiographic changes are not easily confused. In this condition the jaw is affected in ninety-five per cent of cases. Periosteal reactions are also found in congenital syphilis and scurvy but both conditions are easily diagnosed. Epiphyseal separation does occur if vigorous physiotherapy is used to avoid contractures in neurologically abnormal limbs, for example in the lower limbs of children with spina bifida. However, the lack of sensitivity can be demonstrated.

Head injuries

Skull fractures

Infants and children may fall or be dropped on their heads and crack their skulls, but it is occasionally discovered that infants are swung by the leg and their skulls crack against the wall. The diagnosis of fractured skull can usually be made without difficulty from a radiograph, although aberrant suture lines can sometimes closely mimic a fracture. The management and prognosis is that of the associated brain damage. The infant may be killed immediately, or may die due to progressive intracranial bleeding without gaining consciousness, or may initially recover well only to deteriorate because of continued bleeding in the head. The nature of the injury says little of the way it occurred.

Sub-dural haematomas

However, infants can begin to bleed beneath the skull and around the brain following injury without the skull being fractured. The bleeding may be very slow to develop and the diagnosis, therefore, very difficult to reach. It was the recognition of the association of sub-dural bleeding with bony injuries elsewhere which led Caffey to suggest that both may be due to a non-accidental injury (Caffey 1946).

A sub-dural bleed may follow a sharp bang on the head, particularly on the front or back, but it is also possible that rapid shaking of the head may tear the fine veins which travel inwards over the surface of the brain to the large mid-line drainage vein (Figure 4) (Guthkelch 1971). Infants

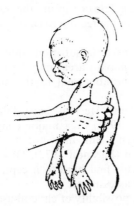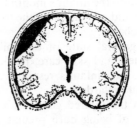

Figure 4. Rocking the head rapidly from front to back may tear delicate veins and cause bleeding around the brain—a sub-dural haematoma.

with sub-dural haemorrhages may start to fit or vomit or become unduly drowsy or unwilling to feed. On the other hand, the lesion may only come to light when it has harmed the brain sufficiently to interfere with the child's mental and physical development. The doctor examining such infants may find the soft spot (anterior fontanelle) between the skull bones to be bulging and there may be bleeds in the retina at the back of the eye,

E

the head may be unduly large or rapidly enlarging. Again blood may press on and damage the underlying brain causing palsies of the eyes and limbs (Russell 1965).

Once the condition is recognized a needle can usually be put into the haematoma and the pressure released. This can be repeated as long as pressure is present (McLauren 1971). Very occasionally more extensive procedures may be required.

The possibility that the child with a sub-dural haemorrhage has been damaged should always be considered. However, the injury could be accidental and occasionally similar lesions can follow infections around the brain. Also it is not known to what extent anatomical anomalies and variations may predispose to cerebral vein rupture.

Other clinical features

A wide variety of injuries have been reported in infants following assaults by their guardians, including rupture of viscera (liver, spleen, kidneys), eye injuries with subsequent impairment of vision and a variety of skin lesions as well as obvious abrasions and burns. Instruments may be pushed into the infant's mouth to injure the palate or rupture the frenulum (i.e. the fold of skin under the tongue) or into the rectum to cause bleeding and discharge.

The general state of the child with respect to nutrition, infestation, cleanliness and skin care, particularly the napkin area, may be unsatisfactory. The infant's responsiveness may be abnormal to the point of appearing retarded.

Often the injured child has other problems. He may have difficulties because of being born prematurely (Klein 1971) or a major congenital anomaly requiring surgery. A close maternal link may not have been established in the critical period after birth (Faranoff 1972). Or he may have an unsightly anomaly which his parents find hard to accept. These features should also be noted in the initial assessment.

Once clinical features have suggested the possibility of child abuse, then it is important to expand the clinical history, with certain aspects in mind. The following features many of which may be found in the illustration, would suggest that the child has been injured by the parents.

1. There is an unexplained delay from the time of the injury to the time when the child is brought to medical attention.
2. It is highly improbable that the accident which the guardians described could have led to the injury found or features of the story as given by the parents or guardians are known or found to be untrue.

3. The child has frequently been taken to other doctors and other hospitals for a variety of problems.
4. The mother confesses that at times when the baby has been irritable or annoying that she has felt she wanted to shake it, or the parents hint that one of them might have injured the child.
5. The parents are sick, withdrawn, or behave in an inappropriate way, or perhaps always communicate physically.

In medical practice we often make decisions on the basis of the probability of a suspected diagnosis. These criteria are not adequate when a diagnosis has got to be established by law. It is, therefore, necessary for us to consider what is acceptable as medical evidence of child abuse in the law courts. To take a child into care it is necessary to establish in all probability that the child has been wilfully injured and that, in simple terms, means excluding all other possibilities. This requires sometimes doing investigations which under other circumstances would not be considered reasonable, for example tests to exclude bleeding diseases when a child is bruised. It is often important to decide early in the management of a child whether or not the diagnosis has been established in the legal sense.

Once the diagnosis is entertained, it is necessary from the legal as well as medical point of view to document carefully the injuries observed and the story as presented by the parent and to obtain a full and detailed social history.

References

CAFFEY, J. (1946) Multiple Fractures in the Long Bones of Infants Suffering from Chronic Subdural Hematoma', *Amer. J. Roentgenol.* **56,** 163–73.

FARANOFF, A. A., KENNELL, J. H. and KLAUS, M. H. (1972) 'Follow up of Low Birth Weight Infants—the Predictive Value of Visiting Patterns', *Paediatrics,* **49,** 287–90.

GUTHKELCH, 'Infantile Subdural Haematoma and its Relationship to Whiplash Injuries', *Brit. Med. J.,* **7,** 430.

KLEIN, M. and STERN, L. (1971) 'Low Birth Weight and the Battered Child Syndrome', *American Journal of Diseases of Childhood,* **122,** 15–18.

MCLAUREN, R. L., ISAACS, E. and LEWIS, H. P. (1971) 'Results of Non-operative Treatment in Fifteen Cases of Infantile Subdural Haematoma', *Journal of Neurosurgery,* **34,** 753–9.

RUSSELL, P. A. (1965) 'Subdural Haematoma in Infancy', *Brit. Med. J.,* **2,** 446–8.

10 After abuse: the medical interview
M. H. Hall

If the preliminary history and examination raises the possibility of a non-accidental injury further information must be obtained from the parents. This initial interview should be carried out as soon as possible by a person with experience of these cases. The object is to make a preliminary assessment of the family situation and to try and discover what stresses or strains may be present. It is NOT to discover who is responsible for the injuries, though in the course of the discussion this might become apparent.

It should be held in a room where interruptions can be avoided. A cup of tea can go a long way to easing the atmosphere. A senior member of the nursing staff should be present and the child should whenever possible be looked after by the nursing staff. If both parents are present the writer prefers to leave the child in the care of one of the parents whilst the other is being interviewed. They can then change places and after both have been interviewed a joint interview can be held.

The whole discussion should be 'low key'. Admissions, criticism, blame and accusations must be excluded however difficult this may be. There is no place for any emotional involvement by the doctor. A useful opening approach, especially towards the mother, is to ask her 'How are things with you?' or 'when did you last have a good night's sleep?'

Once the initial strain has subsided it is frequently found that it is difficult to stop the parent talking. The sense of release that can be obtained from a sympathetic non-accusing initial interview can go far to make the subsequent management an easier matter. On occasions the parents may be aggressive and rude; to react in a similar manner however mildly, increases the hostility and renders management of the situation at a later stage a much more difficult undertaking.

The length of the interview must be assessed by the response of the parents. If they appear co-operative and anxious to talk it is advisable to allow the interview to continue until no further information is forthcoming. If, however, the response is hostile it is better to terminate the interview as soon as the essential facts have been obtained.

The doctor must be quite open in his dealings with the parents. At the beginning of the interview he must explain that he is concerned about

---

HALL, M. H. (1974), 'The diagnosis and early management of non-accidental injuries in children', *The Police Surgeon*, October, pp. 21–2.

the discrepancies between the history and the injuries found and that he is anxious to investigate the matter further. Unless, at the conclusion of the interview, he is completely satisfied that the child's condition is due to a true accident the child must be admitted to a place of safety. When treatment or investigation is required this is usually the hospital wards, but occasionally a local authority or foster home may be appropriate.

The reasons for this step must be explained to the parents and if they are not prepared to agree to it being carried out on a voluntary basis then a 'Place of Safety' order must be obtained by the Local Authority Social Services, the National Society for the Prevention of Cruelty to Children or a Police Officer not below the rank of Inspector.

The doctor must provide a short certificate stating that he has examined the child, has found certain injuries and recommends removal to a place of safety. This certificate is placed before a magistrate who issues an order which allows the child to be taken into care for a period of up to twenty-eight days after which the order must be discharged or the matter brought before a court.

If the child is admitted to hospital on a voluntary basis and the parents subsequently decide to remove him before the investigations are completed, it is necessary to obtain a similar order. There is indeed, much to be said for obtaining such an order in the majority of cases as it avoids the attempted removal of the child in the middle of the night and simplifies the explanation as to why the child cannot be discharged, even though he appears perfectly fit.

11 After abuse: the social worker's interview
The NSPCC Battered Child Research Team

Crisis intervention and how we introduced ourselves

It would be true to say that the first interview was a time of crisis for the child, the parents and equally for the worker. We had to try to convey to the parents that we were there to help and not to punish them. We were therefore very cautious in our initial approach, as we did not wish to jeopardize our chances of continued success with them. With the first few cases, this brought about initial hesitancy in introducing ourselves as social workers from a child protective agency, involved because of the child's injuries. Other cases presenting particular difficulties to us were those in which recent injuries were not visible on referral, or where parents had not been informed about our involvement. To these parents we tended to introduce ourselves as social workers from a small research team, who wanted 'to try and help families who had similar problems to them with their young children.' However, these 'problems' were not made explicit. One worker remarks, 'I was desperate to give a plausible and fairly honest account of why I was there, but expected from what others had said that the mother would be hostile; I was afraid of threatening her and being denied access.' The first interview with this mother was conducted on the doorstep, the worker being greeted by the abrupt words, 'What do you want?' Another worker who decided that the first interview with a very resistant mother was 'the wrong time to come clean', subsequently wrote her a letter explaining 'the hospital asked me to see you because your baby had a couple of injuries and it can be difficult to be a young mother on your own a lot, with a young baby and maybe not know whom to turn to if you need help.' As we grew more confident, and as later cases tended to be those with serious referral injuries, we were less hesitant about identifying ourselves and our agency during the first contact with the parents. We also made early reference to our specialised interest in helping families where young children had been injured.

Probably at no time were we more concerned to convey ourselves to the parents as a caring, undemanding presence than during the first interview when stress was at or near its peak. A dramatic illustration is provided by

BAHER, E. et al. (eds.) (1976) *At Risk: An Account of the Work of the Battered Child Research Department*, NSPCC London, Routledge, pp. 137–9.

a family referred before midnight. The baby had just been admitted to hospital in a critical condition and the mother was waiting in the ward. The social worker visited within the hour and sensed that the mother could not face what was happening or what had led to the child's admission. The mother wanted to talk about mundane topics such as the price of vegetables and simply have someone wholly with her. The worker stayed chatting with her for most of the night until the mother felt comforted enough to allow exhaustion to take over and was driven home to bed. The development of a good therapeutic relationship was dependent to some extent on the circumstances surrounding our intervention. . . . Undoubtedly prompt referral and prompt visiting as in the above case made for much better initial contact. In contrast delays in referral of only a few days seemed to foster avoidance and resistance in the parents.

The help we offered in the crisis period was obviously dependent on the particular problems presented by individual cases and the emotional state of the parents at the time of intervention. However, the primary focus in all cases was on providing a 'life line' for the parents . . . 'I gave her my card, described how the on-call system worked and suggested that as she got to know me better, she might feel able to call and get someone to visit if she was feeling at the end of her tether with the kids or wanted company.' Another important focus was the provision of relief in caring for the children in the home, usually through the offer of alternative care for them . . . 'my first offer of help was a day nursery placement for a purported hyperactive child.' During this early crisis period our offers to approach other agencies on their behalf were an important means of gaining the parents' trust, while often the offer of practical help was the first acceptable way of demonstrating our concern for them. In all cases, we felt that one of our most valuable functions was attentive listening and providing the opportunity to share anxiety and release pent up emotions.

There is no doubt that in some cases, our anxiety about the initial contact was exacerbated by difficulty in communicating with the parents. A few interviews were described as 'the hardest half hour of my life . . .'; 'an uphill task . . .'; 'fraught and difficult'. This applied equally to interviews with one parent alone or with both parents. However, a few joint interviews were particularly difficult, either because of the parents' constant competition for our attention, or the complete withdrawal of one partner. However, in most cases, our caring approach and the nature and immediacy of help offered seemed to facilitate communication, relieve pressure and pave the way for further contact.

12 Paediatric implications of the battered baby syndrome
C. Henry Kempe

Who batters children?

... In our understanding of the battered child syndrome, we have focused on families from the upper and middle social classes because we felt that individuals favoured by education and the usual amenities and not stressed by crowding, poverty, ill health, and poor education would give us more insight into the underlying dynamics of the disease. We have come to feel that perhaps 5 per cent of battering families have one parent who has a psychosis which may be of a frankly delusional or depressive kind while some are 'encapsulated' as regards a specific child at a specific time. It is not easy for a psychiatrist to diagnose such an 'encapsulated psychosis' in a single one-hour session, and many visits, over a period of weeks, are often required to make a proper diagnosis. Children in these families tend to have bizarre injuries. Such was the case of Jody who was 4 years old when her parents brought her to Colorado General Hospital. She had suffered from severe abuse all her life and showed one of the most severe cases of malnutrition that we had seen. She weighed only 7.7 kg and was covered with bruises and abrasions. Radiological studies revealed fractures of the skull and arm and two fractures of her hands. She also presented a high intestinal obstruction due to a haematoma in the lumen of the duodenum. For years Jody's mother had expressed to her husband and other members of the family and community her concern about this child and the manner in which she was able to care for her. No one had been willing to accept this responsibility, and no help was offered the mother. Four sibs were well and happily cared for. The scapegoated child was the only one the mother saw as 'bad', indeed she was, and remained, the only one the mother saw as being like herself. Shortly after Jody was admitted to the hospital, the mother was told that we would not recommend that Jody be sent home because of our concern for her welfare. Without hesitation the mother in a very relieved tone stated, 'I would be more frightened than you if she were sent home.' Jody's progress in the hospital was dramatic. During the six months after discharge she grew 15 cm and showed considerable developmental improvement. Parental rights were

KEMPE, C. H. (1971) 'Paediatric implications of the battered baby syndrome', *Archives of Disease in Childhood*, vol. 46, no. 245, pp. 28–37.

permanently terminated by the Juvenile Court and the child was successfully adopted. None of the remaining children was subsequently
scapegoated.

Another 5 per cent of parents appear to be aggressive psychopaths.
These are individuals, mostly men, who beat everyone: their wife, their
friends, their children, quite indiscriminately. They speak little and communicate through bashing people. Our therapeutic results in both these
groups have been dismal while the child remains in the home. We are left
then with 90 per cent of battering mothers and fathers who seem to have
serious problems in mothering.

Professor Brandt F. Steele, who is our collaborating psychiatrist and a
pioneer worker in this field, feels that basic in the abuser's attitude toward
infants is the conviction, largely unconscious, that children exist in order
to satisfy parental needs. Infants who do not satisfy these needs should be
physically punished in order to make them behave properly. Further, this
demand for satisfying behavioural response from the infant to parental
need is highly premature and expressed very early in the infant's life. As
an inevitable corollary, there is parental disregard of the infant's own
needs, wishes, and age-appropriate abilities or inabilities to respond
properly. It is as though the infant were looked to as a need-satisfying
parental object to fill the residual, unsatisfied, infantile needs of the
parent.

Myth of unfailing love of child

Let me stress here that while your country and mine [UK and USA] are
obsessed with teaching 'mother-craft', very little is taught to young girls
and boys about 'mothering', and motherliness is thought, wrongly, to be
instinctive and universal. By 'mothering', we mean the sensitive, generous,
and individualistic approach to the young child by a very tender mother
or father prepared to give promptly and predictably whatever the baby
needs in the way of individual attention, food, and comfort. It is regret-
table that our concept of mothering is so influenced by our idealized view
of the mother as a madonna, sweetly smiling on her young child. This
madonna-like mother of infinite patience is in the mind's eye of many
physicians and the public at large. But in fact, every parent knows better.
It is unlikely that any mother or father can be loving and generous 24 hours
a day, seven days a week. The ability to be unfailingly generous to the
child, particularly if the child is not easy to care for, varies widely. In our
experience perhaps 20 per cent of all young mothers have serious problems
in mothering, sufficient to require a great deal of support on the part of
husbands, health visitors, and physicians. Of this group perhaps 1 in 5
does not know how to turn on mothering ever, and in this situation func-

tions of mothering are often taken on by other people in the family or else the child will receive insufficient mothering and be damaged for life. We must somehow learn to 'titrate' the amount of supplemental mothering a given child needs. . . .

When does battering occur?

The dynamics of the *immediate* outbursts towards the child are often related to the very quality of mothering being brought into question by the child's behaviour. The baby cries and the mother feeds if, it cries more, the mother changes it, it still cries, and there comes that dreadful moment in every parent's life when love and desire to care for the child is mixed with incredible disappointment, anger, and even hate. It is surprising not that there are so many battered babies but that there are so few. Happily, there are many safety valves which prevent batterings in most situations. These include the capability of the mother to withdraw at this moment of great rage from the child by closing the door, finding help from an understanding husband or neighbour, or communicating with some other person who can help by phone. Typically, the battering parent cannot withdraw from the child who cries because the crying child is saying to her (the parent) something quite specific. 'If you were a good mother, I would not be crying like this'. At the moment of attack, the child is seen as 'bad', 'naughty', 'wilful'—in fact, exactly as the attacker was viewed by his or her parent. In this sense, the attack on the child is an attack on the person of the attacker himself—a form of suicide.

The bashing often relates to the immediate feeling of frenzy about the inability to stop the crying, but other triggers may exist, including soiling, or rejection of feedings.

Diagnosis

. . . A leisurely and sympathetic psychiatric evaluation of the parents often yields useful information. Such information includes answers to these five questions: (1) How does each parent see this child? (2) How much and what do they expect of this child? (3) How were both parents raised? (4) Was there a personal or family crisis at the time? (5) Do the parents have effective help in crises from friends or family—a rescue operation? These must be considered by physicians and by the courts as important and hard data comparable to x-rays and photographs.

If on a skilled interview there emerges a picture of an emotionally deprived childhood in one or both of the parents, if the child is pictured in a negative way, if the parent's attitude is one which is too demanding and full of unreasonable expectations, and if there was a crisis, then all this information can be added to the medical 'grey area' and intervention can proceed on firmer ground. This cannot be done, in most cases, by the paediatrician alone, nor, however, should it be simply turned over to the child psychiatrist or the social worker. All professionals together are needed to get a consensus in consultation, to consider what the family pathology is, and what might best be done. The decision is often one of life and death as far as the child is concerned. *Sharing* the decision will decrease the anxieties of all professionals and, in time, lead to certain improvement in their skills and judgement.

This country [USA] rightly has had a long-standing love affair with the detective story. The temptation is certainly large for the physician to decide who the culprit is. In fact, I see much time wasted on trying to find out 'who did it'. It is now clear to us that the important question for the physician to answer is 'did something happen?' If he thinks something happened he must then assume that he is dealing with at least four sick individuals: the baby, the father, the mother, and himself. Each in their own way are debilitated by the event and need treatment. For every battering parent mother or father, there is a spouse who abets, condones, and covers up the battering. Marriage partners tend to be very protective of one another. Often they are both severely deprived individuals who cling together for very inadequate support.

The potential for child abuse is greatest among the parents who were both emotionally deprived through lack of early mothering. These parents seek to get an unrealistic amount of love, gratification, and satisfying care even from their very small children.

> 'I've waited all these years for my baby and when she
> was born she never did anything for me.'
> 'When she cried it meant she didn't love me; so I hit her.'

... Battering parents tend to see the child not as he is but see him as they themselves were seen by their parents early on—as slow, bad, selfish, defiant, hard to discipline. These parents often demand the impossible from very young children. Characteristically, the parents tend to be depressed and isolated and lack a lifeline to a giving parent, friend, or professional person who can help in moments of crisis.

Some children may be more vulnerable to abuse than others. Among them are the hyperactive and precocious, the premature, the adopted, and the step-child. In addition some children from the earliest day seem to be singularly unrewarding to the mother no matter how hard she tries, though it is not easy to know in a given situation whether the primary problem lies mostly with the baby or with the mother. The act of battering is a final common pathway. For it to occur there must be (a) the potential

75

for abuse, (b) the characteristics of the particular child as seen by the particular parent, and (c) there must be a crisis. . . .

Predicting and managing insufficient or pathological mothering

How is it possible to predict mothering ability and to assist in mothering where it seems to be deficient, since it certainly is not an all or none proposition? We think there are certain useful leads in trying to pick out women who have serious difficulties in mothering. These can often be discovered in the prenatal period, begin to become quite obvious in the immediate postpartum period, and are often well recognized by the time the child is 6 to 8 weeks of age. Clearly, health visitors, midwives, general practitioners, and paediatricians may have an opportunity to suspect what may be one of the most important diagnoses in paediatrics. We have come to feel that certain questions may be highly predictive. They are (1) does your child cry a lot? How do you manage your baby's crying? Does it upset you when you are unable to stop the crying or comfort your baby? How do you feel inside when the baby cries? Does it ever make you feel like crying? (The answers to these questions relate to anxiety and anger or feelings of despair.) (2) Does it upset you when you are left alone? Have you ever been afraid to be alone with your baby? (During stressful periods parents may express many fears of being alone.) Can you usually call someone to help at these times? (Absence of life-line.) Does it make you anxious to have someone watch you feed your baby? Do you ever get the feeling that others are critical of how you feed or take care of the baby? Do other people understand the problems you have with your child? (These questions reveal the amount of pressure these people have felt all their lives to respond to somebody else's needs.) When do you feel children are old enough to understand what is expected of them? How well do you feel your children understand you? Can they tell when you are upset and do they help? (These reveal how the parents may be turning to a very small child for satisfaction of their own needs.)

If we understand that mothering will not be turned on ever in some situations no matter how hard one tries, we will then stop pushing some babies at their mothers who tell us, with every verbal and non-verbal way they know how, that they cannot and will not take care of their child. It is clear to me that one of the urgent needs in our society is to provide, without waiting for injuries, for the baby who cannot receive all its mothering from the biological mother. A great variety of therapeutic approaches is needed. For the mother who can be competent 14 but not 24 hours a day at a given moment in time, there should be day help, day nurseries, mother's groups. In moments of personal or family crisis, a 'safe place' should be known to exist in each community where, on the decision of the mother alone, and with no delay or red tape, the child could be received for a few hours or a few weeks.

But when that is all done there will still be mothers who will not be able to turn on mothering no matter what support is given. Society will have to accept the fact that mothering does not occur spontaneously because of the biological fact that the child has been through the birth canal. Excellent mothering can occur from women who have never had a baby and, of course, from the vast majority of fathers as well. On the other hand, we know mothers who have had seven or eight babies, none of whom has received even minimum mothering. We seem to say to these mothers: 'you have had your fun, now take care of it.' Along with this there is a terrific fear on the part of society that if mothers were free to dump their child who is for one reason or another not wanted, there would be thousands upon thousands of unwanted babies deposited at the doors of local authorities to be cared for by society. It is a serious moral question as to whether in the long run it would not be wiser to provide these children with well-paid foster homes. . . .

Later management

It is simply unsafe to have a small child who has been injured returned to parents, if one of them is either suffering from major mental illness or is an aggressive psychopath. On the other hand, in the majority of cases, where one is dealing with maternal deprivation of the parents it is often possible to introduce a therapeutic person while allowing gradual return of the child to the family under continuing treatment. Eighty per cent of children under our care are back with their parents within 8 months of initiation of treatment, but 5 per cent have parental rights permanently terminated and the children are adopted. The treatment of the deprived parent is another attempt at 'mothering', so that emotional dependency on the child and isolation are lessened and feelings of trust are developed.

It is not easy to take on another adult as a friend offering love and support and reliable, predictable human resource. These patients tend to wear one out emotionally, they are challenging, and often almost ask to be rejected. It takes a high degree of generosity to permit a marked early dependency upon the therapist which is required in such treatment. In our experience while professional training does not hurt, it does not seem to help either. We have had very excellent results with therapists who were psychiatrists, social workers, nurses, paediatricians, and our untrained 'foster grandmothers' and 'mothering aides'. I might add, that we have had some very bad luck with some highly trained professionals who simply are not prepared to give of themselves in this therapeutic experience of loving a very deprived parent.

Treatment consists of weekly or twice weekly home visits devoted to patient listening, understanding, and uncritical approval, with focus on the parent's need rather than on the child's. It must be stressed that it is our experience that if the parents' basic needs are met the child will be safe. Interpretive psychotherapy has, in fact, very little to offer to these very damaged parents, and it is generally dangerous and contraindicated. Early on they tend to do better with male than with female therapists, but we provide a choice and we allow the patients to go back and forth between members of our team. In any event we provide a telephone lifeline 7 days a week, 24 hours a day for moments of stress.

The plan of treatment once the diagnosis is suspected is: (1) child admitted to hospital for diagnosis; (2) child temporarily separated from parents for protection; (3) begin plan to make home safe for child's return through 'mothering' therapy; and (4) gradual return of child to home or family foster care. . . .

13 Treatment: a medical perspective

Arnon Bentovim

In no condition in medicine in recent years has the medical model shown more limitations than in the treatment of the abused child. . . . The medical profession has had to realize that parental ambivalence is a real quality. Doctors need to question the expressed feelings of a parent who seems unusually accepting or co-operative—for instance about a multi-handicapped child. The parent who can look after the child and his physical needs so carefully can be the same parent who can abuse and be violent to that child in a moment of severe emotional stress. What is needed is a change in the frame of reference, from that of an illness lodged in a child who happens to have a family, to a family which has a child in it with an illness.

If this family, or personal approach to illness is adopted, familiar mistakes will not be made. The parent returning to accident and emergency or outpatients departments or to a general practitioner will not be sent away when repeated complaints are made of a child's screaming, sleeplessness or poor feeding. A depressed mother in the first few months after the birth of a child in a position of strain, marital discord and loss of a family lifeline will not then be sent away with reassuring noises. There will not be an acceptance of empty, superficial explanations of injury. Doctors, particularly in hospitals, need an altered view to encompass the needs of the whole family rather than just a view of disease alone.

Mutual support among hospital staff

To dare to ask questions about the wider context of the child and his family is anxiety-provoking, and the organization of the hospital ward and its structure of action and communications has evolved to reduce the anxiety of staff (Menzies 1960). The result is cautiousness, a need to have the same opinions and limited self-expression by junior staff. All this tends to reduce the staff's sense of personal responsibility and involvement. In this way, painful feelings about a child, parent or family can be reduced and the staff can function in the face of the intolerable anxieties of nursing

BENTOVIM, A. (1974) 'Treatment: a medical perspective', in Carter, J. (ed.) *The Maltreated Child*, London, Priory Press, pp. 75–88.

very ill children and their parents. By contrast an open system of communication permits honest observation and self-expression, views differences between members of groups as natural and offers an equal voice to all members of staff. Such responsibilities to observe and discuss what is occurring honestly, can produce a backlash of anxiety.

Expression of this may be found in the ward sister who cannot stand having an abused child on her ward, the nurse who finds the questioning of a parent intolerable or who is so angry at the thought of the parents' violence that she rejects them. There is the doctor who refuses to perceive that a child with a fracture with very little explanation needs to be admitted to hospital and the parents confronted, because he feels it is too embarrassing to doubt the parents' word.

All this means that if a new framework of perspective is to be adopted, then a new framework of support for staff has to be developed. This can be carried out in three ways. First, a place needs to be provided within the hospital where staff of all disciplines and ranks can discuss cases which concern them. This should be a regular, informal meeting, preferably weekly, set up with the agreement of the appropriate executive committee and chaired by a staff member—paediatrician, psychiatrist or social worker—in whom is lodged the responsibility for the care and management of the abused child, or child at risk, in the hospital. Not only can the obvious problems be discussed, such as children with fractures, bruising, failure to thrive, but this group will have the authority to ask a reluctant consultant to come to discuss the 'borderline' case in his unit which his sister and medical social worker may be concerned about, or to ask a casualty officer about a young child with a fracture sent home. Such a meeting can ask for follow-up data on cases already discussed, or become a time for an official case conference involving all hospital staff and community agencies concerned with the case so that decisions about future management can be made. . . .

Strategy for effective co-operation

Guidelines summarizing the hospital policy need to be issued so that the frontline junior medical staff, changing frequently over the years, can know what their roles need to be in that particular hospital. . . .

After initial investigations, the consultant or his deputy gives the parents—both if possible—an account of the objective findings and of the steps to be taken, for example, referral to the local authority social services department. He should give the parents an opportunity to explain the injuries. . . .

Once an organization sets in motion a group of staff responsible for the investigation, management and treatment of abused children in hospital, it is interesting to note how many more cases are seen to be 'at risk', because there is a group that can help to deal with the anxiety of staff. Unexpected cases discussed during the first year's functioning of such a group, included those parents whose unusual religious responses to a profoundly handicapped child prevented the children having adequate emotional support, parents who refused necessary corrective operations for their children, children whose care was so obsessionally perfect that intense feelings of rejection masked potential breakdown. Such a group can help individual staff members to make and take decisions which are painful. For instance, there is sometimes the need for a child to be separated from its family through juvenile court proceedings. There is the awareness that a child with congenital malformations who has been in hospital for a long period can become a 'ward pet' and lose touch with his family and be at risk after his return home. Staff can be helped to dare to acknowledge that their handling may have put the child at risk. Also it enables staff to ask why a child is not thriving, not growing, or to wonder why a parent is visiting rarely. A support group can help to clarify issues such as the understandable desire for punitiveness towards a parent who has hurt a child, or to reassert the child's need to be cared for and protected despite sympathy towards a parent who is obviously attached to her child. Salutary lessons can be learned when a child is returned to the parents and then rebattered despite considerable discussion and thought. . . .

Aims of medical treatment

Careful diagnosis of parental psychiatric state, social situation and personal history have to be made. Whatever the diagnosis and specific treatment necessary, decisions have to be made as to possible separation from parents to achieve the meeting of primary needs, or whether the parents, with help, can provide sufficiently for the child.

The parents whether they continue to care for their children or not, need to have the emotional experience of being held, contained and cared for by another human being. This may begin to reduce the strength of the painful negative experiences which have led to abuse. This positive experience may need to be continued over several years—a lengthy period of distortion cannot be righted overnight. Social factors such as poor housing, financial privation, and isolation which militate against coping need to be countered. Also it should be ensured that as good a marital relationship as possible can be fostered between couples, which may involve helping a couple who are mutually destructive to separate, or bringing another couple together when anxiety about the ability of the other prevents mutual dependency. Decisions have to be made about whether such changes can ever take place.

Once the aims are decided, the first step in medical case planning is to ensure that an arrangement is created where the child is as safe as is reasonably possible from further re-injury. It has already been stressed that decisions need to be made about where the child should be, whether returned to the family or placed in local authority care. It is important to be clear about who should be responsible for the medical oversight of the case—examinations and checks to make sure that the child is not being re-injured, whatever the setting he is in. The decision about separation or not is one of the most difficult decisions to take and needs the backing of the whole group involved and a consensus to be reached by all. Without this the forces of inertia, complacency and blindness to the facts can ensure a wrong decision. . . .

Care of the parents

The second part of medical case planning is to do with the treatment of the parents. Planning to help parents relates to the very complexity of the pathology which leads parents to be violent, and can only take place on the basis of as full an understanding of the parents' problems as possible. A subnormal, psychopathic, young parent with an unstable electro-encephalogram who attacks child, mother and hospital staff is very different to a sophisticated parent with an emotionally distorted but materially comfortable childhood which led to a subtle sadomasochistic bond between parent and child. However, both situations can lead to the same end state as far as the child is concerned.

Questions have to be asked in medical case planning about the resources available. This not only refers to the need for psychiatric treatments for parents, the availability of sophisticated psychotherapy or caretaking, primary mother-aiding and casework, but also to who is available, what staff resources can be offered to a particular family and who and what will match their expectations and needs. As well as the planning of who should be doing what with the parents, there is the need to plan to whom the people carrying out the primary treatment can turn for help.

Deprived parents who turn to their children to act as parents to themselves, or who attempt to control their children's needs because of being unable to meet them, vent their frustrations by criticisms and aggression (Steele 1968). They are likely to show similar attitudes to those who are trying to help them. The strain of trying to parent a parent can be enormous. The feelings projected on to whoever is doing therapeutic work are intense: the explosiveness and infantile demandingness can in turn provoke a caring person to rage and frustration and to repeat again symbolically, what happened to the parent as a child.

This is likely during holiday breaks, at times of illness, under additional strains such as a new pregnancy, or during a marital crisis. There can be an intense testing out of the resolve of the caring and concern for the therapist or caseworker. The workers need to have a resource of understanding, containment and acceptance of the burden of care to whom they can turn. The treatment of deprived people, or those who have had severely distorted parenting, is a major therapeutic effort extending over a long period and it is often helpful if more than one person is involved with care.

As well as personnel available for the parents the whole question of what is available for the child must also be considered, since the needs of a child with a considerable disturbance, is very different to a young infant or child who is basically normal and not damaged by abuse.

Psychiatric care

The question of where people are helped seems important. Whilst often cases can be managed within general paediatric services, others may need more specialized psychiatric care. One useful setting is the psychiatric day centre for infants and pre-school children (Bentovim 1973)—whether these cater for all problems or specifically for children at risk. In these settings, mothers' groups should be available and joint marital work should be possible as well as individual casework. Necessary observations and care of the children can be carried out in this setting. It has been observed that the children themselves either imitate the parents' own explosiveness or respond in an overly passive way, both of which may need intervention. It is possible in a day setting to meet both the parents' and the child's needs for containment and the sharing of burdens. Others have felt that an in-patient setting may be necessary so that twenty-four hour care, concern and parenting can be offered (Ounsted 1975). . . .

Specific psychiatric treatment is often necessary where there is a discrete psychiatric entity such as a long term depression becoming more severe after the birth of a child. In-patient units taking in the whole family may be particularly useful for the child who is markedly at risk (Barnes 1968). . . .

At times the parents of the parents might be involved, to undo a faulty adaptation between a parent and her own parents. During a crisis a new basis of interaction can develop. . . .

It is of interest to note that in recent years to a marked extent in the child-psychiatric field and rather less in the adult field, there has been a change in focus from the individual and his own pathology to the family and the factors which cause it to break down. Techniques have now been developed to meet with the family as a group in an attempt to help them communicate better, to provide more for each others' emotional needs, to take appropriate roles of mothering and fathering and to reduce distorted beliefs and expectations about what parents and children should do for each other.

Time-scale of medical follow-up and planning

Medical follow-up will depend on the plans that have been made by the group involved with a particular case and who has the prime responsibility for work with the case. However, one important aspect must be the assessment of the child's physical state and development over time. The child at risk should be assessed regularly by a doctor for several years, intensively at first and less so at a later date.

If the main aim of treatment is to modify the parental attitudes and child-rearing practices and mediated by non-medical personnel, such as social workers, health visitors, mothering aids, day nurseries or special centres, then a doctor has to be deputed to evaluate that the child is progressing physically. Related to this is the assessment of a child, who has become, or who may be in danger of being handicapped from brain injury, partial sight or other problems. This doctor may well be the paediatrician, general practitioner, or doctor in a local child health clinic. . . .

Prevention

To be complete, prevention would have to extend right back to the very childhood of parents themselves and to the very preparation for parenthood. More use should be made of crisis periods when people make routine contact with medical agencies. For example the antenatal period is a particularly good time. Although some parents who abuse their children have not attended antenatal classes or clinics, this does not apply to all. At present there is still too much emphasis on the physical well being of the infant and mother in the antenatal period, with the stress on relaxation. Perhaps insufficient attention is paid to the crisis and vulnerability of the parent during the period of change. During this time there can be the possibility of a corrective relationship which may make a difference to the eventual relationship between mother and baby. Parents' groups are used insufficiently for these purposes. Too often mothers together in waiting rooms and clinics tend to lie back and relax rather than be helped to discuss the emotional feelings and anxieties that are so commonly experienced: the fears of losing the self one was, one's figure, aspirations, hopes, fears of difficulties in marriage, the knowledge that one's own experiences in childhood may militate against the possibility of relating to an infant. These are factors which may be dealt with satisfactorily in groups carried out on group-therapeutic lines (Wilson 1968). The period of birth itself is again one where intervention may become possible. It has been shown that even a short period of supportive contact between mother and infant in the first hours after birth can improve the communication, handling and contact between a mother and her infant for several months after this and maybe even for a longer period (Klaus 1972). Nursing skills in maternity units and perhaps the intervention of social workers can help in promoting this first bond between mother and infant; thus mitigating some of a mother's earlier emotional problems. Care in helping mother to make feeding an emotionally satisfying relationship for mother and infant can also make a difference here, as can involvement of fathers. All this implies attention towards the personal setting of events, of childbirth or pregnancy, rather than just to the events themselves.

The birth of a mildly handicapped, more obviously of a severely handicapped child is an obvious area of prevention (Bentovim 1972). The parents of a child need to be helped through the understandable mourning and grief for the loss of a normal child to begin to accept the child they have and to deal with the inevitable separations if the child has to be hospitalized for treatment. Adequate attention to this stage may prevent the situation that arose after the birth of a deaf, partially-sighted rubella baby. The parent twenty months later when he was very much at risk said with much feeling that she felt that her child had not yet been born. He was not the perfect expected child she was still waiting for and so could not be acknowledged as he was. Even periods of brief separation in incubators can make a significant difference to the contact between mother and infant (Klaus 1970).

Another period of possible intervention is the early months after birth when mothers attend welfare clinics. This is a period of intense concern and maternal preoccupation about the welfare of the child. If parents have already had the experience of talking about problems in a group, then, instead of the anxiety being centred on the weight of the baby, or the feed, real feelings can be carried and tolerated. The early months are so vital for the mother to be able to put herself sensitively just where her infant can find her. To be preoccupied with marital worries or problems of support, as the single mother is, makes it impossible to provide the setting that enables a baby to be cared for so well that the baby is not at first aware that there has to be anybody there to do it (Winnicott 1958). In one case where a mother was preoccupied with supporting herself, the result was irritability and increasing misery. Eventual bruising and failure to thrive led to the baby being admitted, the mother's depression treated, and the long term social support and supervision necessary for the baby's physical and emotional growth provided. Even this careful planning was insufficient and the baby was readmitted with a sub-dural haematoma having been shaken and smacked to stop her crying, necessitating placement away from mother.

Education is important to help health visitors, general practitioners and hospital outpatient departments to be aware of the signs. The infant who has difficulties feeding, the crying infant, the non-sleeping infant, the depressed mother or frantic mother over-arousing her baby, the sudden appearance of worries about her spouse, social isolations, loneliness or absence of a grandparent or friend. All these can lead to the sort of loneliness, desperation and the start of a struggle between mother and infant which can lead to tragedy.

Above all there needs to be a source of support for the professionals so that they can dare to see what is in front of them, rather than trying desperately to pretend that it does not exist.

References

BARNES, D. (1968) *Psychosocial Nursing*, London, Tavistock.

BENTOVIM, A. (1972) 'Emotional Disturbance of Handicapped Preschool Children and their Families', *Brit. Med. J.*, 3, 579 and 634.

BENTOVIM, A. (1973) 'Disturbed and under five', *Special Education*, 62, 31.

KLAUS, M. and KENNELL, J. H. (1970) 'Mothers separated from their newborn infants', *Paediatric Clinics North America*, 17, 4.

KLAUS, M., JERAULD, R., KREGER, N., MCALPINE, W., STEFF, M. and KENNELL, J. H. (1972) 'Maternal Attachment, Importance of the First Five Postpartum Days', *New England Journal of Medicine*, 286, 460.

MENZIES, I. (1960) 'A Case Study in Functioning of Social Systems against Anxiety', *Human Relations*, 13, 2.

OUNSTED, C., OPPENHEIMER, R. and LINDSAY, J. (1975) 'The Psychopathology and Psychotherapy of the Families, in A. White Franklin, (ed.) *Concerning Child Abuse*, London, Churchill.

STEELE, B. F. and POLLOCK, C. B. (1968) 'A Psychiatric Study of Parents who Abuse their Small Children', in Helfer, R. E. and Kempe, C. H. (eds.) *The Battered Child*, Chicago, University of Chicago Press.

WILSON, A. R. (1968) 'An Investigation into the Psychological Aspects of Pregnancy and the Puerperium Using the Technique of Group Analysis, *Journal of Psychosomatic Research*, 12, 73.

WINNICOTT, D. W. (1958) *Through Paediatrics to Psychoanalysis*, London, Tavistock.

14 Treatment: a social perspective
Ron Jones and Carolyn Jones

Immediate fear and revulsion tend to make a pariah of the battering parent. . . .

We are sometimes inclined to deal with the disquieting manifestations of human behaviour by dissociating ourselves rather than by developing our understanding.

Currently, disproportionate attention is being given to the improvement of procedures for identifying abused children and the overall management of cases. In comparison there has been little consideration of the actual treatment resources available once children have been identified. There seems to be a very real danger of professional workers merely limiting their involvement to the discussion of cases at review committees while nobody is very keen to get close to the families themselves and engage them in treatment.

'Social work operates at the storm centre of conflict' (Younghusband 1970). In cases of parental violence towards young children there are obvious clashes between the rights and interests of different people interwoven in the same situation, particularly the rights of the parents and the welfare of the child.

Most family aggression is private and privileged but when it comes to the attention of community agencies in the form of an injured baby, social workers have not only a right but a duty to intervene in order to protect the defenceless, inarticulate child from being damaged seriously, or even destroyed by its natural protectors. From a social work viewpoint this duty can be extended to the frightened, inadequate parents who need protecting from their own violent, impulsive actions.

Unlike the researcher, the busy practitioner operates in conditions which are far from ideal, yet research can suggest ways of improving practice. Before discussing what can be done when time is at a premium, the results of specialized projects will be reviewed. Preference will be given to those approaches which recognize the chronic nature of the problem and concede the difficulties of establishing a firm diagnosis. Because ideas about the cause of child abuse influence strategies for treatment, some reference to causation seems necessary. . . .

JONES, R. and JONES, C. (1974) 'Treatment: a social perspective', in Carter, J. (ed.) *The Maltreated Child*, London, Priory Press, pp. 89–99.

Action research into treatment methods

Several research projects have begun with a therapeutic commitment to abusive families and their findings offer illuminating insights and guidance which can be used immediately at the individual case level. For example, from a clinical study in depth of sixty abusive families, Steele and Pollock in Denver noted the high incidence of psychoneuroses and character disorders in the parents together with the almost universal presence of some degree of depression, but found wide variations in their psychiatric symptoms. In a subsequent review of his work, Steele writes: 'Child abuse cannot be considered an integral part of any of our usual psychiatric entities, but is best understood as a particular type of parent-child interaction which can exist in combination with any other psychological state' (Steele 1970a). For him the key factors in the cause of abuse are the lack of motherliness in these families, 'role reversal' in which the parents expect the child to take care of their emotional needs, and a model of aggressive parenting (Morris 1963a and Morris 1963b). Their view is not a narrow one, and their colleague Kempe highlighted five factors which he believes are necessary for abuse to occur: the psychological make-up of the parents which predisposes them to batter; collusion on the part of the spouse; social isolation or the absence of an effective lifeline in the form of someone to whom the parents can turn; real or attributed provocation from the child; and some kind of precipitating crisis (Kempe 1971). Steele has discussed in detail the broad cultural factors which serve as a backcloth to the problem in America (Steele 1970b).

In the view of the Denver team, the essence of therapy is the provision of a corrective, nurturing experience for the parents which encourages them to seek the satisfaction of their needs from other adults rather than their own offspring. The dangers of attempting this without first removing the child from the abusive setting of the home are stressed. Efforts are also made to relieve the effects of social stress on the family.

The Denver school has demonstrated the effectiveness of caring and intimacy in the treatment of abusive parents. Often this meant a long period of profound dependency on the therapist and a corresponding investment of considerable time and energy by the treatment team. Subsequently they often found it possible for professional therapists to be supplemented by carefully selected lay workers, except when parents were thought to be mentally ill. These lay workers are called parent aides and work under close supervision at befriending and mothering the parents. Therapy is directed at improving the basic patterns of child rearing within the family by providing intensive individual support for the parents, not aimed at developing insight, but more '. . . a kind of repetitive patterning in which the worker assumes the "good mother" role which the parents so desperately need and which is such a crucial element in the healing process (Alexander 1972). The team observed that the majority of parents responded positively over time in the sense of being able to perceive and treat their children more realistically and less punitively.

In Britain the NSPCC Battered Child Research Department based its treatment methods with modification on the Denver approach (Court 1970 and Jones 1973). Both the Denver team and the NSPCC team, while identifying extensive marital problems amongst the families, found great difficulty in trying to engage both partners in therapy. Their immature and powerfully competitive needs for attention made it very hard for the worker to relate to both parents at once. Equally, separate sessions for the parents, even with a second therapist, seemed doomed as this required a formal recognition and acceptance of problems by both parents, a situation which is rare in these families. It may be that the latter approach is too threatening to what are, at best, tenuous marital relationships.

Group therapy

In the early literature on the battered child syndrome there were few references to group therapy as desirable treatment for the parents, but recently parent groups have been used in the development of child protective services. For instance in Boston, the Parents Center Project for the Study and Prevention of Child Abuse consists of two separate but co-ordinated efforts: a therapeutic day centre to which the children are brought in specially provided transport and a parents group which meets one evening a week under the leadership of a male and female therapist. All families have agreed voluntarily to accept help from the project. Parents are encouraged to participate in the daily care of their children in the centre, and the staff extend 'an accessible presence' to the parents (Galdston 1971). The project workers do not provide regular individual casework or material aid but they do offer themselves as persons who are available as needed by telephone, for office interviews or home visits.

Starting from the belief that the basis of child abuse is the transfer to the child of parental self-hatred, the group therapists aim at getting the parents to recognize the destructive effects of this process. This differs from the Denver aim of providing for the parents the 'good mothering' experience which was lacking in their own early development. Although both teams adopt a psycho-dynamic frame of reference, their premises are dissimilar. Indeed Galdston believes that the parents' problems stem from unresolved sexual conflicts about their right to reproduce.

Clearly the two projects presuppose different levels of emotional development in the parents. In Boston the parents require motivation to attend voluntarily, to develop self-awareness in the groups, and to call on workers when in need. This excludes those families in which the parents lack fundamental emotional resources. As many battering parents appear to fall into this latter category, the Boston service is likely to be of value to only a limited number of families.

The Boston team concluded from daily observations of the children over three years that their approach prevented the recurrence of physical abuse to the child and promoted his growth and development. Significant improvement in the children's disturbed behaviour were noted within as little as three weeks' attendance at the centre. The parents too responded through their own participation by expressing spontaneous pleasure in their children. The children became much less vulnerable emotionally to the parents' swings in mood and improved relationships between husbands and wives following group therapy reduced the level of domestic tension. This therapeutic service has been described as '. . . authenticating parenthood. It is a process by which a belief is conveyed in attitudes and practices that allows a parent to establish herself the sense of validity of her parenthood' (Galdston 1973).

Paulson and his colleagues in Los Angeles marshal a wide range of theoretical approaches to the problem, to which they directly attribute their success. 'It was postulated that a learning theory approach, combined with a therapy that enhances emotional growth and improves the parents' self image, was a fruitful and desired approach' (Paulson 1973). Psychoanalytic theories including those of Freud, Adler, Erikson, etc., are combined in a treatment programme which includes the use of direct teaching, demonstration and confrontation.

As in Denver, intervention begins frequently with placing the child in a safe residential setting away from home. Group psychotherapy is provided for the parents in addition to a parent training programme run by nurses. As many of the parents revealed marked anxiety about the everyday care of their children, this programme aims at instructing the parents in basic child care skills and fostering their understanding of infant and child development. The nurses also act as supportive co-therapists, making frequent home visits to sustain the parents when the child is allowed home, at first for a few hours and gradually for longer periods. Paulson's comment again underlines the importance of offering the parents a nurturing experience in treatment: 'for many of our abusive parents the need for love and acceptance, the desire for physical care and protection, and the opportunity for emotional stimulation and affective interchange became the working material of many group therapy sessions.'

In Britain a family centred therapy scheme involves sheltering the whole family in a supportive residential milieu by admitting the child and family to hospital (Ounsted 1975). Careful evaluation distinguishes those parents who are unlikely to benefit from this form of treatment in which case permanent separation for the child is recommended. The reason for admission is made quite explicit to the parents from the outset and they are encouraged to acknowledge their part in the battering incident. This usually leads to a crisis in which the therapists can convey their empathy and concern. As well as relieving the burden of guilt on the parents, this fosters the much broader aim of replacing the closed family relationships, laden with fantasy, with more open communication. After discharge, continued support is offered by the hospital staff to the parents, and the child may remain the subject of a care order. . . .

Separation of parent and child

Some people think that separating the child from his parents for a limited period may be an adequate protective measure. If battering is associated with youthful parenthood, the risk may diminish as the parent gets older (Smith 1973). On the other hand some battering incidents occur only during specific developmental stages in the child which activate at that time associated conflicts in the parents (Milowe 1965), for example, the helplessness of tiny babies may evoke strong hostile feelings in parents with problems of dependence but the same parents may find the child much easier to care for when he is walking, talking and generally being more responsive.

Temporary removal of the child to hospital, even if the injuries are not serious ensures his immediate protection and gives the social worker some opportunity for assessing the acute and chronic stresses in the family and the parents' capacity to care for the child. It may be necessary to obtain a place of safety order at this stage but very often the parents will agree to the child's admission to hospital. Furthermore, in a few cases the parents may actually request or agree to the child's reception into care for a longer period to relieve the strain in a difficult family situation. In practice, this rarely proves satisfactory for long, as the parents' fundamental ambivalence towards the child invariably leads them to change their mind about the placement and suddenly take the child back home where once again he is at risk.

In many cases, after careful consideration of all available information at a case conference, a decision may be reached to apply to the juvenile court for a care order. If the application is successful this ensures that the child can be separated from the parents for a longer period of time, but it must be remembered that the parents still have a right to appeal and can also apply for a revocation of the order at some future date. In other words, our current legislation may permit permanent removal of the child from its parents in some cases, but it by no means guarantees permanent separation in all cases.

Even if the battered child is removed from the home, there is still the question of how to protect other young children in the family who are likely to be at risk. Also, the parents may react to the removal of one child by immediately conceiving another. The provision of a day nursery place for young brothers and sisters should afford some measure of protection. This is also a useful alternative for the battered child if, for various reasons, he is not placed in residential care.

An attempt to secure the removal of the abusing parent from the home is another course of action to be considered. It is tempting to believe that to adopt a controlling, regulatory approach will somehow dispense with the problem. In practice most legal measures such as a prison sentence or compulsory admission to psychiatric hospital offer only temporary safeguards, are unlikely to modify abusive attitudes in the parents, and in the majority of cases cannot be applied. Probation is a more positive alternative provided that this is not seen as obviating the need to consider placement of the child as well, but the compulsory nature of the relationship between the probation officer and client may make therapeutic progress more difficult by engendering compliance rather than trust in the parents. . . .

References

ALEXANDER, H. (1972) 'The Social Worker and the Family', in Kempe, C. H. and Helfer, R. E. (eds.) *Helping the Battered Child and his Family*, Philadelphia, Lippincott.

COURT, J. and OKELL, C. (1970) 'An Emergent Programme to Protect the Battered Child and his Family', *Intervention*, **19**, 16–21. Association of Professional Social Workers, Quebec.

GALDSTON, R. (1971) 'Violence begins at Home', *Journal of the American Academy of Child Psychiatry*, **10**, 336–50.

GALDSTON, R. (1973) 'Preventing the Abuse of Little Children', in *Annual Meeting of the American Psychiatric Association*, Hawaii (unpublished).

JONES, R. A. (1973) 'Battering Families', *Health and Social Service Journal*, **83**, no. 4321, 313–14.

KEMPE, C. H. (1971) 'Paediatric Implications of the Battered Baby Syndrome', *Archives of Disease in Childhood*, **46**, 28–37.

MILOWE, L. D. (1965) 'Child Abuse and Injury', *Military Medicine*, **130**, 747–62.

MORRIS, M. G. and GOULD, R. W. (1963)a 'Role Reversal: A Concept in Dealing with the Neglected/Battered Child Syndrome', in *The Neglected/Battered Child Syndrome*, New York, Child Welfare League of America.

MORRIS, M. G. and GOULD, R. W. (1963)b 'Role Reversal: A Necessary Concept in Dealing with the "Battered Child Syndrome" ', *American Journal of Orthopsychiatry*, **32**.

OUNSTED, C., OPPENHEIMER, R. and LINDSAY, J. (1975) 'The Psychopathology and Psychotherapy of the Families', in A. White Franklin (ed.) *Concerning Child Abuse*, London, Churchill.

PAULSON, M. J., SAVINO, A. B., CHALEFF, A. B. and SANDERS, W. (1973) 'Group Psychotherapy: A Multidisciplinary Group Therapy Approach to Life Threatening Behaviour', *Journal of Lifethreatening Behaviour*, **4**, 1.

SMITH, S. M., HONISBERGER, I., and SMITH, C. A. (1973) 'E.E.G. and Personality Factors in Battered Baby Cases', *Brit. Med. J.*, **2**, 20–2.

STEELE, B. F. (1970)a 'Parental Abuse of Infants and Small Children' in Anthony E. J. and Benedek, T. J. (eds.), *Parenthood: its Psychology and Psychopathology*, London, Churchill.

STEELE, B. F. (1970)b 'Violence in our Society', *The Pharos of Alpha Omega Alpha*, **33** (2), 42–8.

YOUNGHUSBAND, E. (1970) 'Social Work and Social Values', *Social Work Today*, **1**, 6.

15 Parents' reactions to hospital care
The NSPCC Battered Child Research Team

Typically a child's admission to hospital, whatever the circumstances, is a time of crisis for the family. Undoubtedly, for parents who have injured their children, it is a very stressful time, but the child's admission to hospital actually may be welcomed in that it provides them with a much needed break from caring for the child. However, it became clear to us that for most of our parents, who were highly aware that the focus of professional concern was the child's injury and future safety, any feelings of relief were marred by their anxiety about what would happen next, both to them and the child. This was particularly true of the six families whose children were detained in hospital under a Place of Safety Order.

Separation from the child was particularly hard for those parents who closely identified with the child and wanted him home, in contrast to their partners who showed little feeling for the child. We were aware that this led to a tremendous build up of tension between such couples, who were quite unable to acknowledge openly their feelings to one another. Some parents understandably felt that the detention of their child in hospital under an order implied condemnation of them as parents and became obsessed with getting the child home. It was evident that one young mother wanted her child home in order to make reparation. She was unrealistic when the worker tried to point out the enormous stresses which she still faced. She tended to idealise the child in his absence, yet in practice found it difficult just to cope with his feeds when visiting him in hospital and quickly became overwrought. The father, who had a horror of residential care, was equally unrealistic and was preparing to fight the order as his wife had set her heart on having the child home. However, after the mother had received constant reassurance and support from her psychiatrist and social worker that she needed rest and respite from the demands of the child, at least on a short-term basis, she was able to acknowledge that there were some advantages in transferring the child from hospital to a residential nursery for a few months.

In over half the cases, workers remarked on the parents' apparent lack of affection for the child, lack of concern for the child's suffering if there were injuries, and inability to sympathize with what the child must be

---

BAHER, E. et al. (eds.) (1976) *At Risk: an Account of the Work of the Battered Child Research Department, NSPCC*, London, Routledge, pp. 116–117.

feeling on finding himself in strange, new surroundings. Ironically, some parents were noted to be more interested in and empathetic towards other children in the ward than their own. In two cases, the mothers were described as strikingly emotionally detached, negative and hostile towards the children, almost as though they were blaming them for being injured and causing so much fuss. Some mothers expressed that they were missing their babies and felt empty or without a purpose in life, but they were preoccupied with their own needs rather than the babies'.

A number of the parents were very critical of the care provided by the hospital, including the food, clothes and routine. Some blamed the hospital for their children's unhappiness and boredom, but were quick to sabotage any plans proposed by the hospital staff to alleviate this. Clearly, these were parents who felt powerless and threatened by the situation so that resorting to criticism was the only way of hitting back. Some parents commented, with good reason, to their workers that they felt that the hospital staff were withholding information from them, or felt hounded by doctors who were anxious to seek information from them, 'nobody tells us anything, but everybody keeps asking us the same questions and there doesn't seem any point in it.'

16 The predicament of abused children
Carolyn Okell Jones

Even without damage from trauma, even without the
associated effects of poverty, parental mental illness, neglect,
under-nutrition or deprivation, the child cannot be expected
to thrive in a home in which fear of bodily harm is an
unrelenting spectre. It has long been recognised that
imagined fear of physical harm affects the developing psyche.
Abused children live with a continual fear of harm, that is
not a fantasy but an ever present reality.

Martin et al., 1974

1 Introduction

1.1 When one surveys the rapidly increasing volume of world literature
on child abuse, it is striking how relatively few publications have focused
on the experiences and development of the surviving affected children
and their psychotherapeutic needs. Yet, on reflection, it is very understandable. In the decade following the publication of Kempe's (1962)
classic article on the battered child syndrome, which drew attention to its
high mortality rate and the associated brain injury, the main concern was
to protect the child from lethal physical harm and the main thrust of
professional intervention was directed towards life-saving procedures.
Emphasis was placed on clinical manifestations in order to improve diagnosis, on the complex legal issues, and on the psychodynamics of the
abusive parents in relation to the type of psychiatric and social work
treatment that they could use with benefit. It was soon recognized by
practitioners that these parents could rarely tolerate the child becoming
the focus of attention and were quick to sabotage any arrangements made
on the child's behalf unless their own dependency needs were being met
first.

1.2 Regarding the children, the tendency was to make theoretical
generalizations about their development and to stereotype them in terms
of their characteristics and behaviour on the basis of early anecdotal data.

JONES, C. O. (1977) revised version of 'The predicament of abused children' in
White Franklin, A. (ed.) *The Challenge of Child Abuse*, London, Academic Press
(in preparation).

Although clinical observations suggested that many of the children were considerably damaged emotionally as well as physically by the time they came to professional attention, direct work with the children was, in the main, neglected. Also overlooked, when their physical safety was so much at stake, was the potentially damaging effect on the children's personality and emotional development of separating them from their parents, placing them in hospital often for extended periods, and moving them from one caretaker to another.

1.3   It is only now, in the second decade of child abuse research, that professionals have begun to ask, 'for what are we saving these children and what is the quality of their subsequent life?' Knowledge about abused children's long-term development is still limited but the depressing data from existing follow-up studies on their neurologic, cognitive, social and emotional development have prompted us to acknowledge that there is an urgent need to broaden our therapeutic goals.

2   Developmental problems of abused children

2.1   In order to appreciate some of the problems of abused children this paper will give an overview rather than detailed consideration of the follow-up studies. Apart from identifying common consequences of abuse some consideration will also be given to what extent these are consequences of:

1.   The physical injuries per se.
2.   Other malevolent environmental influences of the kind frequently associated with abuse, each of which is already known to have the potential to impair and disrupt the growing child's development. These include under-nutrition, emotional and physical neglect, social and/or economic disadvantage, emotional disturbance in the parents and family instability.
3.   Professional intervention and treatment planning.

2.2   The literature shows that common sampling problems have been met by most of the researchers conducting follow-up studies of children diagnosed as abused. Abusive families are difficult to trace because of their frequently high mobility rate; parents resist evaluation of their children; the children may have died or been placed far away from their family of origin in institutions or adoptive or foster homes. While the morbidity in children who are traced has been shown to be serious, one feels even more pessimistic about the fate of many of the other children, who were not available for study, as they are likely to be living in considerably worse environments with minimal or no professional intervention.

F

2.3 Other methodological problems associated with the follow-up studies include failure to employ matched comparison groups so that the findings may be skewed by uncontrollable variables such as social class, and failure to document the type of intervention the families have received. Methods of assessing the children vary from study to study, some researchers having used a range of formal and developmental tests whereas others have relied mainly on clinical impressionistic data.

2.4 In spite of the difficulties described above, the findings of a variety of follow-up studies in different countries, concur that abused children are clearly at high risk for damage to the central nervous system and maldevelopment of ego function. Mental retardation, learning disorders, perceptual-motor dysfunction, cerebral palsy, impaired speech and language, growth failure and emotional disturbance are documented with depressing frequency (Elmer, 1967; Elmer and Gregg, 1967; Birrell and Birrell, 1968; Johnson and Morse, 1968; Terr, 1970; Martin, 1972, 1974, 1976; Sandgrund et al., 1974; Morse et al., 1970; Smith and Hanson, 1974; Baldwin and Oliver, 1975; Straus and Girodet, 1976; Kline, 1976). However there are conflicting findings on the extent to which such physical or developmental deviations antedate abuse and are of a congenital nature or are the result of rearing in an abusive environment.

2.5 The hard data from follow-up studies relate chiefly to mortality and significant intellectual and neuromotor handicap. Considerable variation has been noted in the type and severity of neurologic damage sustained by abused children. Physical assault on the head may itself be the cause of the child's neurologic handicap but it is important to emphasize that a young child can suffer significant damage to the brain through violent shaking (Caffey, 1972, 1974) with no outward sign of damage to the head such as bruises or fractures of the skull. Martin (1974) reports that as expected neurologic dysfunction is highly related to IQ and a history of head trauma. However he emphasizes that some children with serious head injury were not retarded and that significant neurologic dysfunction occurred in 16 children with no obvious explanation of the cause and no documented history of head trauma. Hence Martin, Baron (1970) and others conclude that the nervous systems of abused children are also at risk from the psychological and environmental stresses to which they are exposed, and that neurologic dysfunction may be an adaptation to the abusive environment. Galdston (1975) on the basis of observations of abused children recently admitted to a day care centre, reports that some children were so retarded in their development and that their movements were so clumsy and uncoordinated that brain damage was suspected. However after a short period of daily attendance at the centre the same children demonstrated such rapid improvements in motor activity that the diagnosis of organic brain damage was precluded.

2.6 In a number of studies under-nutrition has been reported in approximately 30–35 per cent of abused children at the time abuse was recognized (Elmer, 1967; Birrell and Birrell, 1968; Martin, 1972). Martin (1974) refers to convincing evidence that under-nutrition during the first year of life can and does result in permanent effects on the nervous system, including motor dysfunction and mental impairment; and in older children may reduce the child's ability to focus on, orient to or systain interest in learning tasks. Martin's (1972) report of 42 abused children as well as Elmer's (1967) report indicate a significant difference in intellectual prognosis when under-nourished, abused children were compared with well-nourished abused children. It appears that children who are under-nourished as well as physically abused have a much poorer prognosis in terms of mental function and neurologic integrity.

2.7   The psychological damage sustained by abused children has been, in the main, the subject of speculation. For example, Green (1968) postulates that early physical abuse which occurs in a matrix of overall rejection and stimulus deprivation may enhance the development of pain dependent behaviour. The children may become accident prone, indulge in self-destructive behaviour or establish a pattern of inviting harm and playing the victim (Bender, 1976). The latter may be one reason why some children get rebattered in foster homes. Other writers have emphasized the tendency of the children to identify with aggressive parents and pattern themselves on the parents' behaviour. Clinical experience suggests that the young child physically abused at a pre-verbal stage of development is particularly prone to develop violent behaviour as a character trait (Galdston, 1975). The most detailed study of the emotional development of abused children to date has been completed by Martin and Beezley (1976). The nine characteristics and behaviour noted with impressive frequency and intensity in the 50 children studied included:

1.   Impaired capacity to enjoy life.
2.   Psychiatric symptoms (e.g. enuresis, tantrums, hyperactivity, bizarre behaviour).
3.   Low self-esteem.
4.   School learning problems.
5.   Withdrawal.
6.   Opposition.
7.   Hypervigilance.
8.   Compulsivity.
9.   Pseudo-mature behaviour.

Over 50 per cent of these abused children had poor self-concepts, were sorrowful children and exhibited a number of symptomatic behaviours which made peers, parents and teachers reject them. Martin and Beezley's data do not confirm any relationship between the type of injury nor the age at which it was inflicted with subsequent emotional development. Psychiatric symptoms were on the other hand significantly correlated 4.5 years after abuse with environmental factors such as the impermanence of the subsequent home, instability of the family with whom the child was living, punitiveness and rejection by caretakers and the emotional state of the parents or parent surrogates. Elsewhere Martin et al. (1974) noted that even the intelligence of abused children, when brain damage was controlled for, correlated quite highly with the subsequent stability and punitiveness of the home.

2.8 Scant attention has been paid to the siblings of abused children in the existing literature yet the psychological effects of witnessing or being aware of repeated ill-treatment are likely to be profound. A few studies that have involved siblings of the presenting children indicate that they are also at risk of physical abuse, be they older or younger, and that they often appear as deviant in their functioning as the child identified as abused (Johnson and Morse, 1968; Skinner and Castle, 1969; Baldwin and Oliver, 1975; Smith and Hanson, 1974; Baher et al., 1976; Straus and Girodet, 1976). It would seem that these children have few healthy ways of adapting to the abusive environment. However variations in the inherent equipment of the child, which determine his capacity to adapt to these stresses or to surmount the damaging influences of earlier developmental insults when placed in more favourable environments, warrant further exploration.

2.9 A major mechanism of survival for an endangered child is modification of his behaviour according to his surroundings. Malone (1966) has noted that pre-school children living in dangerous environments (including danger of abuse from their parents) have certain areas of overdeveloped ego functioning, areas of advanced ability. These include extreme sensitivity to parental moods and discomfort and role reversal with parents such as making decisions for them or taking care of younger siblings; such 'precocious' behaviour is constantly reinforced by the parents. While the child's ability to cope and his areas of overdeveloped ego-strength are highly adaptive and assets to survival, they are weaknesses insofar as they contribute to the child's literalness and inflexibility. Similarly Martin and Beezley (1976), out of their total sample of 50 abused children, identified a group of 10 pseudo-adult children who demonstrated precocious behaviour and a group of 11 children who demonstrated marked compulsivity. Both groups tended to have a high frustration tolerance and were extremely attentive and co-operative in the testing situation. Martin and Beezley stress that although these behaviours appeared to be more successful modes of adaptation they are not necessarily healthy ways of coping. 'The compulsive and pseudo-adult children were locked into styles which are not conducive to age appropriate enjoyment or flexibility. Compulsivity, by definition, connotes rigidity and inflexibility. The

pseudo-adult child has forfeited his right to feel and act like a child, instead planning his life for the pleasure of adults rather than for himself.'
2.10 The above examples describe the behavioural characteristics of a small group of children who appear to have learnt certain adaptive coping mechanisms in order to survive in dangerous environments but at considerable cost to themselves. However we can no longer assume that the abusive environment results in either a specific personality or a neurologic profile. Some abused children have been observed to be passive, withdrawn, unresponsive and apathetic while others present as hyperactive, aggressive, attention seeking and extremely provocative (Baher et al., 1976; Martin and Beezley, 1976). Some with extremely high intelligence do well at school and keep pace with their parents' high expectations, but they more commonly present with school learning problems (Martin, 1974; Martin and Rodeheffer, 1976; Kline, 1976).

3 The effects of professional intervention and treatment planning

3.1 Another basis for the varying effects of abuse is related to what happens to the children after the diagnosis of physical abuse. Hospitalization, separation from parents, frequent home changes and poor quality foster homes or institutional placements may be more damaging to the child in the long term than the physical trauma itself. Martin and Beezley (1974a) discuss how professional intervention and treatment planning often contribute to the abused child's difficulty in developing a sense of object constancy or a concept of self. In Martin's own study (1976) seventeen children had from three to eight home changes from the time of identified abuse to follow up (mean of 4.5 years). The more seriously maladjusted the child, the more likely he was to have had three or more home changes. Similarly the more maladjusted a child was, the more likely he was to have perceived his present home as lacking permanence. Martin comments 'there is no data to show that any of these study children had been physically injured in foster homes but we know that in foster care they were frequently subjected to inappropriate discipline, indifference, rejection or seductiveness. Moreover efforts to reunite the family may prevent consideration of the optimal home placement for the child in foster care. Many children were placed back with their parents on a trial basis repeatedly.'
3.2 Baher et al. (1976) emphasize the urgent need for information on the relative merits of various type of protective placements for abused children in comparison with the home environment. They describe the difficulties that arise when choice of placement is governed not only by the extent to which it will meet the child's emotional needs but also by the extent to

which it will encourage and enhance the parent–child relationship. They comment 'with hindsight, we now feel that in several cases, the child's interest might have been better served if the focus of our intervention had been on helping the parents to accept permanent separation rather than on working towards rehabilitation.' Baher et al. (1976) also note that disrupted caretaking featured prominently in the childhood of many of the abusive parents studied.

3.3 Besides considering the possible damaging effects on the child of professional intervention, what needs examining is the extent to which such intervention is capable of improving the abusive home environment. The intervention by many child protective agencies still seems concentrated on the prevention of recurrence of physical assault with little attention to improvement of the home environment. As soon as the home seems reasonably safe for the child from the standpoint of physical abuse, professionals tend to decrease their visits and support. However it is distressing to those who are concerned about the abused child that the few studies that have attempted to evaluate progress in families in relation to the type of therapeutic intervention experienced, suggest that even intensive long-term treatment programmes have had little ostensible impact so far on the parents' distorted views of the child or on the aberrant child-rearing practices.

3.4 In 1970, Morse et al., reported a follow-up study of 25 children who had been hospitalized three years previously for injuries or illnesses judged to be the result of abuse or gross neglect. During that three year period one-third of the children were again neglected or abused. The data from this study are discouraging. Only 29 per cent of the children were within normal limits intellectually and emotionally at the time of the follow up; 42 per cent were considered mentally retarded and 28 per cent were significantly emotionally disturbed. Ten out of 19 children were below the tenth percentile in height and weight. The study attempted to relate the degree of agency intervention to the status of the abused children at the time of the follow-up study. No pattern of relationships could be found. The authors comment, 'neither the amount of time nor skill expended by agency workers and nurses was predictive of how well the children progressed'. In fact the only characteristic common to the majority of children who appeared to be developing normally was a good mother–child relationship *as perceived and reported by the mothers*. Additional data from Morse's study suggest that the milieu of the abused child and more specifically the parents' perception of the child are critical influences on the child's development.

3.5 Martin and Beezley (1976a) also report on the relationship between the therapy received by the abusing parents and the subsequent developmental status of 58 abused children at a mean of 4.5 years after abuse had first been documented. They comment 'It was disheartening to note the current behaviour of the parents towards the previously abused child'. Parents of 21 of the children had had psychotherapy as part of their treatment programme; 90 per cent of the children of these parents were still living in the biologic home. Even though the children were no longer being battered in the technical or legal sense, 68 per cent of them at follow-up were still experiencing hostile rejection and/or excessive physical punishment. However, these children were faring much better than those whose parents had received no formal treatment. Of those parents who had received only casework or services from a public health nurse, only 43 per cent of the children were living with them at follow-up. Thirty-six per cent were still in foster care and 21 per cent had been adopted. The families where no formal treatment had been instituted for the parents were even less satisfactory. In this group of children only 40 per cent were living with the parents, and of those, 83 per cent were the objects of rejection and excessive physical punishment. In all three groups of parents there remained considerable chaos in the family function. As already stated in this paper, the severity and frequency of psychiatric symptoms in the children correlated significantly with unstable family function and punitiveness and rejection by caretakers.

3.6 Baher et al. (1976) have evaluated the progress made in families referred to the Battered Child Research Department of the NSPCC, after a substantial period of intensive therapeutic intervention. This was of value to the abusive parents and improvements in several aspects of family functioning are reported. Also the supportive, intensive care provided, was, in the main, associated with an absence of rebattering or a reduction in its probable severity. The findings on the cognitive development of the children are encouraging. They show that the Department's system of care helped to restore the child's overall developmental status in most cases with those in the special therapeutic day nursery showing the greatest improvement of all. However, psychological assessment also indicated that these children's family relationships remained distorted, especially their relationship with their mothers, and differed from those of non-abused but deprived controls. This was substantiated by the fact that only slight positive changes were noted in most aspects of parent–child interaction, leaving many doubts about the effectiveness of the treatment service in improving the quality of parenting. The majority of the children were still living in homes where empathy and sensitivity to their needs were still lacking, where inconsistent and often harsh discipline remained the mode, where parental expectations remained inappropriately high and where little positive reinforcement took place.

3.7 In the author's estimation only eight out of twenty-three children seemed to be making reasonably satisfactory and *sustained* emotional development at the time of final evaluation. Of the remainder, a few had serious emotional problems which caused grave anxiety about their future development. A few were like weathervanes who reflected the moods of their parents by regressing or displaying disturbances when the home situation was particularly stressful. The authors comment '. . . we now feel that our dual and interlinked emphasis on treatment of the parents and protection of the children, neglected an important area, the psychotherapeutic treatment of the children, which could well be provided in a day care setting'.

4 Implications for future therapeutic intervention on behalf of abused children

4.1 It is apparent from the material presented in this paper that abused children (and frequently their siblings) undergo considerable physical and emotional suffering and that their proper development is impaired in a variety of ways for a variety of reasons. We still have a long way to go in devising methods of intervention that will improve the quality of life for these children. In future professionals must concern themselves with the needs and rights of the child in a broader context than that of physical safety. We must try to find ways of counteracting other malevolent aspects of home life which result in emotional disorder, inhibited intellectual capacity and a propensity to resort to violence in adult life (Curtis, 1963; Silver et al., 1969; Steele, 1970).

The need for child abuse treatment programmes to include comprehensive developmental assessment of all battered children at the time abuse is diagnosed cannot be over emphasized. Only then can their special needs be recognized and appropriate services such as speech therapy, occupational therapy, play therapy and psychotherapy be provided. Subsequently all abused children should be required to be kept under periodic review by medical, psychological and social work staff so that their development can be closely monitored. In accordance with the current interest in child advocacy it would be helpful if a key worker for the child could always be designated at the initial case conference. This person would then assume special responsibility for reporting on the child's development and representing his interests at subsequent reviews.

We can no longer cling to the assumption that treatment of the parents will automatically improve the quality of life and relationships for the child. Direct work with the children is essential since their whole personality organization is endangered. Some children may benefit greatly from short-term support from a sensitive, understanding adult such as their doctor, nurse, social worker, concerned teacher or friend, who can help them deal with the immediate stress of physical injury, hospitalization, court hearings, separation from parents and placement with substitute caretakers. Other abused children will undoubtedly require more intensive therapy to assist them with persistent and deep-seated problems. For example, they may need help in improving their self-concept; in dealing with their own anger; in loosening their inhibitions; in learning to enjoy age-appropriate pleasures, that adults can be trusted and that love is not always conditional on the gratification of adult needs.

4.4 Dr. Ruth Kempe (1975) has discussed the relative merits of individual and group psychotherapy for the pre-school abused child. She describes the difficulties of engaging pre-school children in individual therapy, not the least being parental resistance. She has found group therapy in a special nursery setting easier to arrange and more appropriate for this age range. Individual therapy is often more suitable for the school age child for two reasons. Firstly, the school age child is already used to coping with two environments and sets of relationships and making the shift from one to the other. Secondly school-age children are more able to verbalise, more aware of their difficulties and are perhaps better motivated towards treatment. Group therapy for latency age abused children and their siblings is currently being investigated as a mode of help at the National Center for the Prevention and Treatment of Child Abuse and Neglect in Denver.

4.5 Bearing in mind the acute shortage of child psychiatrists and psychotherapists, play therapists and social workers skilled in communicating with young children, we must enlist other personnel, such as experienced nursery nurses and carefully selected, sensitive foster parents to help meet these children's needs. At the same time the stress on those workers who become involved in the treatment of the children and are able to share in the horror and pain that many of these child clients have experienced, should not be overlooked. They, in turn, need regular support and consultation themselves.

4.6 Ideally the workers treating the parents and those involved in providing therapeutic day care for the children should be based under the same roof. Galdston (1975), Ten Broeck (1974), Ounsted et al. (1975), Bentovim (1976), Alexander et al. (1976) have discussed the great value of special day or residential family centres in which a multi-faceted treatment programme can be offered, including vital work on the abnormal and distorted parent–child interactions. For example, this may include individual and/or group therapy for the parents, parent self-help groups, specific therapeutic attention for individual children in a day-care setting and joint play therapy sessions for parents and children. This kind of setting also helps to facilitate close communication, mutual understanding and support between all staff involved in the treatment process.

4.7 The parents may also benefit from direct education in alternative methods of child rearing (Paulson and Chaleff, 1973; Savino and Saunders, 1973; Smith et al., 1973). However it is important for practitioners to recognize that many abusive parents suffer from an emotional rather than an intellectual block to understanding their children's needs and development and that their receptiveness to instruction on child management is highly contingent on the establishment of a relationship of trust with the workers involved. Jeffrey (1975) describes a very interesting programme based on education and behaviour modifications for changing parent–child interaction in families of children at risk. Practical techniques utilised in the homes of abusive parents include: interventions to change the negative quality of general interaction between children and care givers, interventions to change attitudes and interventions to change the children's responses.

4.8 Undoubtedly permanent separation of the child from his family is another therapeutic option which should be considered more frequently than it is at present in child abuse cases. Clarke and Clarke (1976) have collated evidence that against expectation even severe deprivation can be reversed. They include Koluchova's reports (1972, 1976)[1] on a pair of identical twins in Czechoslovakia who, after being isolated and cruelly treated from the age of 18 months to 7 years by their stepmother, have made surprisingly good progress since placement in a therapeutic foster home. Reference is also made to Kadushin's (1970) work on the successful placement of older children for adoption despite earlier neglect and ill-treatment. While it is impossible to lay down rigorous rules of thumb regarding decisions over permanent removal, the need in some cases remains not only to ensure the child's safety but also to facilitate his development in the broadest sense. In the recent move in child care thinking towards a greater emphasis on the rights of the child as an individual (Goldstein, Freud and Solnit, 1973) there has been a tendency to assume that it is relatively easy to decide that a child has no long-term future with his family. In the experience of practitioners, however, such a prognosis may be difficult to make until the family has been known for some time, and yet only if decisions about separation are made early in the casework process, can frequent disruptions of caretaking for the children be avoided. Of help here would be the setting up of more residential assessment centres similar to the one at the Park Hospital, Oxford, England or the Parental Stress Centre, Pittsburgh, USA, where the whole family could be intensively observed in a safe place over a period of weeks or months. The family's response to efforts to augment their caretaking capacities and capacity for change could then be evaluated as well as the quality of parent–child interaction. At the same time the child is protected and assured optimum growth and development by means of a stimulating environment. Another goal would be to establish more scientific and

---

[1] [Papers 29 and 30 in this Reader.]

legally acceptable criteria for court determination and disposition than are available at this time. This seems vital in view of many of the provisions of the Children Act (1975), for example, the provision which brings in, as additional ground for dispensing with parental agreement to adoption that the parent or guardian has seriously ill-treated the child and, because of the ill-treatment, or for other reasons, the rehabilitation of the child within the household of the parent or guardian is unlikely.

4.9   In conclusion, it has to be acknowledged that detailed study of the phenomenon of child abuse forces us to consider uncomfortable issues relating to the status and treatment of children in the population at large. Regardless of whether they have been physically abused, many children who may never come to professional attention are living in sub-optimal environments and experiencing the kind of inadequate parenting described in this paper which could permanently impair and disrupt their development. Abused children as a group are currently the focus of much public and professional concern in many different countries. It is to be hoped that by devoting considerable attention and resources to them and their families, we shall learn more about preventing the transmission of all kinds of damaging patterns of child rearing from one generation to the next.

References

ALEXANDER, H., et al. (1976) 'Residential Family Therapy', Ch. 19 in Martin, H. P. (ed.) *The Abused Child—A Multidisciplinary Approach to Developmental Issues and Treatment*, Cambridge, Mass., Ballinger.

BAHER, E., HYMAN, C., JONES, C., JONES, R., KERR, A., MITCHELL, R. (1976) *'At Risk' An Account of the work of the Battered Child Research Dept, NSPCC*, London, Routledge.

BALDWIN, J. A. and OLIVER, J. E. (1975) 'Epidemiology and Family Characteristics of Severely Abused Children', *Brit. J. Prev. Soc. Med.*, **29**, 205–221.

BARON, M. A., et al. (1970) 'Neurologic Manifestations of the Battered Child Syndrome', *Pediatrics*, **45**, 1003–1007.

BENDER, B. (1976) 'Self-Chosen Victims: Scapegoating Behaviour, Sequential to Battering', *Child Welfare*, **LV**, no. 6, 417–422.

BENTOVIM, A. (1976) 'A Psychiatric Family Day Centre Meeting the Needs of Abused or At Risk Pre-school Children and their Parents', *Paper presented at the first International Congress of child abuse and neglect, W.H.O., Geneva*.

BIRRELL, R. G. and BIRRELL, J. H. W. (1968) 'The Maltreatment Syndrome in Children: A Hospital Survey', *Med. J. Aust.*, **2**, 1023–1029.

CAFFEY, J. (1972) 'On the Theory and Practice of Shaking Infants: its

C. O. JONES

Potential Residual Effects of Permanent Brain Damage and Mental Retardation', *Am. J. Dis. Child*, **124**, 161–169.

CAFFEY, J. (1974) 'The Whiplash Shaken Infant Syndrome: Manual Shaking by the Extremities with Whiplash-induced Intracranial and Intraocular Bleedings, Linked with Permanent Brain Damage and Mental Retardation', *Pediatrics*, **54**, 396–403.

CLARKE, A. M. and CLARKE, A. D. B. (1976) *'Early Experience: Myth and Evidence'*, London, Open Books.

CURTIS, G. C. (1963) 'Violence Breeds Violence—Perhaps?', *Am. J. Psychiatry*, **120**, 386–387.

ELMER, E. (1967) *'Children in Jeopardy'*, Pittsburgh, University of Pittsburgh Press.

ELMER, E. and GREGG, G. S. (1967) 'Developmental Characteristics of Abused Children', *Pediatrics*, **40**, no. 4 Part I, 596–602.

GALDSTON, R. (1975) 'Preventing the Abuse of Little Children', *Amer. J. Orthopsychiat.*, **45**, no. 3, 372–381.

GOLDSTEIN, J., FREUD, A. and SOLNIT, A. J. (1973) *'Beyond the Best Interests of the Child'*, London, Collier–Macmillan.

GREEN, A. H. (1968) 'Self-Destructive Behaviour in Physically Abused Schizophrenic Children', *Arch. Gen. Psychiat.*, **19**, 171–179.

JEFFREY, M. (1975) 'Therapeutic Intervention for Children at Risk and their Parents' in *Proceedings of First Australian National Conference on the Battered Child*, Western Australia, Department of Community Welfare.

JOHNSON, B. and MORSE, H. A. (1968) *'The Battered Child: A Study of Children with Inflicted Injuries'*, Denver Department of Welfare.

KADUSHIN, A. (1970) *'Adopting Older Children'*, Columbia University Press.

KEMPE, C. H. et al. (1962) 'The Battered Child Syndrome', *J.A.M.A.*, **181**, 17–24.

KEMPE, R. (1975) 'Individual and Group Psychotherapy of the Pre-School Battered Child' in *Proceedings of First Australian National Conference on the Battered Child*, Western Australia: Department of Community Welfare.

KLINE, D. F. (1976) 'Educational and Psychological Problems of Abused Children', *Paper presented at the first International Congress on Child Abuse and Neglect, W.H.O., Geneva.*

KOLUCHOVA, J. (1972) 'Severe Deprivation in Twins: A Case Study', *J. of Child Psychol. Psychiat and Allied Disciplines*, **13**, 103–106.

KOLUCHOVA, J. (1976) 'The Further Development of Twins after Severe and Prolonged Deprivation: A Second Report', *J. of Child Psychol. Psychiat. and Allied Disciplines*, **17**, 181–188.

MALONE, C. A. (1966) 'Safety First: Comments on the Influence of External Danger in the Lives of Children of Disorganised Families', *Amer. J. Orthopsychiat.*, **36**, 3–12.

MARTIN, H. P. (1972) 'The Child and his Development' in Kempe, C. H. and Helfer, R. E. (eds.) *Helping the Battered Child and his Family*, Philadelphia and Toronto, Lippincott.

MARTIN, H. P. et al. (1974) 'The Development of Abused Children', *Advances in Pediatrics*, **21**, 25–73.

MARTIN, H. P. and BEEZLEY, P. (1974)a 'Prevention and Consequences of Child Abuse', *J. of Operational Psychiat.*, **VI**, no. 1, 68–77.

MARTIN, H. P. and BEEZLEY, P. (1976) 'The Emotional Development of Abused Children', accepted for publ. *Devel. med. Child Neurol.*

MARTIN, H. P. and BEEZLEY, P. (1976)a 'Therapy for Abusive Parents: Its Effect on the Child', Ch. 20 in Martin, H. P. (ed.) *The Abused Child—A Multidisciplinary Approach to Developmental Issues and Treatment*, Cambridge, Mass., Ballinger.

MARTIN, H. P. and RODEHEFFER, M. (1976) 'Learning and Intelligence', Ch. 8 in Martin, H. P. (ed.) *The Abused Child—A Multidisciplinary Approach to Developmental Issues and Treatment*, Cambridge, Mass., Ballinger.

MORSE, C. W. et al. (1970) 'A Three Year Follow-up Study of Abused and Neglected Children', *Am. J. Dis. Child.*, **120**, 439–446.

OUNSTED, C. et al. (1975) 'The Psychopathology and Psychotherapy of the Families: Aspects of Bonding Failure', Ch. 4 in White Franklin, A. (ed.) *Concerning Child Abuse*, Edinburgh, Churchill Livingstone.

PAULSON, M. J. and CHALEFF, A. (1973) 'Parent Surrogate Roles: A Dynamic Concept in Understanding and Treating Abusive Parents', *J. Clin. Child Psychol.*, **11**, 38–40.

SANDGRUND, A., et al. (1974) 'Child Abuse and Mental Retardation: A problem of Cause and Effect', *Amer. J. of Mental Deficiency*, **79**, 327–330.

SAVINO, A. B. and SAUNDERS, R. W. (1973) 'Working with Abusive Parents: Group Therapy and Home Visits', *Amer. J. Nursing*, **73**, 482–484.

SILVER, L. B. et al. (1969) 'Does Violence breed Violence? Contributions from a Study of the Child Abuse Syndrome', *Amer. J. Psychiat.*, **126**, 404–407.

SKINNER, A. E. and CASTLE, R. L. (1969) '78 Battered Children', *A Retrospective Study*, London, NSPCC.

SMITH, S. M., HANSON, R. and NOBLE, S. (1973) 'Parents of Battered Babies: A Controlled Study', *Brit. med. J.*, **4**, 388–91.

SMITH, S. M. and HANSON, R. (1974) '134 Battered Children: a Medical and Psychological Study', *Brit. med. J.*, **3**, 666–70.

STEELE, B. F. (1970) 'Violence in our Society', *Pharos of Alpha Omega Alpha*, **33**, no. 2, 42–48.

STRAUS, P. and GIRODET, D. (1976) 'Three French Follow-up Studies of Abused Children', *Paper presented at the first International Congress on Child Abuse and Neglect*, W.H.O., Geneva.

TEN BROECK, E. (1974) 'The Extended Family Center: A Home Away from

Home for Abused Children and their Parents', *Children Today*, **3**, 2–6.
TERR, L. (1970) 'A Family Study of Child Abuse', *Amer. J. Psychiat.*, **127**, 125–131.

17 Consumer's viewpoint
A battering parent

Most people become users of social services through no fault of their own. They may be poor, sick, homeless, grief-stricken, frightened or even aggressive—but their pride is usually intact. However, I am a consumer because I am a battering parent, and my child is in care. So for me, guilt replaces pride as an additional factor. My guilt inevitably colours my attitude to social services.

Initially, I sought help myself, now I am writing this because I am concerned that people in a similar situation—my peers—also receive adequate help. I worry too about breakdowns in communication, because I know how easy it is for my mood to be misinterpreted, and how it is possible to manipulate someone in authority. These 'breakdowns' have occurred elsewhere, with sickening consequences, and will I am afraid, occur again. A layman can sometimes spot a potential batterer a mile off, yet a trained social worker may miss one at five paces. We all know at least one person without the necessary 'O' levels, who has the insight to see 'underneath' a problem. There is an enormous gulf between tea and sympathy and the social worker's case-notes. To err is human, social workers are human, and inevitably there will be tragic mistakes.

The hardest path I tread is the one between support from social services and an over-dependence on them. I find my confidence can easily be undermined, albeit by well-meaning people. Occasionally I wish they would foster my independence, and curb my leaning. On the whole however, I receive a balanced service. For example, the delay experienced in being allowed to care for my son by having him at home for reasonable periods of time, ideally coincided with my own feelings of ability to cope. There have been occasions where milestones have been reached too slowly, and conversely sometimes, too quickly, but my frustration has been shared with my social worker.

Social services take over where the family unit left off. Sometimes, as in a family, there is a conflict of personalities, between worker and client. Guilt makes me concede that my ensuing unhappiness is fair retribution, but at times I become rebellious. The family unit recognizes such conflict, but social services surrogate parents know no such bounds. So at one

ANONYMOUS (1976) 'Consumer's viewpoint', by a battering parent, *Social Work Today*, vol. 7, no. 3, p. 78.

point I hated my child, my social worker and myself. Most of these feelings are now resolved, but it was a painful experience for us all. However, I do now have a viable relationship with my son.

In an 'ideal' society, I'd like to see a surfeit of social workers, so personalities could be matched more closely. In four years I have come across intelligent, intellectually inferior, patronizing, understanding, moralistic, punitive and even supercilious social workers. The same can be said for doctors, police, health visitors, and other officials. I feel ambivalent about all these agencies, because of the variation in my experiences. By reacting differently to all these approaches, I became more unsure of my *own* identity. Also, the workers' reactions differing so greatly made co-operation difficult to say the least. One social worker's undisguised abhorrence of what I had done to my son, initially made me feel like a monster. Then I rationalized that as she was a mother herself, but unable to identify with even a small part of my hate towards my son, then she was the freak not me. After all, isn't it a now widely accepted fact, that all parents hate their children at times?

Sometimes I overcame this 'holier-than-thou' attitude by showing my superiority in other ways. Intellectually I could run rings around some of the social workers, and took delight in doing so. They would flounder in my sea of words, and I would go away triumphant. My only net gain though, was a bolstered ego, because the time wasted inevitably made slower my rehabilitation as a mother. The only recurring pattern to emerge from these varied confrontations, is my guilt.

I'd like a generic worker, who could deal with any aspect of her clients' problems, whether germane or not, without referring me to another agency. She would also deal with the problems of other members of the family herself—after all, these invariably interact with your own problems. For example my daughter was at a school for emotionally disturbed children, but my social worker was unwilling to discuss her case with me, although I needed to talk about the feelings aroused, by having her temporarily 'beyond my care'. A further example of a non-generic worker's drawbacks, is the NSPCC inspector (who dealt with my case previous to social services) who refused to discuss my ailing marriage but referred me to the Marriage Guidance Council.

In addition to possessing a compatible personality, I'd like one worker to see a case through from start to finish. As I am now working with my sixth social worker, I am well aware of the pitfalls in the lack of continuity. I realize that when people move this is not always feasible, but could the case-notes be forwarded quickly, too? Could the social worker make herself known to the family, soon after the move, in a supportive role and not as an obvious deterrent? Sometimes families are determined to disappear behind a mask of anonymity, despite all efforts to keep track of them. It is for this reason that I am all in favour of a central register of both confirmed and suspected batterers. The information would be computerized, and housed in one building. Ideally it would be continually updated with information from all branches of the medical profession, and associated services, and the police and other agencies, possibly even extending to teachers. Care would have to be taken that only authorized persons could have access to these records. Even over the telephone some way would have to be evolved to stop undesirables, i.e. the press, from obtaining this information. There would of course be 'teething problems' and there may also be administrative problems that I have not foreseen.

I would also like to see more group therapy (although I had a very satisfactory one-to-one therapy), more attention to those 'silent' cries for help and more 'safety nets'. By safety-nets I mean 24-hour relief centres where you can temporarily, and voluntarily relinquish responsibility during a traumatic period. These would be like a creche, but with trained social workers to initially advise the parent, as well as offering temporary relief. Also, more short term fostering or short stay accommodation in a place of care, i.e. hospital, or a children's home, to ease the burden, while the parents receive help. A general vigilance is needed by all concerned with child welfare, possibly aided by more films and lectures on the subject of child abuse.

Greater liaison and the following up of information may lead to a reduction, but I believe the nearest thing to a cure of society's ills, especially that of cruelty to children, is to be found in our own communities. If we ever revert to the time when generations of families lived in the same neighbourhood, then things may be different. If, once again the grandparents become the hub of the family, acting as midwives, health-visitors, baby-sitters and general advisers, baby battering may be reduced. Social services could well be replaced by the family incorporate.

Part Four   Psychotherapeutic and Psychiatric Aspects

Attitudes to abusing adults vary greatly and this adds to the responsibility faced by doctors and therapists in their diagnosis and treatment of battering parents.

Two opposing views are presented in this section, one is an extract from a report of studies carried out in America and the other in England. Steele and Pollock believe that abusing parents are sick people whose behaviour can be modified by treatment directed towards improving the pattern of child rearing; Smith takes the view that a high proportion of abusing adults have personality deviations or psychiatric disorders which are resistant to modern methods of treatment.

The papers by Ounsted et al. and Reavley and Gilbert describe treatment techniques which have been used with abusing families. This is further dealt with in Part Six.

18 General characteristics of abusing parents
B. F. Steele and C. B. Pollock

[During a five and a half year period Steele and his colleagues studied 60 families in which significant abuse of infants or small children occurred. The families were referred through various services and agencies.

The group is not thought to be useful for statistical proof of any concepts, it was not picked by a valid sampling technique, nor was it a 'total population'. The researchers believe that their data have particular significance because their haphazardly selected group provides a spectrum of child abusing behaviour which negates in many respects stereotypes of the 'child beater' popularly held.]

. . . The ethnic background of most of our families was Anglo-Saxon American. There were also a few whose backgrounds were Scandinavian, Irish, German, Eastern European, and Spanish-American. We saw only one Negro family very briefly, but we draw from a population which is less than 10 per cent Negro. There were children of immigrants but no immigrants. True alcoholism was not a problem except in one family, and many were total abstainers. Among those who did use alcohol, drinking was occasionally a source of marital conflict but bore no significant, direct relationship to episodes of child beating.

The actual attack on the infant is usually made by one parent. In our series, the mother was the attacker in 50 instances and the father in 7 instances. We were unable to be sure which parent was involved in two families, and in one family both parents attacked.

These general characteristics of the parents in this study, as described above, are significantly different from those reported by Elmer (1964, 1965) and others (Young 1964 and Greengard 1964). The incidence of poverty, alcoholism, broken marriages, and prominence of certain racial groups is not significant in our series. We do not believe our data are any more accurate than those of other reporters, but that different reports reflect the inevitable result of using skewed samples. Social agencies, welfare organizations, and municipal hospitals will inevitably draw most of their child beaters from lower socioeconomic strata. Our institution

---

STEELE, B. F. and POLLOCK, C. B. (1968) 'A psychiatric study of parents who abuse infants and small children', in Helfer, R. E. and Kempe, C. H. (eds.) *The Battered Child*, Chicago and London, University of Chicago Press (2nd edn. 1974) pp. 93-7, 112-16.

116

serves a wide range of socioeconomic groups and is closely associated with physicians in private medical practice. Obviously, our sample will be skewed in a quite different way. Our data show a great majority of women as child beaters. Other reports show a roughly fifty–fifty distribution between male and female, and some a significant predominance of men. We suspect that our low incidence of male attackers is related in part to a low incidence of unemployment among the males in the group. . . .

Similar comments may be made concerning the other social, economic, and demographic factors mentioned above. Basically they are somewhat irrelevant to the actual act of child beating. Unquestionably, social and economic difficulties and disasters put added stress in people's lives and contribute to behavior which might otherwise remain dormant. But such factors must be considered as incidental enhancers rather than necessary and sufficient causes. Not all parents who are unemployed and in financial straits, poor housing, shattered marriages, and alcoholic difficulties abuse their children; nor does being an abstaining, devout Christian with a high IQ, stable marriage, fine home, and plenty of money prevent attack on infants. These facts are well recognized by most of those who work in the area of child abuse. We have stressed them, however, because large segments of our culture, including many in the medical profession, are still prone to believe that child abuse occurs only among 'bad people' of low socioeconomic status. This is not true.*

Psychopathology of the attackers

General characteristics

As noted in the previous section, the parents in this study were not at all a homogenous group from the standpoint of their general descriptive characteristics. In respect to psychopathology they were equally heterogenous. They do not fall into any single one of our usual psychiatric diagnostic categories. On the contrary, they present the wide spread of emotional disorders seen in any clinic population—hysteria, hysterical psychosis, obsessive-compulsive neurosis, anxiety states, depression, schizoid personality traits, schizophrenia, character neurosis, and so on. It was not possible to make a simple diagnosis in most patients. They

---

* It would be hard to find a group more deprived and in more socioeconomic difficulty than the Spanish-American migrant agricultural workers. We spent some time running down rumors of child abuse in this group and were unable to document a single instance. Possibly some cases do occur, but we were unable to find them.

presented mixed pictures such as 'obsessive-phobic neurosis with marked masochistic features and mild depression.' A majority of the patients could be said to be depressed at some time. Psychosomatic illnesses such as asthma, headaches, migraine, colitis, dysmenorrhea, urticaria, and vomiting were significant in several patients. Sociopathic traits such as passing bad checks were quite rare. The diagnosis of sociopathy was entertained in one case but could not be firmly established. We would not agree with the concept that by definition anyone who abuses a child is a sociopath. No doubt sociopaths have attacked children many times, but certainly, sociopathy and child abuse are not closely related.

It is our impression that with few exceptions our patients had emotional problems of sufficient severity to be accepted for treatment had they presented themselves at a clinic or psychiatrist's office. As noted before, a few of our patients were picked up in the clinic or hospital during treatment undertaken for reasons other than child abuse. One patient had been treated for depression during adolescence and again for a mild postpartum psychosis a year before she abused her child and came into our study. Most of our patients had been living for years with a significant amount of emotional difficulty, feeling it was not worthwhile or not possible to look for help from anyone. They had not been able to engender in their environment any useful, sympathetic awareness of their difficulties.

Child abusers have been described as 'immature', 'impulse ridden', 'dependent', 'sado-masochistic', 'egocentric', 'narcissistic', and 'demanding'. Such adjectives are essentially appropriate when applied to those who abuse children, yet these qualities are so prevalent among people in general they they add little to specific understanding. Categorical psychiatric diagnoses contribute little more, and do not answer the crucial question of why a certain parent abuses children.

Instead of trying to associate child abuse with a specific type of psychiatric disorder or a commonly accepted character-type description, we have searched for a consistent behavior pattern which can exist in combination with, but quite independently of, other psychological disorders. Although we constantly dealt with the whole gamut of emotional turmoil, we persistently focused on the interaction between caretaker and infant. From direct observation of parents with children and the descriptions given by them of how they deal with their offspring, it is obvious that they expect and demand a great deal from their infants and children. Not only is the demand for performance great, but it is premature, clearly beyond the ability of the infant to comprehend what is wanted and to respond appropriately. Parents deal with the child as if he were much older than he really is. Observation of this interaction leads to a clear impression that the parent feels insecure and unsure of being loved, and looks to the child as a source of reassurance, comfort, and loving response. It is hardly an exaggeration to say the parent acts like a frightened, unloved child, looking to his own child as if he were an adult capable of providing comfort and love. This is the phenomenon described as 'role reversal' by Morris and Gould (1963). They define this 'as a reversal of the dependency role, in which parents turn to their infants and small children for nurturing and protection.' We see two basic elements involved—a high expectation and demand by the parent for the infant's performance and a corresponding parental disregard of the infant's own needs, limited abilities, and helplessness—a significant misperception of the infant by the parent. . . .

Examples of his high parental demand combined with disregard of the infant are the following:

Henry J., in speaking of his sixteen month old son, Johnny, said, 'He knows what I mean and understands it when I say "come here". If he doesn't come immediately, I go and give him a gentle tug on the ear to remind him of what he's supposed to do.' In the hospital it was found that Johnny's ear was lacerated and partially torn away from his head.

Kathy made this poignant statement: 'I have never felt really loved all my life. When the baby was born, I thought he would love me; but when he cried all the time, it meant he didn't love me, so I hit him.' Kenny, age three weeks, was hospitalized with bilateral subdural hematomas.

Implied in the above vignettes and clearly evident in the tone of voice of the parents as they told us these stories, is a curious sense of 'rightness'. We have often called it a 'sense of righteousness' in the parents. From early in infancy the children of abusing parents are expected to show exemplary behavior and a respectful, submissive, thoughtful attitude toward adult authority and society. Common parental expressions were: 'If you give in to kids, they'll be spoiled rotten.' 'You have to teach children to obey authority.' 'I don't want my kids to grow up to be delinquent.' 'Children have to be taught proper respect for their parents.' To be sure, such ideas are extremely prevalent in our culture and are essentially acceptable ideals of child rearing. Parents feel quite justified in following such principles. The difference between the non-abusing and the abusing parent is that the latter implements such standards with exaggerated intensity, and most importantly, at an inappropriately early age. Axiomatic to the child beater are that infants and children exist primarily to satisfy parental needs, that children's and infants' needs are unimportant and should be disregarded, and that children who do not fulfill these requirements deserve punishment.

We believe there exists in parents who abuse children this specific pattern of child rearing, quite independently of their other personality

119

traits. It is not an isolated, rare phenomenon but rather a variant form, extreme in its intensity, of a pattern of child rearing pervasive in human civilization all over the world. . . .

It is this pattern of caretaker-child interaction and style of child rearing with which we will be concerned in the following sections. . . .

Secondary factors involved in abuse

Contributions made by other elements of parental psychopathology

Up to now we have concentrated on those basic psychological factors essential to the pattern of abuse. There are other factors which are not essential ingredients but are potent accessories in instigating abuse and in determining which infant is selected for attack. Three such factors are intense unresolved sibling rivalry, an obsessive–compulsive character structure, and unresolved Oedipal conflicts with excessive guilt. Following is a clear example of sibling rivalry precipitating abuse.

Naomi was a fourth child raised largely by baby sitters until age six and then by a grandmother whom she felt did not love her. She did not think either mother or father really cared for her, especially mother. An older sister was the only person she loved or felt loved by. A three-year-old brother was the family favorite, and she felt her life was ruined by being neglected while he got everything. She hated and envied her father, brother, husband, and all men. A belligerent sense of rightness in her behavior thinly covered deep feelings of being inadequate and worthless as a mother. Her first child, a girl, was raised strictly and became very submissive, obedient, and cooperative. However, Naomi said, 'I'd beat her, too, if she rebelled or got angry at me.'

An unwanted pregnancy produced a boy two years later. Naomi said, 'He came too soon after the girl and cheated her out of her childhood. I weaned him at two and a half months because nursing him upset her. I hate him; the mere sight of his genitals upsets me. I don't have time for him; I wish he'd never been born or that I could give him away to someone who'd love him. I want to hit him, hurt him, shake him, get him out of the way.' She also said she saw all her own undesirable qualities in him. Naomi did slap, bruise, and rough up her baby boy, and by age two he had had three head wounds requiring stitches.

Obviously Naomi's sibling rivalry abetted by her envious anger toward males was important in the release of attack on her baby boy. Yet it is equally clear from her story that she had the underlying attitude of demand and criticism characteristic of the abusing parent. Only the fortunate accidents of sex, time of birth, and ability to respond correctly had spared her first child from attack.

Obsessive–compulsive personality traits often channel parental expectations and disapproval of infant behavior in specific ways. The conflicts over dirt and messiness lead to excessive early demand for the baby to eat without slopping and smearing food around and to control excretory functions too soon. Inability of the infant to comply will arouse parental ire. The inevitable tendency of older infants to strew toys around and to get fresh clothing dirty will also cause trouble if the parent is overly concerned with neatness and cleanliness. We postulate that the infant's behavior stimulates the parent's unconscious and threatens a breakthrough of his own unacceptable impulses to be messy. Defensive control must be instituted by aggressive repression in the parent and by aggressive action against similar bad behavior in the baby. . . .

Zilboorg (1932) in discussing parent–child antagonism accents the part played by Oedipal conflicts. He is describing older children, and we would agree that abuse of children over three or four, especially beginning at that time, is profoundly influenced by parental concern over sexuality and competitiveness. We are in complete accord with Zilboorg's statement that

> . . . the stronger the parents' 'conscience', that is, the
> stronger their inhibitions, the greater will be their hostility
> against the child's freedom. To put it in technical terms: to
> the unconscious of the parents the child plays the role of the
> Id; the parents follow it vicariously for a time and then hurl
> upon it with all the force of their Super Ego; they project
> onto the child their own Id and then punish it to gratify the
> demands of their uncompromising Super Ego.

In the context of abuse of infants, however, we are more involved with the earliest pregenital determinants rather than Oedipal residues.

Usually only one parent actually attacks the infant. The other parent almost invariably contributes, however, to the abusive behavior either by openly accepting it or by more subtly abetting it, consciously or unconsciously. An example of this is the strong support given each other by parents in their protestations of innocence, although it is clear both knew injurious abuse was occurring. Even though one parent openly accuses the other and righteously documents the other's abusive behavior when it has come to the attention of authorities, on investigation it is obvious that he or she has previously condoned it.

More direct instigation of abuse occurs when a spouse expresses opinions that the infant is being spoiled and needs more discipline or should be punished to break excessive willfulness and be brought under control. Similarly, one parent feeling overwhelmed and frustrated may turn the infant over to the other with admonitions to do something more drastic to stop the baby's annoying behavior. The non-abusing parent may show undue attention and interest toward an infant which stimulates feelings in the spouse of envy, abandonment, and anger leading to attack on the baby.

A husband's direct criticism of his wife's baby-caring ability, pointing out her errors and inadequacies, can trigger her attack on the child. Such husbands seem aware, at least on an unconscious level, that this will happen; yet they do it repeatedly.

Behavior which in any way signifies rejection or desertion is a potent stimulus to the attacker. If the abusing parent's own needs are neglected or rebuffed, there is an immediate turning to the infant with increased demand, and attack is likely. One woman told her husband she was uneasy about being alone with her previously injured baby and asked him to stay with her. He ignored her request and left the house. Shortly afterwards the baby was hit, resulting in a subdural hematoma. Less overt desertions can have a similar effect.

The various actions of the non-abusing parent become quite understandable when it is discovered that he or she had much the same life experience as the abuser and has developed a similar set of attitudes about parent–child relationships. Present in lesser intensity are the same feelings of unheeded yearnings for care, inferiority and hopelessness, coupled with the basic tenet that children should satisfy parental need. Thus, unknowingly, the marriage has become almost a collusion for the raising of children in a specific way. One parent is the active perpetrator; the other is a behind-the-scenes cooperator. Such parental tendencies become obvious when under treatment an abusing parent becomes gentler and the previously non-abusing parent starts being abusive. In a sense the infant becomes the scapegoat for inter-parental conflicts. Inability to solve their frustrated dependencies and antagonisms with each other leads them to turn for comfort to the child who is then attacked for failure to assuage the needs. It is obvious that treatment is often needed for the spouse, as well as for the overtly abusing parent.

The contribution made by the attacked child

There is no doubt that the infant, innocently and unwittingly, may contribute to the attack which is unleashed upon him. An infant born as the result of a premaritally conceived pregnancy or who comes as an accident too soon after the birth of a previous child, may be quite unwelcome to the parents and start life under the cloud of being unrewarding and unsatisfying to the parents. Such infants may be perceived as public reminders of sexual transgression or as extra, unwanted burdens rather than need-satisfying objects. An infant may also be seen as 'uncooperative' or unsatisfying by having been born a girl when the parents wanted a boy or vice versa. Babies are born with quite different behavioral patterns. Some parents are disappointed when they have a very placid child instead of a hoped-for, more reactive, responsive baby. Other parents are equally distressed by having an active, somewhat aggressive baby who makes up his own mind about things when they had hoped for a very placid, compliant infant. A potent source of difficulty is the situation in which babies are born with some degree, major or minor, of congenital defect, therefore requiring much more medical as well as general attention. Often such infants are fussy, crying, and difficult to comfort and are limited in their ability to respond as a normal, happy baby should. Intercurrent illness may produce a similar picture. Babies born prematurely require much more care and offer less response soon enough to satisfy the parents' needs. A case which illustrates several of these points is as follows.

Jerry and Connie had their first baby, a boy, as the result of a pregnancy which was instrumental in leading them to get married. Unfortunately, this otherwise quite healthy little boy was born with a congenital stricture of the bladder neck which required two long hospitalizations with surgery during the first six months of his life. Not surprisingly, he was a fussy, whiney, difficult to care for baby, requiring much more than average care and offering less happy, rewarding behavioral response to his parents. When he was eight months old, his father returned home late from an unusually hard day at work and found his wife terribly upset and irritable because of conflicts arising with his mother. His wife, in an effort to assuage her own turmoil, left the baby with Jerry and went to visit her own mother. Jerry, tired, feeling quite needy, deserted by Connie, was faced with caring for a crying baby. After several attempts to comfort and feed the baby, he became out of patience, angry, and struck the baby, fracturing its skull. There were no serious consequences, fortunately, from this injury. Jerry came under our care some three years later because of his worry over the fact that he was still very punitive toward Willie and often spanked him and slapped him to an unnecessary degree. By this time, a second boy, Benny, had been born and was now nine months old. Jerry spoke of his attitude toward Benny being extremely different, and when asked why responded with, 'Well, Benny's just the kind of a kid I like. Whenever I want to wrestle with him, he wrestles. He does everything that I want him to do.'

Thus, it is obvious that characteristics presented by the infant, such as sex, time of birth, health status, and behavior are factors in instigating child abuse. An interesting presentation of the role of the child is that of Milowe and Lourie (1964) with its accompanying discussion. Often stated in support of the idea that it is somehow 'all the infant's fault' is the fact that occasionally battered children have been attacked and injured again in the foster home where they have been placed for protection. We have not had the opportunity to study such an event nor have we seen any report of an adequately thorough study; but our other experience leads to doubt the assumption that only the child is at fault.

Despite the contributions which infants make toward the disappointments and burdens of their parents, they can hardly be used as an excuse or adequate cause for child abuse. They are part of the inevitable hazards all of us face in being human and in being parents. The essence of the problem is again the excessively high demands which parents impose upon infants, disregarding the inability of the infants to meet them. . . .

Summary

Our treatment of those who abuse infants has been directed toward improving the basic pattern of child rearing. It is based upon the hypotheses derived from the study of the psychology of the abusing parents in our study group. We were able to establish useful contact with all but a few of the sixty families, and of this treated group well over three-fourths showed significant improvement. Some changed a great deal, some only moderately, some are still in therapy. We considered it improvement when dangerously severe physical attack of the infant was eliminated and milder physical attack in the form of disciplinary punishment was either eliminated or reduced to a non-injurious minimum. Of equal significance was a reduction in demand upon and criticism of children accompanied by increased recognition of a child as an individual with age-appropriate needs and behavior. Further signs of improvement in the parents were increased abilities to relate to a wider social milieu for pleasurable satisfaction and source of help in time of need rather than looking to their children for such responses. We did not always try nor did we always succeed in making any change in all of the psychological conflicts and character problems of our patients. These were dealt with only as much as the patient wished or as far as we thought necessary in relation to our primary therapeutic goal. Our philosophy of the value of treatment is twofold; first, it deals in the most humanitarian and constructive way we know with a tragic facet of people's lives; second, therapeutic intervention in a process which seems to pass from one generation to the next will hopefully produce changes in patterns of child rearing toward the lessening of unhappiness and tragedy.

References

ELMER, E. (1964 and 1965) *The Fifty Families Study*, Unpublished reports from The Children's Hospital of Pittsburgh.

GREENGARD, J. (1964) 'The Battered Child Syndrome', *Med. Sci.* **15**, 82–91.

MILOWE, I. and LOURIE, R. (1964) 'The Child's Role in the Battered Child Syndrome', *J. Pediat.*, **65**, 1079–81.

MORRIS, M. G. and GOULD, R. W. (1963) 'Role Reversal: A Concept in Dealing with the Neglected/Battered Child Syndrome' in *The Neglected/Battered Child Syndrome*, New York, Child Welfare League of America, 29–49.

YOUNG, L. (1964) *Wednesday's children: A study of child neglect and abuse*. New York, McGraw-Hill.

ZILBOORG, G. (1932) 'Sidelights on Parent–child Antagonism', *Am. J. Orthopsychiat.*, **2**, 35–43.

19 Psychiatric characteristics of abusing parents
Selwyn M. Smith

[The following discussion paper is based upon research undertaken by Smith and his colleagues.

Index cases
Over a period of two years 134 battered infants and children under five and their parents were studied. All the parents had either confessed to battering or could give no adequate explanation of their child's injuries. Ninety-one (68 per cent) were referred from eight hospitals. Eighteen (13 per cent) were prison cases. Twenty-five (19 per cent) came from other sources.

Control Group
The controls comprised 53 children under five years, emergency admissions to hospital and where there was no question of battering, accident and trauma cases were excluded. Parents of these children were matched with the index group on the basis of the mother's age and the age of the infant. Other variables were held constant.]

Age

The young age of mothers closely compares with the age distribution described by other authors (Gil 1968*b*; Skinner and Castle 1969). On average index mothers were aged 19.7 years at the birth of their first child. This compares strikingly with the national average of 23.3 years (Registrar General 1972*a*). Even in the lowest social class the average was 22.6 years (Newson and Newson 1963). Index mothers were thus nearly 4 years younger than the national average when they gave birth to their first infant. Considering that most battered babies were first or second born and that more than half were under 18 months old when battered it may be concluded that battering is associated with youthful parenthood. This argument is further exemplified by the infrequent occurrence of battering in older parents with large families observed in this and other series

---

SMITH, S. M. (1975) *The Battered Child Syndrome*, London, Butterworth, pp. 197–202, 213–15.

(Bennie and Sclare 1969; Lukianowicz 1971) and suggests that the risk of battering diminishes with parental age.

Social class

The parents in this series were predominantly from the lower social classes. The association of low social class with battering parents has been commented on by several other workers (Young 1964; Skinner and Castle 1969). No support was found for the statement that all social classes are represented (Kempe 1969). Of the index group 76 per cent were from social classes IV and V compared with only 32 per cent in the Birmingham population (City of Birmingham 1972). It may be argued that such a large discrepancy is due to the youthfulness of the parents and type of admission (emergency) of the children. Nevertheless, despite allowing for these important factors it was found that the control group also contained 33 per cent of social class IV and V. This strongly suggests that battering is mainly a lower social class phenomenon. Furthermore, as the criteria for referral of cases were medical it may be reasonably assumed that if more children from high social class families had been admitted with unexplained injuries then consultant paediatricians would have referred them.

Abnormal personality

Abnormality of personality was a significant finding among the parents of battered children. The less severe types of personality disturbance were more commonly found among the mothers, who in general had features of emotional immaturity and dependence. Many of these mothers had in addition little concept of appropriate child-rearing practices. Battering may at best be regarded as an ineffectual method of controlling their child's behaviour. Techniques of teaching child-rearing skills based realistically on their low intelligence should perhaps be explored further as a possible means of correcting such ineffectual parent care.

Among the fathers studied 33.3 per cent were psychopaths. The association of battering with psychopathy has been commented on . . . (Birrell and Birrell 1968; Lukianowicz 1971; Scott 1973) but contrasts with Kempe's (1969) finding that psychopathy is a feature in only 2 or 3 per cent of battering parents. . . .

Criminal records

Twenty-nine per cent of the fathers had a criminal record. Though the follow-up period was brief, nevertheless 6.7 per cent went on to commit subsequent crimes. Furthermore though 19 per cent of the children's siblings had been previously battered only 1 per cent of the parents had been charged with cruelty or neglect, highlighting the capriciousness of the legal system towards parents who batter babies. Criminality and recidivism particularly if associated with a psychopathic personality should caution against an optimistic outcome, and invoking a care order is essential if further battering incidents are to be prevented. No association was found with alcoholism or drug addiction, which agrees with Steele and Pollock's (1968) findings but differs from those of Young (1964) and Gil (1968a) who maintained that battering is precipitated by alcoholism.

Neurosis

It was found that mothers were neurotic by three different measures. Fifty-eight per cent were non-psychotically disturbed on Goldberg's General Health Questionnaire and 48 per cent were diagnosed as neurotic at interview—the usual symptomatology being depression, anxiety or a mixture of both. The diagnosis of neuroticism on the Eysenck Personality Inventory lends some support to the clinical finding of neurosis and the questionnaire results. Thirty-four per cent reported having an unhappy childhood. In general neurotic mothers—in contrast to psychopathic fathers—confessed to harming their children and expressed willingness to discuss their difficulties further. For this particular group of mothers the combination of symptomatic relief with a programme of social re-learning conducted by skilled therapists seems to the author to be far more beneficial than relying solely on programmes of 'mothering' and other methods (Kempe and Helfer, 1972) that tend to reinforce their dependent behaviour.

Neuroticism was also found to be an important characteristic of those mothers who confessed to battering their children. Among the fathers neuroticism was masked by the high proportion who denied battering the child. However, among the fathers who were identified as perpetrators the mean scores on both the Eysenck Personality Inventory and the General Health Questionnaire were abnormally high. The need for these parents to act out their hostility was not detected for the sample as a whole but emerged when only those who confessed to battering were singled out. This is not surprising considering that items on this scale would be particularly pointed for a battering sample—for example, 'When I'm angry I feel like smashing things'.

Hostility

Foulds has shown that as a general rule the hostility of neurotics is of the introverted kind (Caine, Foulds and Hope 1967). The results from this study, however, showed that baby batterers who were neurotic were not predominantly intropunitive, but were characterized equally by extra-punitiveness. The most clear-cut for both mothers and fathers were the bizarre forms of hostility, hitherto found only in psychiatric populations (Philip 1969) namely projected hostility and guilt. While guilt and remorse have often been dismissed as symptoms unrelated to actual circumstances in psychiatric populations and as glib sophistication among psychopaths (Hare 1972), there is no reason to suppose that the guilt experienced by the sample is not reality-orientated or genuine, considering recent events. Considering their impaired relationships their high level of paranoid hostility is perhaps also understandable. . . .

Self-criticism was also not detected for the sample as a whole, so that on first inspection of the results the pattern of significant types of hostility was most reminiscent of psychopaths who 'may regard themselves as hot-tempered, cynical, interestingly mad or diabolically wicked; but . . . draw the line at appearing faintly inferior or incompetent' (Philip 1969). However, those who confessed to battering did not draw the line in their self-descriptions. This group of baby batterers may possibly, as previously suggested (Smith, Hanson and Noble 1973, 1974), be more amenable to treatment.

Thus the results depict baby batterers as neurotic—chiefly depressed—and characterized by all kinds of hostility directed against both others and themselves. This description resembles that of the depressive psychopath (Sattes 1972). Indeed in the backgrounds of the sample there was considerable evidence of psychiatric disturbance; childhood neurotic symptoms, childhood unhappiness, a family history of psychiatric illness, physical handicaps, head injuries and lack of school success. Despite such adversities very few baby batterers had received any formal psychiatric treatment.

Psychomotor performance

The spiral maze

A test of risk-taking while under pressure has demonstrated that delin-quents have relatively fast and careless performances, while behaviour disordered children are likely to be either fast and careless or slow and careless (Gibson 1964). West and Farrington (1973) have pointed out that clumsiness, although significantly predictive of both juvenile delinquency

G

and recidivism, seems to be 'of importance only because of its association with low intelligence'. It was found that index and control mothers did not differ on the 'quick and careless (to slow and accurate)' dimension but that index mothers were more slow and clumsy. The prevalence of depression in this sample probably contributed something to the slow tempo (Mayo, 1966) but the clumsiness may be regarded as a reflection of low intelligence. The relative effects of personality and intelligence on the psychomotoi behaviour of baby batterers deserves more attention. However, risk-taking when under pressure does not appear, from the results of the Spiral Maze Test, to be a characteristic of battering parents.

Psychosis

The findings confirm the view that only a minority of battering parents are psychotic (Steele and Pollock 1968). The bizarre nature of the injuries inflicted by psychotic parents suggests that they form a separate sub-group among baby batterers whose management must differ accordingly.

Abnormal EEGs

Because the numbers who underwent EEGs are on the small side, tentative conclusions only may be drawn from this aspect of the study. Nevertheless, the prevalence of abnormal EEG findings strongly suggests that some baby batterers at least are much more closely related to other groups committing acts of violence than they are to the general population. This is borne out also by the results of psychological testing, particularly of the group with abnormal EEGs, which also showed a consistent variation from the normal population. It would, therefore, seem clear that baby batterers are not a homogenous group about whom it is safe to generalize. Whereas in some instances battering may be a response to unusual and excessive stress situations—though this needs further investigation—the presence of a definitely abnormal EEG in almost 25 per cent of cases points to what may well be a separate sub-group to which special attention should be paid. This is further borne out by a demonstrable relationship between personality diagnosis and abnormal EEGs. Indeed five female batterers and one male batterer all with abnormal EEGs could undoubtedly be classed not only as having a personality disorder, but as aggressive psychopaths (Walton and Presly 1973). The male subject also had a criminal record. The two other female patients exhibited a personality disorder though this was not primarily of an aggressive type.

Violence breeds violence?

Steele and Pollock (1968) have suggested that baby batterers were deprived both of basic mothering and of the deep sense of being cared for from the beginning of their lives. Some of the findings from this study are at variance with this suggestion. Significant proportions of index mothers said they were physically maltreated in childhood and that their parents were unreasonable, rejecting and harsh. High proportions of index fathers also experienced punitiveness from their own parents, and significant proportions said their parents were unreasonable in their disciplinary methods, supporting those authors (Gibbens and Walker 1956; Tuteur and Glotzer 1966; Steele and Pollock 1968; Fontana 1968) who suggested that such child-rearing practices reflected childhood experiences. On the other hand the sample did not report lack of affection to any greater extent than others of low social class. Considering the parents were willing to report unreasonable discipline, there is no reason to assume that lack of affection was not reliably reported. Such inconsistencies may be realistic illustrations of the backgrounds of baby batterers. . . .

Management aspects

Recent comments (New Society 1973) have suggested that social workers have been 'too soft' and have often misjudged situations because of their enthusiasm for keeping the child and family together. Medical personnel are, however, also reluctant to notify authority particularly if they consider that this might result in parents being prosecuted. This reluctance may, of course, partly be due to the fact that medical and social welfare considerations on the one hand, and legal rights and safeguards on the other, are often hard to reconcile. However, by reserving to themselves this discretion of whether to pass on relevant information the doctor or social worker concerned may deprive the child of his legal rights of protection.

The results showed that there was a failure to ensure protection of the child. It was disconcerting to observe that the majority of cases were not brought to the attention of the juvenile court, reliance instead being placed on voluntary supervision. In view of the high mortality and morbidity reported in this and other series (Helfer 1968; Hall 1975; White Franklin 1975) and the high frequency of re-battering that occurs, it is alarming to observe that no arrangements for supervision took place in 21 instances. It is the author's opinion that local authorities are failing in their statutory role of protecting the child by being reluctant to institute care proceedings.

The quality and quantity of supervision available varies in different areas, and may, of course, influence a local authority's plan of management. Nevertheless, supervision whether it be voluntary or by court order does not overcome the inherent difficulty in managing these cases—namely, that no supervisor can be with the child or his family for more than a fraction of the time. Social workers in their desire to help parents and keep families together may embark upon a programme of casework. Considerable emphasis has been placed upon intensive casework with families since the passing of the Children and Young Persons Act 1963. The success of this has never been systematically evaluated. Furthermore management at present is hampered, in the author's opinion, by the local authorities' practice of imposing a dual role on the social worker. By appearing as the person who had made an application to deprive the parents of their parental rights the social worker's task of establishing and pursuing a therapeutic relationship is made even more difficult. In the light of the findings from this study it is already apparent that casework will not succeed in many instances and that trusting the parents unduly may have damaging consequences to the child.

Management of the problem has in the past too often been plagued by a tendency to rely on the case conference on the assumption that discussion alone is in the child's best interests. It has been the author's experience, however, that this method is often extremely inefficient. I would propose instead that a regional team, hospital based, consisting of a paediatrician, psychiatrist, social worker and psychologist should be established to tackle the overall problem.

An alternative but somewhat complementary scheme has been proposed by Bevan (1975) who suggests that a new office of 'Children's Guardian' should be created. The guardian would be a social worker with some legal training whose primary duty would be the protection of children's rights. Either of these appointments would perhaps improve the poor liaison that presently exists between the various agencies which concurrently and sequentially are involved in managing a case. It would also circumvent the unilateral action that often occurs through these agencies and go some way towards overcoming the present practice of returning the children home where re-battering takes place.

Other remedies rest with the courts. The case in the juvenile court is a civil and not a criminal one. It is not the court's duty to establish whether a particular individual has inflicted the injuries. It is only necessary to prove that a state of neglect or injury exists and that the parents are not preventing this. At present juvenile court magistrates have no powers to either request a psychiatric report or to recommend where appropriate that parents attend a treatment centre. It is the author's belief that improvements in child care would come about if magistrates were granted these powers.

In deciding upon an appropriate sentence, the court can follow the

Criminal Justice Act 1972 (and its amendments) which gives it wide powers—particularly if the accused has not previously been in prison. In order to decide whether other measures are more appropriate in dealing with the offender—for example, probation with a condition of treatment—the court is empowered to obtain psychiatric and social reports. This procedure allows an opportunity for reaching a sentence determined in the best interests of all concerned.

The methods used by the courts in sentencing baby batterers in this study varied. Probation with a condition of psychiatric treatment was the most frequent method used in the case of the mothers, while for fathers, imprisonment was the more likely outcome. This difference in sentencing may be due to the higher incidence of previous criminality among the fathers. It could be argued that as adult courts already have these wide powers there is no need to provide juvenile court magistrates with similar ones. However, the hesitation of doctors and social workers to facilitate criminal investigation procedures, the legal rights of the parent to remain silent and to have certain prejudicial evidence excluded and the high burden of proof on the part of the prosecution to prove their case, may all go some way towards explaining why the majority of these parents did not appear in the adult courts. Observations during this study revealed that a surprising lack of liaison occurs between the juvenile and adult courts. Furthermore, a mistaken belief is often apparent that it would be improper to mention any other proceedings in connection with the same set of facts. It is the author's belief that if the juvenile court also had the power to request psychiatric reports on the parents it would overcome some of these difficulties.

References

BENNIE, E. H. and SCLARE, A. B. (1969) 'The Battered Child Syndrome', *Am. J. Psychiat.*, **125**, 975–979.

BEVAN, H. (1975) 'Should Reporting be Mandatory' in A. White Franklin (ed.) *Concerning Child Abuse*, London, Churchill-Livingstone.

BIRRELL, R. G. and BIRRELL, J. H. W. (1968) 'The Maltreatment Syndrome in Children: A Hospital Survey', *Med. J. Aust.*, **II**, 1023–1029.

CAINE, T. M., FOULDS, G. A. and HOPE, K. (1967) *Manual of the Hostility and Direction of Hostility Questionnaire*, London, University of London Press.

CHILDREN AND YOUNG PERSONS ACT 1963, Part I, Section I, London, H.M.S.O.

CITY OF BIRMINGHAM (1972) ABSTRACTS OF STATISTICS (1970–1), City of Birmingham, Central Statistics Office.

FONTANA, V. J. (1968) 'Further Reflections on Maltreatment of Children', *N.Y. St. J. Med.* **68,** 2214–2215.

GIBBENS, T. C. N. and WALKER, A. (1956) *Cruel Parents,* London, Institute for the Study and Treatment of Delinquency.

GIBSON, H. B. (1964) 'The Spiral Maze. A Psychomotor Test with Implications for the Study of Delinquency', *Br. J. Psychol.,* **55,** 219–225.

GIL, D. G. (1968)a 'California Pilot Study' in R. E. Helfer and C. H. Kempe (eds.) *The Battered Child,* Chicago, University of Chicago Press.

GIL, D. G. (1968)b 'Incidence of Child Abuse and Demographic Characteristics of Persons Involved' in R. E. Helfer and C. H. Kempe (eds.) *The Battered Child,* Chicago, University of Chicago Press.

GOLDBERG, D. P. (1972) *The Detection of Psychiatric Illness by Questionnaire. A Technique for the Identification and Assessment of Non-Psychotic Psychiatric Illness,* London, Oxford University Press.

HALL, M. H. (1975) 'A View from the Emergency and Accident Department' in A. White Franklin (ed.) *Concerning Child Abuse,* London, Churchill-Livingstone.

HARE, R. D. (1972) 'Depression' in H. J. Eysenck, W. A. Arnold and R. Meili (eds.) *Encyclopaedia of Psychology,* London, Research Press.

HELFER, R. E. (1968) 'The responsibility and role of the physician' in R. E. Helfer and C. H. Kempe (eds.) *The Battered Child,* Chicago, University of Chicago Press.

KEMPE, C. H. (1969) 'The Battered Child and the Hospital', *Hosp. Pract.,* **4,** 44–57.

KEMPE, C. H. and HELFER, R. E. (eds.) (1972) *Helping the Battered Child and his Family,* Philadelphia and Toronto, Lippincott.

LUKIANOWICZ, N. (1971) 'Battered Children', *Psychiat. Clin.,* **4,** 257–280.

MAYO, P. R. (1966) 'Speed and Accuracy of Depression on a Spiral Maze Test', *Percept. Motor Skills,* **23,** 1034.

NEWSON, J. and NEWSON, E. (1963) *Patterns of Infant Care in an Urban Community,* London, Allen and Unwin (Penguin Books, 1972).

NEW SOCIETY (1973) 'Caring for Children', **24,** 542.

PHILIP, A. E. (1969) 'The Development and Use of Hostility and Direction of Hostility Questionnaire', *J. psychosom. Res.,* **13,** 283–287.

REGISTRAR GENERAL (1972)a *Statistical Review of England and Wales for 1970 Part 2,* London, H.M.S.O.

SATTES, H. (1972) 'Psychopathy' in H. J. Eysenck, W. A. Arnold and R. Meili (eds) *Encyclopaedia of Psychology,* London, Research Press.

SCOTT, P. D. (1973) 'Fatal battered baby cases', *Med. Sci. Law,* **13,** 197–206.

SKINNER, A. E. and CASTLE, R. L. (1969) *Seventy-eight Battered Children: A Retrospective Study,* London, National Society for the Prevention of Cruelty to Children.

SMITH, S. M., HANSON, R. and NOBLE, S. (1973) 'Parents of Battered Babies: A Controlled Study', *Br. med. J.,* **IV,** 388–391.

SMITH, S. M., HANSON, R. and NOBLE, S. (1974) 'Social Aspects of the Battered Baby Syndrome', *Br. J. Psychiat.*, **125**, 568–582.

STEELE, B. F. and POLLOCK, C. B. (1968) 'A Psychiatric Study of Parents who Abuse Infants and Small Children' in R. E. Helfer and C. H. Kempe (eds.) *The Battered Child*, Chicago, University of Chicago Press.

TUTEUR, W. and GLOTZER, J. (1966) 'Further Observations on Murdering Mothers' *J. forens. Sci.*, **11**, 373–383.

WALTON, H. J. and PRESLY, A. S. (1973) 'Abnormal Personality', *Br. J. Psychiat.*, **122**, 259–268.

WEST, D. J. and FARRINGTON, D. P. (1973) *Who Becomes Delinquent?* (Second Report of the Cambridge Study in Delinquent Development) London, Heinemann Educational Books.

WHITE FRANKLIN, A. (ed.) (1975) *Concerning Child Abuse* (Papers presented by the Tunbridge Wells Study Group on non-accidental injury to children) London, Churchill-Livingstone.

YOUNG, L. (1964) *Wednesday's Children: A Study of Child Neglect and Abuse*, New York, McGraw-Hill.

20 Aspects of bonding failure

Christopher Ounsted, Rhoda Oppenheimer,
Janet Lindsay

Diagnosis

The first step in therapy is that the diagnosis should be made and maintained with equanimity. The parents are told at our first interview that the injuries are such that they must have been inflicted by an adult. We find that the parents often accept this with relief, though the relief may not be explicit until therapy has advanced. . . .

Diagnosis of other disease in the proband

We have found that many children who are battered have unrecognized physical and/or behavioural abnormalities, or are thought to have them by their mothers. This obtained in about one-half of all the Park Hospital group of treated families. The abnormalities were very varied. For example, one child had had seven hospital admissions before it was found that he was blind and hence could not gaze-fixate his mother. The parents had maintained a totally defensive attitude until they were told that their child was blind, and had been from birth; then their defences fell. 'He cried and cried and he never looked at me' said the mother. The father said 'It's my fault. I knew what was happening really. I should have stopped it'. They asked the physician—'Could you have done it?' (battered the baby). He answered 'Yes', and this empathic answer led to an open relationship. This second stage in diagnosis is also therapeutic. One shares with the mother and father those features of the child's development and behaviour which could provoke anyone to abuse.

Diagnosis of the parents

A thorough, delicate and psychiatrically sophisticated diagnosis of both parents is essential. It must be a progressive process.

OUNSTED, C., OPPENHEIMER, R. and LINDSAY, J. (1974) 'Aspects of bonding failure: the psychopathology and psychotherapeutic treatment of families of battered children', *Developmental Medicine and Child Neurology*, vol. 16, no. 4, pp. 447–56.

Serious mental illness, psychopathy and inadequate personalities were found. Precise statistics cannot be had and we think that statistical treatment of data is likely to mislead more than to clarify.

Diagnosis of the family

The family diagnosis, extending back into the pedigree, should be made in detail. It is well-recognized (and our own data confirm) that parents who abuse their children often come from families in which violence has been the rule for some generations. Both parents must be made conscious of this pattern, then they can see their task as one of breaking what often seems to them to be a family curse extending down the generations. The parents are themselves unloved children, specifically children to whom very little was given but from whom much was demanded. Many of the mothers have a dependent, yet angry and hating relationship with their own mothers. Since in therapy we give to these mothers the mothering of which they have been deprived, it is essential to elicit a clear and precise diagnosis of their own developmental experiences.

Diagnosis of family relationships

All these families are by definition disturbed, but it is desirable as treatment proceeds to try to define the nature of these different disturbances. For example, jealousy is relatively common, by which we mean that one of the parents is morbidly jealous of the other's feelings towards the baby. The father can often feel displaced by the baby in his wife's affections. In one case a social class 1 father came into the maternity ward and saw his wife breast-feeding their new-born infant; he physically tore the infant from the breast and flung it violently across the ward, shouting 'those breasts are mine!'

In-patient service

Both the architecture and the setting of the in-patient service are essential aspects of the treatment we give. The mothers' house consists of a domestic dwelling, closely annexed to a children's hospital. The house contains three comfortable bed-sitting rooms, a communal sitting-room, a dining area, a kitchen, a laundry and the usual offices. It is set in a garden with peaceful views on every side. The hospital where the children and their brothers and sisters are treated has a great diversity of rooms and territories in it. There is an active school, and a large occupational therapy department with a number of environments. The play-rooms are equipped and furnished for children of all ages. There is a separate day-nursery, staffed with experienced nurses and removed from the rest of the day space. The night-nursery is in a different part of the hospital from the day space and from the mothers' unit.

Admission to the unit

When the diagnosis is first made the parents are defensive, thus a crisis arises which must often be resolved by law. This can be a therapeutic action: the doctor and the parents know that the child has been injured, and the child must be put where such injuries will not recur. In the UK, this is done by obtaining a Place of Safety Order, either from the appropriate department of the social services or from the police. The Place of Safety Order names the hospital and gives 28 days in which the plan of treatment can be put into action.

When the Order is obtained, we explain what it means and offer to admit the mother to the Unit, together with any brothers and sisters of the injured child. In the great majority of cases the offer is accepted.

The first few days of therapy are crucial. The mothers and children have been living a life of extreme tension, punctuated often by outbursts of rage. Communication has been by shouts and blows. The families usually have been existing in social isolation.

Almost universally the mothers have felt trapped, unwanted, unloved and unequal to their roles as children, as spouses and as parents. These feelings must be reversed.

In the first few days the mothers and children experience for the first time total care. Without having to ask, they are provided with food, warmth, privacy, tranquillity, and with an undemanding routine and the attentive care of varieties of mature adults.

The standard reaction of the mothers to this experience is one of astonishment. It is a situation quite new to them. We see at first the phenomenon which we have named 'second-day packing': on the second day after admission the mothers often panic and wish to leave. It is a situation analogous to the sudden cessation of chronic pain. Calm intervention by the staff soon overcomes this situation and the mothers settle down to a regular routine.

'Frozen watchfulness'

The abused child must also receive his initial treatment. Once the injuries have received attention the behavioural syndrome remains to be treated.

Repeatedly abused children show a characteristic behaviour which we have named 'frozen watchfulness' (Ounsted 1972). Children with frozen watchfulness make no sounds. If they are toddlers they do not chatter in the presence of adults. If they are approached they stand quite still. They will gaze-fixate but do not smile. They are often silent, even when their wounds are dressed.

We see frozen watchfulness as an adaptation to situations in which the loving and loved parent unpredictably and without provocation becomes transformed into an aggressor, and then immediately reverts to good parental behaviour. Treatment aims primarily to provide care that is predictable. Characteristically, the child with frozen watchfulness has been unable to establish basic trust in the regularity of his life, and this must now be given him. The routine is designedly regular; bed times, meal times, bath times and play times are all on a fixed schedule, and the behaviour of the nurses is equally predictable.

An extreme example of frozen watchfulness and its change under treatment is exemplified by this case history.

> The patient was admitted to hospital at the age of nine months, with his mother. The mother had a chronic schizophrenic illness which had been manifest for at least eight years. The father was unknown. The mother and infant had lived in isolation, and the mother had not allowed any interactions with the infant by any person other than herself. On admission, the child's physical measurements were on the 25th centile for his age. Examination revealed no stigmata. He was well washed. He lay completely immobile. When picked up he made no response, and his body was held in tonic extension. He showed no interest in toys; if a play-thing was placed in his hands he would drop it without a glance. When food was placed in his hand he did not move it to his mouth. He did not react to sounds. There was no stopping response. If sat up, he lay down at once. He did not smile, nor did he vocalize or babble.
>
> He was gently separated from his psychotic mother and given intensive mothering by the staff. His development was dramatic. Within a month he had made at least four months advance. At 25 months his skills were measured on the Griffiths Scale and he performed as follows:
>
> | | |
> |---|---|
> | locomotor scale | 22 months |
> | personal social scale | 21 months |
> | hearing and speech scale | 21 months |
> | eye/hand co-ordination | 22 months |
> | performance | 20 months |

Observation of the child in the presence of his foster-mother showed what appeared to be a natural and warm bonding between the two, and no significant abnormalities in their interactions. The child showed disturbed behaviour at and after visits to his mother in a mental hospital. These were stopped when he was $2\frac{1}{2}$ years old. At the age of $3\frac{1}{2}$ years the foster-parents abruptly rejected him and ended the fostering. They gave no reason.

The 'open relationship'

The parents of battered babies usually have developed an overgrowth of fantasy, not only in respect of the battering, but also in respect of other matters in their lives. The fantasies protect the parents from a reality which they see as unbearable. This perception is often distorted. In the setting of the Unit, these fantasies are not needed. The situation moves forward and during the second week of treatment it is common for clarifications to occur in which with relief, the parents will admit to the assaults and will abreact the emotions they have denied.

The timing of this crisis is critical. Behind the treatment is the Consultant, who does not interfere in the day-to-day therapy. He has to judge when the moment has arrived to see the parents. Both parents are seen together and in privacy. It is usual for them to condense what happened into a few emotive sentences. 'His crying' said the mother of one battered baby, 'seemed to follow me round the house. I could not stop it. I could not escape'. They then go on to tell how alien to themselves the assaultive behaviour seemed to be: 'It did not seem to be me that did it'. They express the feeling that they could not incorporate into their egos the alien behaviour which they had shown.

During the interview, weeping, sobbing and mutual comforting behaviours are prominent. Towards the end of the interview they begin to express their feelings of alienation: 'I did not think that I could be part of the human race'. At this point it is essential for the physician to make clear to them, with empathic communications, that cataclysmic breakdown in parental behaviour is an integral part of the human ethogram. One has to convey that all of us, given adequate provocation, could batter babies. Later it is useful to go over each violent act and elicit in detail what really happened so that the fantasies can be eliminated.

By the end of the second week of inpatient treatment we aim to have established an 'open relationship'with the families. By this we mean that:

1. We have released the proband from his frozen watchfulness. We have let him find a safe and predictable world, in which he can begin to

explore, to learn and to mature, both as an individual and as a social being.

2. We have helped the mother to feel free. She no longer feels trapped in a vicious circle. She begins to mature. She learns by precept and example how to care for her young.

3. We have helped the parental relationships and the intrafamilial dynamics to lose their quality of fantasy.

4. We have let the future be seen afresh with hope for growth and change.

We must here make a theoretical digression to explain our terminology. We use the terms 'closed relationship' and 'open relationship' as analogous to Bertalanffy's (1968) division of general systems into closed and open systems. In the former, the laws of classical thermodynamics apply—a closed system over time proceeds inevitably towards complete disorder, just because it is closed in on itself. These families seem similarly to have been closed in for generations. By removing, both physically and emotionally, all the constraints that have held the family closed, we allow an open relationship to develop. Open systems are those which show increasingly expressed orderliness as they develop over time. The classical example is the realization of the zygote's potential as it evolves into the adult organism through a series of metamorphoses.

We place the families in a highly regressive situation. They are fed, housed and cared for as though they were infants. It might seem a paradox that, in this situation, they can change and mature. But consider how a caterpillar changes into a butterfly—the regression of pupation is essential. Thus we see the simultaneous occurrence of psychodynamic dissolution and psychodynamic developmental advance, not as a paradox but rather as the *coincidentia oppositorum* in Nicholas of Cusa's sense—a resolution by the coming together of opposites.

The therapeutic court

Court-hearings need not damage the open relationship between the hospital and these families. Properly handled, the small drama of the Juvenile Court can itself be a useful catharsis. These parents have been dogged by guilt, denial and fear of exposure. Their upbringing has often been unjust. They have fantasied another world of 'them'—of police, magistrates and parental figures whom they must dread but obey.

They expiate their guilts in reality and this enables them for the first time to feel themselves to be responsible people (Ounsted 1968). After the court-hearing the parents usually express relief. The court usually makes an order placing the child in the care of the Local Authority but in

141

treatable cases this does not mean separation from the parents. It does mean that the parents have an organization which protects both them and the child.

The liberating bond

Another apparent paradox is the notion that firm bonds to mature adults are pre-conditional for the capacity to choose freely and responsibly. Yet analogous concepts are basic to the physiology of stability and change: Claud Bernard's 'La fixité du milieu intérieur est la condition essentielle de la vie libre' expresses the matter precisely (Bernard 1895).

When part of a system is employed in choice, in idiosyncratic development or in movement, then another part of that same system must be stable. The stable bond for the battering parents is with the hospital and its staff. It is important that this trusting bond should not be seen as a kind of 'transference neurosis'. Specifically we make no attempt to end the families' relationship with us, nor do we interpret it to them. In an open relationship mutual courtesy between all parties is the goal. Verbal discussion has limited usefulness, and interpretations of private feelings are apt to destroy the self-respect which we aim to create.

The outcome

No statistics of the results would be meaningful, since both our ideas and our practice are in a state of evolution. In most cases there has been a notable improvement in the intrafamilial dynamics.

Many cases still cannot be treated, and in others only palliation is possible. We now turn to the more hopeful area of prevention.

Out-patient service

Preventive study

Kempe and Helfer (1972) showed that prevention is practicable and effective. We now describe a study of families treated on an out-patient basis.

Referral

The children were referred by their family doctors because of a grossly abnormal mother–child relationship, and because the doctors thought that the children were at risk for battering. From those referred to us as out-patients, we selected for detailed study and treatment 24 families in which the mother and child were of normal intelligence and the child was not older than four years.

Two-thirds of the mothers had complained to their family doctors that the child was driving them crazy. One-third had admitted to hitting the child too often and too hard. At the time of referral 22 of the mothers were on tranquillizers or anti-depressants and 16 of the children were receiving sedatives. Fifty-four separate factors were examined for each of the 24 families and were then arrayed in order of increasing frequency within the sample as a whole.

Parental characteristics

The early biographies of both parents were often distorted. Fifteen of the mothers had had unhappy, emotionally deprived childhoods. The most striking aspect of their personalities was an extremely low tolerance to any form of pain or frustration. Two-thirds of the mothers were labile in mood. Migrainous attacks of sufficient severity to require withdrawal to bed had occurred in 16 of the others. Nineteen of the 48 parents had suffered from Besnier's syndrome (asthma, eczema). Ten of the fathers and 19 of the mothers showed immature and dependent personalities.

In general the families were isolated and lonely. They had made few friends in their neighbourhoods. Many had removed themselves from their own part of the country and were new settlers in the area. Not one of the 24 mothers went out to work.

The mothers were on average 24 years old at the time of the birth, which is two years younger than the median age of maternity in our region at the present time.

Parental relationships

Parental relationships were generally bad. Four mothers had children by men other than their spouse. A further six mothers conceived by their spouse prior to marriage.

In about one-quarter of the sample, housing and work difficulties were prominent. In 10 of the families one parent had been sterilized by the time of referral. Nearly two-thirds of the mothers complained that the fathers lacked understanding of their difficulties and were impatient and un-helpful. Sexual difficulties were an outstanding complaint by 19 of the mothers.

Proband's histories

From the beginning, most of these families had had an unhappy and disturbed mother–infant interaction. Nearly two-thirds of the mothers had complained of and were treated for puerperal depression. The 'colicky child' syndrome (Barrett 1971) was a prominent feature of most of the probands during infancy. One-third of the children were reported to have vomited frequently in the neonatal period. Complaints of tics and other displacement activities figured in 10 of the children. Asthma and/or eczema afflicted 11 of the probands. Sleeping difficulties, 'crossness', excessive crying and irritability were present in two-thirds. This had led to the same proportion of children being treated with some form of sedation or tranquillizers before they were referred to the clinic.

State at referral

At the time of referral the mothers had a multiplicity of complaints about the child. They saw the child as too clinging, too aggressive, too timid, too defiant, and disobedient. They made quite unrealistic demands on the children for obedience and for love. Two-thirds of the mothers complained that the child could not be cuddled.

As part of the general failure in communication which was evident in every case, it was striking that one-half of the children had selective speech retardation.

Thus we were faced in these families with a situation in which the interaction between all members had become distorted and fixed in the pattern of a closed system. This was made explicit by the mothers, often in terms that they felt trapped, or in prison, and were unable to break out except in outbursts of rage. The vicious circle of mal-communication was present in every case.

Treatment

On referral, the parents and the child were seen by the physician. Individual therapy by the social worker was begun for the parents and the child in their own home, as this made it easier to involve the father.

When judged to be ready, the mothers were introduced into a group of between five and eight other mothers. At the same time the child was introduced into a toddler's group. The two groups were run simultaneously in adjoining rooms, with free access between the two. The goal of therapy was to help the mothers with their own problems and, at the same time, to teach them to cope in a more constructive way with all their children.

The groups were found to be therapeutic. The mothers were able to receive support from each other. The mothers were encouraged to telephone to the social worker whenever a crisis arose. As the mothers learned to cope, many of them reported that simply thinking of using the telephone was enough to enable them to regain control.
The mothers were helped to keep a daily diary of the situations in which their child drove them to explosive anger. This was brought along to the sessions with the therapist for detailed discussion.
The children soon learnt to play and explore naturally, and associated these activities with the mothers' presence. The mothers came to be regarded by the children as bringing them to a place where they were safe and free. Babies who were too small to join actively in play activities were involved by being cuddled and loved by any staff member available. The mothers saw their children being handled cheerfully when they showed any signs of the 'colicky child' syndrome or when they soiled, vomited or were angry.

Outcome

The 24 mothers who attended regularly for between one and two years all showed some improvement. In no case did battering occur.
It must be emphasized that this group was a selected one. We deliberately chose those likely to respond to treatment and no generalizations can be made to all parents of battered infants. . . .

References

BARRETT, J. H. W. (1971) in Batstone, G. F., Blair, A. W., Slater, J. M. (eds.) *A Handbook of Prenatal Paediatrics*, Aylesbury, Medical & Technical.
BERNARD, C. (1895) *Introduction a l'Etude de la Médicine Experimentale*, Paris, Ballière.
BERTALANFFY, L. VON (1968) *General System Theory*, London, Penguin.
KEMPE, C. H. and HELFER, R. E. (1972) *Helping the Battered Child and his Family*, Philadelphia, Lippincott.
OUNSTED, C. (1968) in de Reuck, A. V. S., Porter, R. (eds.) *The Mentally Abnormal Offender*, London, Churchill.
OUNSTED, C. (1972) in *Proceedings of the 8th International Study Group on Child Neurology and Cerebral Palsy (unpublished)*.

21 The behavioural treatment approach to potential child abuse

William Reavley and Marie-Therese Gilbert

A considerable amount is known about child abuse. The incidence, how to identify child abuse and factors associated with abusing parents have been reported (Kempe and Helfer, 1968; Smith, Hanson and Noble, 1974). Although identification of the problem and prevention (Richards 1974) have been discussed, there has been little written concerning treatment. Some areas identified as important in treatment include the formation of a 'trusting relationship' (Okell 1969; Holmes et al. 1975) and as the abusing parents are reported to have unrealistic expectations regarding the child's behaviour in relation to its developmental level (Pollock 1968) the therapist has been directed to take an educational role (Holmes et al. op. cit.).

Social learning theory places the educational aspects of treatment into an effective framework and also allows for a detailed analysis of the problem. In general, behavioural psychotherapy aims to develop new acceptable responses to stimuli which previously evoked deviant responses. It is necessary to introduce the new behaviour at the appropriate point, therefore the first stage in treatment is an accurate description of the circumstances and stimuli, both internal and external, which precede and follow the deviant behaviour. Within behavioural psychotherapy a number of flexible techniques and strategies of demonstrated efficacy have been developed to help people cope with a range of difficulties, e.g. tics, phobias, obsessional behaviour, sexual dysfunction. Describing and analysing child abuse in terms and language of a behavioural analysis leads to the application of these effective techniques to the set of problem behaviours subsumed under the heading 'child abuse'.

Although it may appear to be an over simplification, dichotomising maladaptive behaviour into inappropriate emotional responses and problematic instrumental responses gives a framework to the behavioural analysis. The stimulus of the child crying may lead to the response of violence (inappropriate instrumental response) or perhaps anxiety and consequent avoidance of the situation (maladaptive emotional response). Response prevention has been claimed to be very effective in modifying the maladaptive responses of obsessional patients (Meyer and Levy 1973)

REAVLEY, W. and GILBERT, M.-T. (1976) 'The behavioural treatment approach to potential child abuse: two illustrative case reports', *Social Work Today*, vol. 7, no. 6, pp. 166–8.

and is readily adaptable to the treatment of child abuse. In the treatment sessions inappropriate violence is prevented by the therapist's presence.

Should the parent wish to escape or avoid the situation he is encouraged to remain while the therapist models appropriate coping behaviours. As the parent's anxiety diminishes she is guided in her imitation of these coping behaviours. New responses are developed by participant modelling (social learning theory) which are gradually placed under the parent's own control. Gradually the therapist 'fades' out his control of the situation. The parent maintains the newly acquired adaptive behaviour by introducing self regulation procedures.

With child abuse the results of problematic instrumental behaviour are more readily observable and have tended to receive more attention, although it is well recognized that inappropriate emotional responses may be equally if not more damaging. In Case B particularly, treatment was aimed to produce changes in the potentially damaging feelings and attitudes the parent had towards her child. Attitudes as well as behaviour have been shown to be altered by participant modelling (Bandura et al. 1969). Meichenbaum and Goodman (1971) demonstrated that teaching children to talk to themselves helped in developing self control. Impulsive schoolchildren were trained to tell themselves to 'slow down', 'be careful' and 'avoid being hasty'. In our cases the parents were taught to say such things as 'I will not become angry', 'I will not harm my baby', while handling their children.

Meichenbaum's strategies of model rehearsal with commentary followed by patient practice also with commentary were incorporated into the participant modelling programme. The therapist's commentary reduces the ambiguities in performance which are then recognized and corrected by the therapist.

This tactic also serves to present the patient with a 'coping' model, shown to be therapeutically more effective (Bandura 1969). A problem associated with participant modelling is that the patient may come to see the therapist's presence as conditional for the new adaptive behaviour to occur. Any changes in behaviour may be attributed to the reassuring presence of the therapist rather than the patient's own efforts. To prevent this discrimination learning taking place it is necessary for the therapist to be continually alert for opportunities to 'fade out' of the situation.

Experience with agoraphobic groups suggested that the parents' confidence in their ability to cope could be facilitated by their practising soon after termination of the treatment session what they had been doing in that session. (The effectiveness of this approach has recently been experimentally demonstrated (Bandura et al. 1975). With parental child abuse one cannot run the risk of negative consequences (with the possibility of the child being harmed) in the self directed sessions, that one can with agoraphobia. Therefore in both cases the husband was encouraged to take on the therapist's response prevention role as a step on the way to self directed and self maintained changes in behaviour.

To enhance the patients' seeing themselves as contributing to their own treatment they were encouraged to keep detailed records of the treatment sessions and what happened between these sessions. These records also allowed the patients to monitor subtle changes in their behaviour which might otherwise have been overlooked. Information given to the patient concerning his progress has been shown to be of importance in the success of behavioural psychotherapy (Leitenberg et al. 1968). In our cases this feedback was provided by these records. As well as the above, rating scales have been demonstrated to influence people's behaviour, for example, with regard to cigarette smoking (Pyke et al. 1966, Koenig and Masters 1965). Instead of rating how much 'anxiety' was experienced in carrying out target behaviours between sessions the patients were instructed to rate how much pleasure and enjoyment they felt.

One of the essentials in treatment is that the problem is tackled where it occurs—in the patient's home. It must be emphasized that repeated practices of the new behaviours, guidance from the therapist during practice, the graduation of practice exercises, the provision of feedback during the practice are necessary as are favourable conditions for practice. The use of response prevention, participant modelling and self regulation procedures to change and then maintain the changed attitudes and behaviour is described below.

Case A

Sylvia, aged 33, was anxious to build a normal relationship with her daughter Anna, aged 13 months. Anna was born in London in December 1973. While still in hospital Sylvia had difficulty in feeding her baby. The advice she was given then was 'If you pinch her legs she will suck'. Sylvia found once begun that she could not stop pinching Anna's legs. Sylvia became anxious over this and did not take care of her baby until she was discharged from hospital and went home. From this point Sylvia became increasingly worried about harming the baby and could not confide in her husband. When Anna was three months old she was admitted to hospital, where she remained a month, following assaults by Sylvia. After Anna left hospital Sylvia was visited by social services representatives. Sylvia does not recall any advice being given and saw the visits as 'seeing if I had done anything else to Anna'.

When Sylvia was referred she said she was 'frightened of an uncontrollable wish to harm Anna when she cries'. As a consequence Sylvia was avoiding as much contact with Anna as possible. She was depressed at her inability to cope. Her husband found himself taking over the child care role as he was afraid to leave the child with his wife. To enable the husband to attend work the social services arranged for a baby minder who took over the daily care of the baby. At the weekend the husband took care of the baby. As well as reducing the risk of Anna being injured these measures seemed to be increasing Sylvia's feelings of inadequacy. Anna crying was the stimulus for Sylvia to feel like harming the baby. Elaborate steps had been taken to avoid the child being distressed and likely to cry, for example, in the bedroom the light and wireless would be left on and toys left in the cot in case Anna woke in the night. From the beginning of our contact with Sylvia, her husband, social worker and baby minder were introduced to the aims and strategies of the treatment programme. Sylvia was encouraged to play a major part in the identification of her problems and the planning of treatment. As Sylvia reported that when she became anxious and tense she was more likely to hit Anna she was taught an anxiety management technique and given practice on how to employ it on the lines advocated by Goldfried (1973).

A list was made of problem behaviours in ascending order of the amount of anxiety each produced.

1. Play and talk to Anna.
2. Change Anna's nappy.
3. Dress and undress Anna.
4. Feed Anna.
5. Put Anna to bed.
6. Pick Anna up.
7. Bath Anna.
8. Cuddle Anna.
9. Stay in room while Anna, crying, is comforted by husband.
10. Comfort Anna when she cries.

One by one Sylvia was introduced to these 'dangerous' feared situations. The therapist's presence prevented any deviant responses, either hitting or avoiding. The therapist modelled the adaptive behaviours, giving a commentary, and Sylvia observed this while consciously lowering her anxiety. Sylvia then performed the same task as the therapist. After satisfactory completion of any task (which included her elimination of anxiety) Sylvia was encouraged to cuddle Anna for a few minutes so that both could enjoy each other's company. Treatment sessions took place daily, excluding weekends, for two weeks with two therapists taking part. At the end of this period Sylvia was performing the above tasks without modelling or prompting but she maintained a commentary peppered with firmly delivered statements like 'I will not smack Anna', 'I will not shout at Anna'. At this stage the therapists were only supervising Sylvia, a role the husband was able to take over. The child responded well to contact with

Sylvia and this seemed to play an important part in the progress made. Sylvia began to take care of the child all day each week. During the afternoon of that day one of the therapists would call. While Anna was not walking the range of potentially 'dangerous' situations, when she might cry, was comparatively narrow. However within two months of treatment beginning Anna was becoming mobile. It was not possible to rehearse every possible situation with a therapist present therefore Sylvia needed to become her own therapist. The Self Control programme was an extension of the participant modelling commentary. Anxiety management was rehearsed in conjunction with statements she developed herself, like 'I will not run away from the room' and others mentioned above. For a period of fourteen weeks Sylvia was required to carry out the list of tasks compiled for the first phase of treatment. She was asked to rate not how much anxiety she experienced but how much pleasure she gained from performing these tasks.

At the end of this period everyone involved with the family agreed that Sylvia did not need the supervision she had been receiving and could take care of Anna when she was not at work.

Follow up
From July 1975 (three months after beginning treatment) Sylvia was seen by a therapist once a fortnight. She is now seen every two months. Sylvia reports that occasionally she uses the self directing verbal statements. She is very confident about handling Anna and enjoys looking after her in all situations. The husband has no hesitation in leaving the child with Sylvia even when he has to be away from home several days at a time.

Case B

Kathleen, aged 30, married, with two daughters was afraid of harming her elder child physically and emotionally. She had been successful at school and had held several responsible secretarial posts and was working until her elder daughter was born in October 1970. Shortly after the birth Kathleen began to smack and shout at Sarah and when she was three weeks old tried to suffocate her while her husband was at work. Kathleen was admitted to a psychiatric hospital in March 1971 and given the diagnosis 'A puerperal type of depression'. Meanwhile Sarah was cared for by her maternal grandmother. Kathleen was in hospital five weeks and on her discharge, although Sarah lived with them, it was the husband who took on the maternal role. Another daughter Liza, was born early 1973 and Kathleen found herself enjoying the company of this child from birth. This served to make her feel more guilty about her behaviour towards and feelings for Sarah.

At the time of referral, August 1974, Kathleen was never left alone with Sarah whose presence and voice irritated her greatly. Sarah was beginning to react to her mother's behaviour which pressured Kathleen to seeking help. When we met Kathleen she felt that there was little chance of her doing any physical harm to Sarah. She was however greatly concerned for the child's emotional development. Kathleen identified several targets for treatment; interactions she wanted with Sarah but was currently unable to have. The list below is ordered from low to high levels in terms of the anxiety produced.

1. Talking to Sarah;
2. Praising Sarah;
3. Smiling at Sarah;
4. Sitting next to Sarah;
5. Picking up Sarah;
6. Kissing Sarah;
7. Cuddling Sarah;
8. Hearing Sarah's voice.

Kathleen identified these behaviours as being impossible for her as she was confident that should she have close contact with Sarah the child would be more aware of her mother's real attitudes and hence more harmed by them. This feeling of Kathleen's had served to establish complex patterns of avoidance in which the husband played a major part. He took care to arrange his working day to allow this avoidance.

The treatment approach of participant modelling was explained to Kathleen and her husband. The observation that behaviour change preceded attitude change was particularly emphasized. Kathleen was unable to accept this but was willing to try the approach. Unlike the baby in Case A, Sarah could not be handled passively. She was older, active and very much a person in her own right. That she was aware to some extent of her mother's feelings towards her was apparent from the first interview with the family. Twice a week the family home was visited and the therapist and mother 'played games' with Sarah and her sister. As often as possible her husband joined in these prolonged games sessions and continued them, as 'therapist' after and between actual treatment sessions. By Christmas Kathleen could perform the first five of the target behaviours but still had difficulty with physical contact with Sarah. In January Kathleen suffered another depressive episode and was given medication (Insidon 50 mgm tds). As the depression lifted she became more fully aware that she was really enjoying the child's company, including physical contact. Sarah was also responding to the change in her mother's behaviour towards her. Kathleen took to spending increasing amounts of time devoted exclusively to the children.

Follow up
From April 1975 *Kathleen was seen on a monthly basis. At that time (April)*
cuddling Sarah in the morning was still a problem. Kathleen was encouraged
to continue practising this and by August was aware that her feeling of
affection towards the two children balanced. In October 1975 *Kathleen*
referred herself for treatment of her sexual unresponsiveness. This is
proceeding.

Discussion

Lazarus (1973) proposes a 'multimodal behaviour therapy' approach. To
have long lasting effects treatment needs to be directed towards changing
'. . . irrational beliefs, deviant behaviours, unpleasant feelings, intrusive
images, stressful relationships, negative sensations and possible bio-
chemical imbalances'. Not every case requires attention to each of these
facets but this can only be determined by a careful behavioural analysis.
Social learning theory facilitates this multi-modal approach. For example,
parents may well need 'education' but, outside of a framework of an
established collaborative relationship it is easy to see how 'education' may
be perceived as patronizing and unhelpful lecturing. Participant modelling
is a teaching approach in which the patient plays an active part in learning
new behaviours. Reports of behavioural treatments usually pay very little
attention to 'non-specific' variables. Our experience with child abusing
parents suggest that non-specific variables such as the relationships
between therapist and patient are of importance. This is not simply that
the relationship is in itself therapeutic but that without the relationship
the patient would not persevere with 'un-natural' activities such as
practising cuddling their child.

Our experiences do not allow us to identify which elements of treatment
are the most effective in producing changes. However, during treatment
we were impressed by the apparent effectiveness of a procedure a therapist
was minimally involved in; self rating and record keeping. Of particular
interest was the strategy of changing from rating 'anxiety' to rating
'pleasure' for the same items.

Is the approach outlined generally applicable to child abuse problems?
Certainly the routine applications of the 'techniques' discussed is to be
avoided. We agree with Ullman (1972) that one must make an extensive
behavioural analysis and in so doing define the problems to be tackled
and the most appropriate ways for doing so bearing in mind the clients'
wishes and limitations. By merely applying 'techniques' one can achieve
very disappointing results.

Although both sets of parents reported on here may not be typical of
abusing parents the behavioural approach could be used with others in

less favourable circumstances. It is often noted, for example, that the risk of child abuse is greater when the parent feels unable to cope with the child's crying. The probability of crying is increased during certain activities such as bathing and nappy changing. Behavioural treatment could be focused on these areas aiming to promote new 'coping' behaviours while the parents' other problems are concomitantly tackled by more familiar approaches.

References

BANDURA, A. (1969) *The Principles of Behaviour Modification*, Holt, Rinehart and Winston.

BANDURA, A., BLANCHARD, E. B. and RITTER, B. (1969) 'Relative Efficiency of Desensitisation and Modelling Approaches for Inducing Behavioural, Affective and Attitudinal Changes', *Journal of Personality and Social Psychology*, 5, 16–23.

BANDURA, A., JEFFERY, R. W. and GAJDOS, E. (1975) 'Generating Change Through Participant Modelling with Self Directed Mastery', *Behaviour Research and Therapy*, 13, no. 2/3, 141–52.

GOLDFRIED, M. R. (1973) 'Systematic Desensitisation as Training in Self Control' in Goldfried, M. R. and Merbaum, M. (eds.) *Behaviour Change Through Self Control*, Holt, Rinehart and Winston.

HOLMES, S. A., BARNHART, C., CANTONI, L. and REYNER, E. (1975) 'Working with the Parent in Child Abuse Cases', *Social Casework*, January, 3–12.

KEMPE, C. H. and HELFER, R. E. (1968) *The Battered Child*, Chicago, University of Chicago Press.

KOENIG, K. P. and MASTERS, J. (1965) 'Experimental Treatment of Habitual Smoking', *Behaviour Research and Therapy*, 3, 235–44.

LAZARUS, A. A. (1973) 'Multimodal Behaviour Therapy: Treating the "Basic Id" ', *Journal of Nervous and Mental Diseases*, 156, 404–11.

LEITENBERG, H., AGRAS, W. S., THOMPSON, L. E. and WRIGHT, D. E. (1968) 'Feedback in Behaviour Modification; An Experimental Analysis in Two Phobic Cases', *Journal of Applied Behaviour Analysis*, 1, 131–4.

MEICHENBAUM, D. and GOODMAN, J. (1971) 'Training Impulsive Children to Talk to Themselves: A Means of Developing Self Control', *Journal of Abnormal Psychology*, 77, no. 2, 115–26.

MEICHENBAUM, D. H. 'Cognitive Factors in Behavioural Modification', *Research Report* 25, Dept. of Psychology, University of Waterloo, Ontario, Canada.

MEYER, V. and LEVY, R. (1973) 'Modification of Behaviour in Obsessive-compulsive Disorders', in Adams, H. E. and Unikel, I. P. (eds.) *Issues and Trends in Behaviour Therapy*, Springfield, Illinois, Thomas.

OKELL, C. (1969) 'A Battered Child—A Tragic Breakdown in Parental Care?' *Midwife and Health Visitor*, June.

POLLOCK, C. B. (1968) 'Early Case Finding a Means of Preventing Child Abuse' in Kempe, C. H. and Helfer, R. E. (eds.) *The Battered Child*, Chicago, University of Chicago Press.

PYKE, S., AGNEW, N. MCK. and KOPPERUCK, J. (1966) 'Modification of an Overlearned Maladaptive Response Through a Relearned Programme: A Pilot Study on Smoking', *Behaviour Research and Therapy*, **4**, 196–203.

RICHARDS, M. P. M. (1974) 'Non-accidental Injury to Children in an Ecological Perspective', Paper presented at DHSS Conference, June.

SMITH, S., HANSON, R. and NOBLE, S. (1974) 'Social Aspects of the Battered Baby Syndrome', *Brit. J. Psychiat.*

ULLMAN, L. P. (1972) 'Presidential Address: Who Are We?' *Advances in Behaviour Therapy*, London, Academic Press.

Part Five   Legal aspects

Attendance at court can be an alarming experience for the uninitiated. The papers in this section will help the professional without a legal background to understand the complexities of the law and the court procedures in cases of child abuse. Useful guidance is given on the preparation of reports and in the giving of evidence. The lawyer who is inexperienced in cases of child abuse as well as the non-legal worker will find the extracts from 'At Risk' valuable in assisting parents who appear in court.

In the appendix is a short paper 'The Statutory Powers of the Police' with references to the relevant Acts of Parliament.

22 A view from the courts
Winifred E. Cavenagh

. . . Where do the courts come into the picture, if at all? The first point is
that in most cases they don't come in. It is now thought that the baby-
battering, which, as such, comes to the notice of the welfare authorities,
is probably only the tip of the iceberg. The trend in social policy nowadays
is to regard problems relating to children as family problems and to try
and treat them without breaking the family up, and as far as possible
without bringing them before a court. So those that not only come to
notice but do get into court may be thought of as no more than the tip
of the iceberg. The summary courts deal with most of these, but so rare
have they been that the great majority of magistrates have never had to
deal with such cases and are not likely to.

Perhaps the courts ought to be used more, but they have no power to
initiate proceedings themselves. They have to wait until a party making
allegations brings a case into court because it wants something done about
a situation which it has no power to alter on a voluntary basis. It is then
the court's job to listen to both sides, the side that brought the action and
the side that is resisting it, and decide whether the allegations have been
proved and, if so, what degree of compulsion is called for by the actions
committed or the situation revealed. The court does not take the required
steps itself. Broadly speaking, it empowers the appropriate authority to
do so. In Britain the courts, the penal services and the social services are
all separate bodies, and the community has allotted differing roles to
them. The court's role is strictly adjudicatory.

Battered baby cases are brought mainly in one or other of two kinds
of summary court—and sometimes in both. Which court is chosen by the
party bringing the case depends on what it is hoped to achieve. If punishment of the baby batterer is what is in mind, then the case is brought (by
the police) in the ordinary adult court, where the choice open to the court
on proof of guilt usually lies in practice between imprisonment or probation. Since the Children and Young Persons Act 1969 that court has had
no power to make any order relating to the victim. If compulsory powers
relating to the child are required, the case is brought (by the local authority,
police, or NSPCC) in the special summary court for juveniles. Here, on a

---

CAVENAGH, W. E. (1975) 'A view from the courts', *Royal Society of Health
Journal*, vol. 95, no. 3, pp. 153–5.

finding that the case is proved, the court usually chooses between the alternatives of giving the local authority power to supervise the child's care on a compulsory basis or taking the parental powers right away from the parents or guardians and giving them to the local authority social services department instead. The latter then have the sole right to decide where and how the child shall live and be cared for until he is eighteen (or for as long as the grant of powers is not revoked or the order discharged). What the juvenile court cannot do is to make an order relating to the batterers simply as persons, e.g. committing them to prison or putting them on probation. If this is desired in addition, a case must also be brought in the adult court.

There are probably a great many cases in which the authorities concerned would like to get compulsory powers enabling them to protect or treat the child and bring pressure on parents or guardians, or would like to see the parents punished—yet no action is brought. This is usually because they have not got sufficient evidence. Moral certainty on the part of one of the parties to an action is not the same as evidence. The standard of evidence required to prove the case against the batterer in the adult court is particularly high, since the allegation is a criminal charge on which a convicted person may lose his or her liberty and must be proved 'beyond a reasonable doubt' to secure a conviction. This is undoubtedly one reason why many charges are only brought in the form of the civil action in the juvenile court, where evidence which shows clearly the balance of probabilities is enough to prove the case and give ground for the grant of powers to the local authority which will enable them to interfere against the wishes of the parents if necessary.

It should be a sobering thought that parents may lose all control over their own child and see him removed completely beyond their power to have any access at all, because the court (three lay citizens or one legally qualified paid magistrate) is not certain, but thinks that 'on balance', i.e. 'more likely than not', what the complainant says is true. No wonder that the court is likely to give very careful consideration at the post-finding stage to the question whether the case has been made out for a care order as against a supervision order, or not.

Another reason why it is easier to prove the case in the juvenile court is that the emphasis in the case is on the child's present condition and situation and his probable future, and not, except as necessary to show these, on who was responsible for the acts or omissions complained of. Showing that the victim is not likely in the future to get the care he needs unless the court makes an order, does not necessarily turn on knowing exactly who caused the present condition, or indeed whether it was voluntarily caused at all. *Mens rea* would sometimes be impossible to prove, but a series of mysterious 'accidents' may suggest the probable future if power to interfere is not given.

The well-known fact that battering parents may sometimes be loving parents makes the situation particularly confusing. It is in these cases, often concerning attractive young parents, that hard evidence is so important. The evidence must not only exist, it must be put before the court. Ours is an adversary system (still feeling the after-effects of a violent revulsion from the authoritarian interrogatory methods of the Star Chamber). The allegations, and the evidence on which the court is to decide, must be put in the presence of those accused and be open to test by cross-examination. What is not given in evidence is not given, and its absence may lose the case.

Just a few words on evidence. Where the local authority bring the proceedings (in the juvenile court), those proceedings are being brought by a body which is also going to be the caring agency if powers are granted. This may produce a situation in which some of the evidence available is not led for fear of damage to the social worker/client situation. Cases have been lost on this, and there seems much to be said for the police bringing the case and calling the social services as—perhaps unwilling—witnesses. This used to be a role of the NSPCC (though one which that excellent organization found necessary in only an infinitesimal number of cases).

The twofold allegation in the juvenile court case—the child's condition now and the need for the court to make an order if adequate care is to be ensured in the future—opens the door to much relevant material which can be put in evidence before the finding, instead of only in the social background report after, and, if the case is found-proved. Here, in stark contrast to the criminal proceedings in the adult court, relevant previous convictions (e.g. for assault, violence, criminal damage) can be mentioned. Factual evidence about relevant behaviour as observed by the witness, and the conclusions he draws as to the personalities involved in relation to future care may be put in, though such evidence must be either clearly fact or clearly opinion. It must not be hearsay.

Professional people other than lawyers are not usually very familiar with the courts. This applies to generically trained social workers carrying mixed case loads, as well as to doctors. They are used to being listened to as authorities in their own field, and are unprepared for being treated as hostile by the lawyer who has been instructed by the parents, and may question them in an aggressive manner. Both doctors and social workers may have much that is material to say along the lines indicated in the previous paragraph, but may be stopped even by the complainants' lawyer or the clerk to the court, if these are not fully aware of what evidence can be received in these cases. Fortunately, owing to recent publicity, the position is changing for the better in this respect, although many of the lawyers appearing in juvenile courts still have very little experience of them. A witness is not fighting the case for either side and may be called for both, though he is usually only called by one side which thinks it can use his evidence in winning the case. So the giving of evidence is not an occasion for a mud-slinging bonanza but for careful answers to the careful and limited questions which are asked. The witness is not the person who is conducting the case, and it is very important that whoever is the person in question should have adequate conferences beforehand, and that the case should be adequately prepared.

Of course it is very important that the justices listening to the evidence should fully realize its significance. Unfortunately, for this purpose, cases in most courts are comparatively so rare that it is unlikely that the justices will have been well briefed by their own experience. It will be fortunate indeed if they, or one of them, has attended a course on this subject. A heavy burden therefore rests on the prosecution lawyer to lead, and the medical or social worker witness to give, evidence as to the significance of what may appear to the lay person to be insignificant superficial bruises. They can explain clearly what the significance may be of even very slight bruising if this in their view indicates very violent shaking, or banging, with consequent risk to the brain or sight, or is sited in a position where it could well have set up internal haemorrhages. They can emphasize the fact that the juvenile court is concerned with the condition and safety of the child, not the culpability of his parents or guardians. Some local authorities have a 'court officer' amongst their staff, designated to prepare and deal with all court cases in the magistrates court. Local authorities can be encouraged to make sure that the lawyers they employ to conduct these cases are fully aware of what has to be proved, by whom and under what rules, and of the background knowledge which now exists on these subjects. It is not too much to expect that there should be a lawyer attached to the social services department in the larger authorities, perhaps even to the children's side of it, who may become expert in the preparation if not the actual conduct of all care cases or prosecutions for neglect.

Many lawyers appearing in the juvenile court in either criminal or care cases have been surprised to hear that they are there to represent the child and not the parents. There is at present no provision for legal representation of the parents at public expense. In a criminal case the interest of parents and child are likely, at least to those concerned, to appear to be the same. This is not necessarily so in the care case. Indeed, the case would presumably not have been brought if a state of actual or potential conflict was not thought to exist. In every case until very recently (exceptions being very rare, and for obvious reasons only where the juvenile is of an age to be articulate) lawyer and parents behaved as if the legal aid was granted to the parents and for their own benefit. Plans are in hand to make legal aid at public expense separately available to the parents in care cases. But who, you may well ask, is to brief the lawyer who represents a child too young to talk? The social services? But they are a party. There could under these arrangements be three lawyers—one presumably having to argue on the basis of his personal views on the welfare of the child. These might well be rather less useful even than those of the ordinary lay person, unless he is a lawyer who has specialized in welfare fields. It might be better to rely on a *guardian ad litem*, who would explore the facts of the situation from the child's angle and place these before the court for its information. There is a practical difficulty in how to identify suitable people to act as *guardian ad litem* and perhaps an independent lawyer or social worker is the only practicable solution.

Where there is open conflict between the social services department and the child's parents, the adversary system of procedure in court is such as will usually alert the court to the child's angle. But where there is no conflict (as in Colwell), and agreement has been reached beforehand, e.g. that the social services department will not oppose an application for revocation of a care order, nothing may come out which alerts the court to the possibility that the child herself is or could be strongly antagonistic to the proposal, and that this opposition should be brought out into the open and looked at by the court. Of course there is the possibility that a social worker appointed as *guardian ad litem* in a case in which another social services department is a party may tend to take the same professional line, feeling she is really evaluating the work of a professional colleague—giving a second professional opinion—but perhaps the risk is less the more senior the person appointed, or if she belongs to another service, i.e. probation. These matters are under consideration by Parliament at present.

Where a child has been in care for some specified time it might be advisable for there to be a rule that, for example, foster parents should be notified that parents have applied to the court to get the child back. They could be notified of the date of the hearing and have a right to be heard by the court whether or not they themselves were interested in applying for custody.

A very great deal has been heard in recent years about the need for the various services which may be involved in family matters to share their information, communicate their views and co-ordinate action. The advantages which it could be hoped are obtainable in this way are indeed self-evident. But in the present state of the social services, where glaring deficiencies appear to be unavoidable and certain to continue at least for some time, such procedures exclusively approved can be dangerous. They can result in dangerous delays, they can produce a sort of paralysis of action and an abdication of responsibility on a wide scale by each of the services and persons who come into contact with the case. This is a danger which must be avoided. It seems to me important to preserve the notion of personal responsibility. And also to accept that the different organizations which may be involved, e.g. police, NSPCC, teachers, health visitors, do represent different approaches to the problem, according to the role and function which the community has allotted to them. I doubt whether there is a consensus amongst the general public as to the paramountcy of role of any one of these services over that of any of the others, in every case, at all times. But in relation to the battered baby the traditional role of each of these services does, in my view, represent the present opinion of sizeable sections of the public as to the appropriate action, or at least the priorities in a case. It would in my view be a backward step if it were to be proposed that any of the relevant bodies *could never* act independently of the social services department or co-ordinating committees. There should be a continuing and open dialogue.

H

23 Court procedures in child abuse
Anthony Jackson

'You are hereby ordered to attend and give evidence before the Central Criminal Court, Old Bailey, London, E.C.4.' Anyone who has been concerned with cases of child abuse may have received an awesome directive of this type set out in an official document called a witness order. Even more alarming is the ominous warning which accompanies the order: 'Under section 3(1) of the Criminal Procedure (Attendance of Witnesses) Act, 1968 a person who disobeys a witness order without just excuse may be punished with imprisonment not exceeding three months and a fine'.

Much to their relief most members of the medical and allied caring professions do not commonly make personal appearances at criminal courts such as the Old Bailey. However, with the increasing recognition of various forms of child abuse those who work in the field of child care may find themselves involved to a greater or lesser extent in some of the relevant legal procedures. This article is intended to give a simple account, for members of the health professions, of the law concerning child abuse and the resulting court procedures.

Courts of law

The courts of law which deal with child abuse are the Juvenile Court, which is concerned with the welfare and protection of children (under the age of 14) and young persons (aged 14 to 17) and the Criminal Courts, which deal with adults who are accused of offences against children.

The Juvenile Court does not admit the public and sits separately from other courts. It consists of three experienced magistrates one of whom is usually a woman. The Clerk of the Court is a qualified lawyer who advises the magistrates on matters of law. In cases of child abuse the proceedings of the Juvenile Court are designed to determine whether or not the child should be taken into care. The arguments for and against a care order are conducted by lawyers but there is no prosecution or defence. Evidence to the court is given under oath but the court procedure is somewhat less strict and rigid than in criminal courts and the degree of proof

JACKSON, A. (1975) 'Court procedures in child abuse', *Midwife, Health Visitor and Community Nurse*, vol. 11, no. 10, pp. 329–32.

is not required to be as strong as 'beyond reasonable doubt'. The object of the court is to obtain as much factual evidence as possible to make a decision which is in the child's best interests. The Juvenile Court is not required to determine whether or not an offence has been committed or to prove responsibility for any offence. Appeals against the decision of a Juvenile Court are permitted and are heard at a Juvenile Appeal Court.

The Criminal Courts, on the other hand, are not concerned with the care and protection of the abused child but deal with charges brought by the police against adults who are alleged to have committed one or more of several possible offences against the child. These criminal proceedings are heard first in the Magistrates' Court which is permitted to try the less serious cases. The more serious offences must be referred to the higher court, the Crown Court, for trial by judge and jury.

The law concerning child abuse

There are thus two distinct aspects of legal procedure concerning child abuse, the protection of the child and the prosecution of adults who may have committed an offence.

Protection of the child

Under the Children and Young Persons Act 1969, Section 1, a local authority (usually the Social Services Department) and certain other authorized persons such as the NSPCC or police may bring a child before a juvenile court if:

a. his proper development is being avoidably prevented or neglected or his health is being avoidably impaired or neglected or he is being ill-treated;
    or
b. the conditions in a. have been proved in the case of another child in the same household.

In practice the grounds for bringing a child before the court under paragraph a. include a number of situations associated with a risk of non-accidental injury such as emotional deprivation leading to impaired development, inadequate nutrition leading to failure to thrive, repeated insistence by the parents on admission of a child to hospital for trivial complaints, and physical neglect resulting in extensive and severe napkin dermatitis. These are more likely to be accepted by the court as grounds

163

for a care order if they are based on firm factual evidence. For example, failure to gain weight, for which investigation reveals no adequate cause and which is rapidly corrected without treatment after admission to hospital, is almost certainly an indication of neglect at home.

If the court is satisfied on these grounds that the child is in need of care and control which he is unlikely to receive unless the court makes an order, the order will be made. A Supervision Order places the child under the supervision of the local authority usually permitting him to remain with his parents although there may be special requirements such as residence with a named individual. A Care Order, which is more usual in cases of non-accidental injury, commits the child to the care of the local authority until the age of 18 or until the care order is revoked. The court can also make an Interim Order, which is really a postponement of a final decision, and in this case the local authority is required to bring the child before the court again within 28 days.

In circumstances where it is considered that a child is in need of immediate protection a social worker may apply to a magistrate for a Place of Safety Order. This authorizes the retention of the child in a 'place of safety', for example a hospital ward, for up to 28 days. A Place of Safety Order in these circumstances can usually be obtained within 24 hours. In cases of extreme urgency, for example if parents are threatening immediate removal of an injured child from hospital against the judgment of a consultant or if a child seems to be in danger at home, the police should be informed and a police officer may detain or remove the child immediately. During the 28 days following the granting of a place of safety order the child must be brought before the juvenile court which will make an order for care or supervision, or order the child's release.

Criminal proceedings

When the police are involved in cases of child abuse they may decide to take criminal proceedings against persons suspected of criminal acts. These proceedings may be brought under the Children and Young Persons Act 1933 (section 1), which states that any person over the age of 16 who has care of a child and wilfully assaults, ill-treats or neglects that child in a manner likely to cause unnecessary suffering or injury to health is guilty of an offence. Such charges are answered in the Magistrates' Court. More serious crimes involving serious injury or death of a child are dealt with under the Offences Against the Person Act 1861 and are referred on to the Crown Court. It is important to repeat that criminal proceedings against an adult in charge of a child do not deal with protection of the child which must be achieved by a care order granted by the juvenile court.

Giving evidence

It is important that members of professions which deal with children should keep careful records of their observations especially if the possibility of child abuse is suspected. Those who are particularly well placed to assist the courts by their observations are doctors, hospital nurses, health visitors, nursery nurses and school nurses. They are familiar with the clinical signs of abuse such as bruises, physical neglect, inadequate weight gain and impaired development and they have been trained to observe. Too often, however, they do not keep accurate records of their observations. Such documented and dated observations may be of great importance in deciding whether or not there is a case to be made for a care order. Records are also a valuable aid to the memory of those who may be asked to give evidence in court long after the events took place or the observations were made, and are more convincing when quoted in court than hazy uncorroborated recollections.

In the early stages of preparation of evidence for either the juvenile or criminal court a potential witness will often be asked to give a written statement. It is advisable to write a draft of such a statement, using one's personal notes, to ensure accuracy and avoid omissions. This draft can then serve as a basis for the formal statement and be used for revision before giving evidence in court at a later date.

In giving statements or evidence in court it is important to stick to the facts which one has personally observed. It is not necessary, except for those (mostly consultant doctors) who may have to give an expert opinion, to do more than this. One should avoid slanting the evidence for the benefit of one or other side, and present it without bias for the information of the court which has to determine the implications of the facts in making its decision. Evidence given in this way, even in the Crown Court in serious criminal cases, is usually welcomed by both sides and does not engender the hostility of the opposing side.

Those of us who are in the medical and allied professions may hesitate to give evidence to courts or police about families with whom we have a professional relationship. We must remember, however, that the welfare of the child is our main concern and if confidence with parents has to be broken for the benefit or protection of the child then this is an overriding consideration.

The usual sequence of events in determining what has to be done for a child who may have been neglected or injured starts with a case conference. At the conference all the evidence of a number of observers can be put together and after discussion the answers to three important questions can be agreed. 1. Is this a probable case of child abuse? 2. Should a Care Order (or Place of Safety Order) be sought? 3. Should the police be informed?

Depending on the answers to these questions agreement will be reached as to who will be required to give evidence before the juvenile court or to the police in the form of a statement. If the police decide to bring criminal charges evidence may have to be given in the Magistrates' Court or even the Crown Court. . . .

24 Reaction of parents to court appearances
The NSPCC Battered Child Research Team

All the parents found their Court appearances a great strain. In some cases anxiety was increased by a long wait and many adjournments. (In one case, the interval between the Place of Safety Order and the Care Order being made was three months.)

We collected parents from home and drove them to Court and they all clearly showed fear, tension and anxiety on the journey. 'I'm really dreading it. All those people looking at me'. 'I feel ill—stop the car, I'm going to be sick'. One father broke down just before going into Court, saying, 'You just don't know ... you shut your eyes for so long and don't see things you don't want to see . . . but terrible things have happened.'

The frequent period of long waiting on hard benches, in dirty, dreary vestibules and waiting-rooms, eyeing the other witnesses and watching policemen and unhappy looking people going in and out of the Court room increased the strain. Many cigarettes were smoked and one thoughtful social worker took along a miniature of brandy in her handbag to support her clients and herself! In several cases, the stress was worsened by the presence of the child, often crying inconsolably, in the care of residential or hospital staff, whilst the parents looked helplessly and angrily on.

In Court, most of the parents were silent and withdrawn, although there were occasional angry outbursts. Several mothers cried as the medical evidence was read out, hearing the parade of shocking clinical detail perhaps for the first time. They all appeared apprehensive whilst giving evidence themselves.

Afterwards, many parents felt angry at the way the case had been conducted. 'I felt very guilty in there—just like a criminal. We both felt on trial. Why did they have to make it seem as though we were cruel parents?' 'I knew I couldn't win. No one listened to me'. 'Is that all? It wasn't worth it'. '. . . that man up there deciding about children who he hasn't got the faintest idea about'. All felt to some extent alienated and rejected by the experience.

In seven of the nine cases, there was hostility or lack of support evident

BAHER, E. et al. (eds) (1976) *At Risk: an Account of the Work of the Battered Child Research Department, NSPCC*, London, Routledge, pp. 111–115.

between the parents. They were described, after hearing that their child had been taken into care, as 'crying separately', 'making no move to comfort one another', 'unable to cope with one another's grief'.

It is often argued that a Juvenile Court hearing can be experienced by parents as a caring and understanding procedure, since magistrates try to appear human and the proceedings are supposed to be relatively informal and free from the usual pomp and ceremony of the operation of justice. The police are encouraged to change into plain clothes, the press are not allowed to report names and addresses and the public are excluded from Court. However, although one mother appeared to respond slightly to a magistrate's comment that 'you have been through hard times', all the parents found the experience distressing and shaming and felt alienated from the whole procedure.

Parents' legal representation

We found this another very difficult area in taking cases before the Juvenile Court. Workers already struggling with the attempt to separate legal and therapeutic activities, and the inevitable blurring of roles, then found themselves recommending and enabling clients to secure legal representation which might result in children being returned home. Particularly where parents denied injuring children and opposed Care Orders, this action was seen by them as caring and in their interests, thus increasing their trust in their worker, but it made the worker's position as the person most strongly recommending removal of the child even more untenable. It also led to difficulties with the parents' lawyers, who quickly became aware of apparent conflict of role and attitude, and felt confused about whose side the social worker was on. 'I wish I knew what you were playing at', one solicitor said to a worker, 'who are you representing—or don't you know?' In one case, it seemed clear to the solicitors that a Denver House [NSPCC Therapeutic Unit] social worker was hostile to his clients, even though they saw her as friendly, and he advised them to refuse to see her, except in his presence.

In two of the nine cases taken before the Juvenile Court, the parents did not contest the case and were not legally represented.

In a further three cases, the parents consulted a solicitor, but did not contest the case. One father intended to contest, but after listening to the evidence at the preliminary hearing, changed his mind.

In the remaining four cases, the parents opposed the Care Order and employed a solicitor to attempt to demolish the local authority's case for removing their child. All the solicitors were paid from Legal Aid funds. One of these cases was taken to Court after several years of treatment, and since the social worker was able to be open with the mother about his wish to remove the child, he could be equally open in advising the mother to seek legal advice and in communicating with the solicitor.

The involvement of the solicitors in the other three cases proved confusing and counter-productive. It should be noted that none of the lawyers involved was particularly interested or experienced in Juvenile Court work. Denver House workers were instrumental in helping the parents to obtain a lawyer and all found themselves distrusted by them and viewed as opposed to the parents. In one case, the solicitor at first assumed that the Denver House worker was supporting the parents' case and that the local authority worker was against them and he telephoned the Denver House worker on several occasions to vent his feelings of identification with the parents. 'I'm a parent myself and I can't sleep at nights for thinking of how they must feel.' His strong partisanship for their cause increased the parents' hostility to the hospital and local authority and made it even more difficult for them to express their real feelings for the child. However, when the Denver House worker, under threat of subpoena, explained to the parents that he would be giving evidence in the Juvenile Court, recommending the child's removal, the solicitor felt confused and let down and warned the parents not to trust the worker. At the Court hearing itself, the solicitor was shocked at hearing the medical evidence fully detailed and commented upon, and muttered to the worker during an adjournment, 'I don't know what to think now. Do you think the mother did it?' In another case, a solicitor, whom the social worker had previously described as 'crusading on behalf of the parents', whilst questioning the mother, realized that she was giving quite a different story to the one that she had prepared with him. After her evidence, evidently disillusioned, he advised the parents to accept the Care Order 'for the best'. Social workers found themselves feeling acutely sorry for the solicitors as they floundered in previously unknown emotional waters!

In the fourth case, the solicitor also strongly identified with the parents against authority, successfully opposing the Care Order, and the case was found not proved.

Whilst we would strongly endorse the human and legal right of parents in such a situation to be legally represented, we found that the difficulties of attempting to maintain our therapeutic role were increased by the involvement of solicitors and that the conflict between the interests of child, parent and social agency were heightened.

We would strongly recommend that lawyers in child abuse cases should have acquired familiarity with both substantive and procedural law, should have learnt to read and evaluate medical, psychiatric, psychological and social work reports and should have some knowledge of child abuse literature and treatment and placement potentials. As Isaacs (1972) observed, 'it is only by acquiring some insight into the motivations which turn a parent into a child beater that the attorney can achieve the level of understanding and compassion that permits him to serve as an effective advocate and counsellor.'

The separation of legal and therapeutic roles

... We had hoped that it would be viable to separate these roles. The current work on battering parents (for example, Elmer (1967) and Steele and Pollock (1968)) described people whose lives had been a long chain of emotional deprivation and rejection and who consequently were unable to invest trust in other people and particularly those in authority. It was felt that if any kind of helping relationship was to be established, this would be doomed to failure if the therapist had to become involved in questioning the parents about the injury, gathering evidence and assuming responsibility for the removal of the child. We had hoped that it would be possible to divide up social work activities so that the local authority social workers would be responsible for taking Place of Safety Orders, informing the parents and discussing legal implications with them, taking cases to Court, giving whatever social evidence might be necessary, and we would be able to concentrate on forming a therapeutic relationship with the parents.

In practice, this split between the 'good' and the 'bad' did not work out as we had hoped for a variety of reasons. We did not find local authority social workers very enthusiastic about playing the 'bad' role, whatever had been agreed theoretically in advance with seniors in their departments. They were not necessarily convinced by the arguments; they resented, when already over-worked having to give time to cases from which they would derive no reward from clients, and they were sometimes unconvinced of the need to take legal action at all. This is well illustrated by the example of one local authority social worker, whose own impulse was to return the child home, to put the parents 'on trust' and supervise the situation. She was over-ruled by her senior and the Denver House social worker and when the case went to the Juvenile Court she consequently had to act in a way of which she disapproved. She reacted by failing to communicate properly with the Denver House worker and by acting, without consultation, in an attempt to woo the parents. In another case, the local authority social worker felt so resentful about her role that she tried to sabotage the Denver House worker's relationship with the parents. In several other cases, local authority social workers were unwilling to communicate bad news to the parents, such as informing them that a Place of Safety Order had been taken, or discussing legal implications with them, and the Denver House social worker played this role.

We had also not anticipated how often we would be the people most strongly recommending removal of the child. Other workers naturally then resented that we should be assigned the 'good' role. As one Denver House worker wrote, 'my position as the person trying to remain the good therapist and at the same time persuading all the other workers of the need for them to take legal action of which they disapproved became quite untenable at times.

We found that the local authority solicitors bringing cases to Court were even less likely to appreciate the therapeutic necessity for a separation of roles than their social work colleagues. In the early days of Denver House, we tried hard to argue our case for non-involvement, but in every instance found ourselves committed to giving evidence in Court for the sake of getting the Order. We were always able to tell the parents that this was under the threat of subpoena and to discuss our evidence with them in advance, but this did not undo the effect on the parents of hearing their 'good' worker recommend removal of the child, and in two cases give evidence of actual conversations. In one case, the Denver House worker agreed to act as an expert witness and it was thought (rightly) that the parents would find a general discussion of battering more tolerable than a specific focus on them.

In the three cases brought to Court after a period of time in treatment, the parents felt let down by their workers. We had hoped that relationships established over at least two years might be able to withstand the effects of the primary worker removing the child, but this was not the case. 'You're meant to help people, not make it worse.' 'You should never trust social workers—they only bring trouble.' Although again the local authorities initiated and implemented Court action, we were seen as directly responsible and the clients felt betrayed, despite the fact that two of the mothers were obviously relieved that their children were going into care. However, workers in these cases felt that the situation was easier because of the established relationship and that parents could far more easily express negative feelings than to an unknown social worker.

In consequence, the parents were often mystified about the roles of different workers and responded in different ways, depending on their own emotional needs. In one case only did the parents clearly uphold the separation of 'good' and 'bad' worker, despite the fact that the Denver House worker recommended the child's removal in Court and they opposed this. They talked about 'us against them', clearly including the Denver House worker in 'us'. However, they had had previous bad experiences of the local authority before the case was referred. In another case, the split was partially upheld by the mother, although she felt let down that the worker had to give evidence. Her husband apparently felt both agencies were equally responsible for Court action. In three cases, the parents appeared to see all workers involved as reasonably 'good' and did not need to blame or dislike anyone.

We do not think it possible to draw conclusion from our experience of trying to separate the legal and therapeutic roles. We often found the mental and emotional gymnastics necessary a source of strain and guilt, and at times our position was quite untenable. Some of the difficulties we encountered could be removed; it would help if there were a consensus of opinion amongst co-workers on the need to remove a child and if there were greater expertise in preparing evidence and presenting cases in Court. It would obviously be easier to operate a split if the two workers were in agreement and trusted one another, and this might be more easily achieved by two workers from within the same department.

References

ELMER, E. (1967) *Children in Jeopardy. A Study of Abused Minors and Their Families*, Pittsburgh, University of Pittsburgh Press.

ISAACS, J. L. (1972) 'The Role of the Lawyer in Child Abuse Cases', in Kempe, C. H. and Helfer, R. E. (eds.) *Helping the Battered Child and his Family*, 225–41.

STEELE, B. F. and POLLOCK, C. B. (1968) 'A Psychiatric Study of Parents who Abuse Infants and Small Children', in Helfer, R. E. and Kempe, C. H. (eds.) *The Battered Child*, 103–47.

25 The police
Jean Renvoize

In an address to the Royal Society of Health in 1972 a doctor . . . said, 'Few aspects in the management of these children generate such heat as the involvement of the police. . . . The two positions are widely polarized; on the one hand there are the enthusiasts who maintain that under no circumstances whatsoever should the police ever become involved; at the other extreme there are police forces who insist that since the physical injury of a child is a crime, the concealment of these cases is unlawful, and all these injuries to children should be reported to them. Clearly this is an intolerable situation, and the doctor, in the centre of two such clearly differing views, must give serious thought as to the attitude he must adopt in these circumstances.

'In general, the police in these situations receive the co-operation . . . they deserve. If a force is determined to prosecute irrespective of whether it be a deliberate assault or whether it be a battered baby, then they will receive very little co-operation. If on the other hand they are prepared to play their part in the management they can expect to receive the co-operation of the personnel engaged in dealing with the situations.' . . .

That there exist almost diametrically opposite views among policemen is not particularly surprising—no one imagines every policeman to be identical—but the remarkable variability of action taken in different cases may surprise those who are not aware of the extent to which county police forces are autonomous. Each force is responsible to itself only: what the Chief Constable of Northampton decides to do on a particular issue may be identical to or the complete opposite to what his counterpart in Dorset does, the decisions are theirs alone, and unless they are clearly behaving in a bizarre or dishonest manner they will not be interfered with by the Home Office (beyond perhaps being given occasional advice). Nevertheless, in general there is probably less difference in certain basic attitudes among policemen than there is in most professions. There can be few, if any, policemen who do not believe absolutely in law and order and in the value of self control. . . .

It is this basic similarity in attitude among the police which occasionally wrecks the most well-meaning attempts of some of them to come to a working compromise with workers in other fields. . . . From the Director

RENVOIZE, J. (1974) *Children in Danger*, London, Routledge, pp. 107–27.

of Social Services of a large London borough: 'I don't think the police in fact have much contribution to make in a society which gets anguished not only about the injury to the child but also about the pressures on the mother and father which led to that injury. I have talked for hours with the police about the point at which we should tell them we've discovered an injury to a child which might be the result of a battering, but all they seem concerned with is calling the mother into the station and saying, right, this is a chargeable offence'. . . .

Psychiatrists, with the mental health of their patients uppermost in their minds, can be even more outright. One London psychiatrist said, 'The police are just acting as agents of vengeance, that's all, they're acting as society's super-ego conscience to attack those who've done wrong: if you've bashed your child then you must be bashed too. . . . The police's job is to deal with anti-social disorders, and to view a mother–child problem as an anti-social disorder is obviously the wrong frame of reference. For the police to come along to investigate at this stage and decide whether they should make a charge is terrible. . . . As it stands the law is quite adequate: if a child is in danger it can be taken into care without any need for police intervention.' . . .

The psychiatrist's point about the police acting as our agents of vengeance is of course partly true. Few people can be so humane that they will wish no punishment to be meted out to parents who have killed or very severely maimed their children. A psychiatrist spends his day investigating the underlying reasons behind human action: when therefore he considers some terrible act a man or woman has done he looks at it as an end result and judges it accordingly, or, more likely, forbears to judge at all. . . .

A hospital doctor discussing his dislike of calling in the police, explained his own attitude with regard to extreme battering. 'Of course I've not been talking about the dangerously ill, severely damaged children. I think that, although in principle it's the same thing, any doctor would feel that in such a gross situation the community is going to demand that such a parent face criminal proceedings. . . . Somebody who has committed murder must suffer the punishments of the community.'

The decision to bring in the police is easy where a child is clearly dying. But sometimes a head injury might not appear very severe even to the examining doctors, and a child may suffer a relapse some months after the injury. In this case if they were not told of the injury when it happened the police may find it almost impossible to check up on facts. . . .

When I put the police's argument—that they are there to protect the child as much as the parent— to [a] paediatrician . . ., he replied, 'You can't do one without the other, Anyway, it's not true. The police's job is to detect crime and to put it to the court for the court's decision whether to punish or not to punish. *That's* the primary aim of the police, to detect crime, not to protect the child or to see that it's rehabilitated with its family—that's the job of the social workers and the doctors'.

To this the police will reply that very often the families need separating from each other, even if only temporarily while feelings cool down, and that only the police can be sure of succeeding in bringing a case successfully to the Juvenile Courts. . . . Police often prefer to bring cases to the Criminal Courts when they suspect a child is in danger of a really severe battering, as an appeal against a Criminal Court ruling is far less likely to succeed. . . .

The truth is it is almost impossible to know what action is correct in any particular case: only after a tragedy has occurred can we be certain who was right. The cases where gentler treatment was successful and nothing further happened do not make headlines. . . .

The real difficulty lies less with the dramatic kind of case . . . than with those where only mild injuries are involved. Often these are not even definitely recognized as having been inflicted by the parent: several doctors pointed out to me that they have been trained to accept the patient's word, and if his or her explanation sounds reasonable they do not go out of their way to look for trouble. Certainly there seems to be no reason for the police to be involved in mild cases on an active level, though in areas where they are fully co-operating and serve on consulting committees their local knowledge of certain problem families can be invaluable as a source of extra information. However, there are still many policemen and women who would not care to accept a passive role as dispensers of local knowledge, and these will continue to pay for their freedom to take action as they see fit, regardless of the desires of the other bodies involved, by only being informed of the most violent cases.

Perhaps the root of the dissension between the police and almost everybody else involved in the treatment of battering families lies in their differing attitudes to punishment. The situation is further complicated by the fact that many ordinary members of the public are ambivalent about the value of punishment: intellectually, they may decide that punishment is ineffective as a treatment, but they themselves have been brought up to expect punishment to follow wrong-doing and they are uneasy with a situation where this does not happen.

The police are single-minded on the question of punishment. Although they insist their job is the detection of crime and that their prime interest is not punitive, it is unlikely that someone who doubted the virtues of punishment for wrongdoing would join the police force in the first instance. . . .

It is instructive to see what various policemen and women, all of whom are interested in and sympathetically-minded about baby battering, have to say. . . .

'Battering parents expect to get punished, you must realize that. They've

175

been brought up that if they've done wrong they'll get whacked for it, and if they don't then they feel society is saying, it's all right, we don't mind what you've done. Then they go and do it again.' From another area, 'Why shouldn't someone who's broken one of society's rules be punished? What's wrong with punishment? As long as it goes hand in hand with treatment, and when the punishment is over the crime is put away and forgotten. I know that's easier said than done, but it's not the concept of punishment that's at fault, it's society's treatment of the prisoner and his aftercare that's wrong.' ...

Many see the threat of punishment as an important part of prevention. ... 'The object of the exercise is the protection of the child. To achieve that you may need to keep some form of sanction hanging over the parents' head to keep them on the straight and narrow. There's nothing wrong with that, you know. It's the theory of a little bit of healthy fear being good for you. ... With problem families you give all the help you can, but you have to watch they don't become so dependent on social services' help that they can't do anything for themselves. They need that little prod to keep them up to the mark, to stiffen them up, and to my mind that's a thoroughly good thing.' On guilt: 'They end up after psychiatric treatment being able to explain away their battering in psychiatric terms. They learn, you see, they learn how to talk quite glibly about all their childhood problems and they try to justify what they've done *instead of feeling guilt*! All right, so the psychiatrist says guilt is a bad thing, but *why* is it? There may be all sorts of reasons why she's done it, but it's a dreadful thing to do and she ought to realize that. I can't see why psychiatric treatment can't do two things, first make a mother aware of a sense of guilt about what she's done but, having felt that guilt, teach her to understand why it's happened so she can try not to let it happen again.' ...

Who then is right? The point of discussion is far wider than the narrow issue of baby battering. The whole world is going through a period of changing values, and as a nation we hardly know what we think on many issues. ...

It is argued that battering parents have an over-developed sense of guilt, that they sometimes have a positively unhealthy desire to be punished which should not be indulged. ... Until sufficient research is done it is impossible to know who in the long run is right about the value of inflicting guilt. When one meets these parents and gets to know them, it seems pointless to consider doing anything other than attempt to help them. But perhaps the police are right in feeling that, where there are no clear pointers to the way one should behave, many people will find it difficult to impose self-discipline on themselves, and as a result will grow lax and behave badly. Some therapeutic communities are managing to help disturbed people combine self-discovery with self-discipline, and this seems to be the most desirable aim to treatment.

Meanwhile the undoubted dangers of police intervention are summed up by Joan Court: 'Prosecution, if successful, is unlikely to have a deterrent effect on parents who are not capable of controlling their conduct, and merely confirms them in their negative self image. If they are acquitted then they feel vindicated and justified in their conduct, and future therapeutic work with them may prove impossible. Most important of all, perhaps, is that the resultant publicity prevents other parents from seeking help in the early stages. The injured child, who could have been adequately protected through the Juvenile Court, is then in great danger.' . . .

When I talked to [a] Chief Superintendent of Scotland Yard, whose chief concern is the welfare of children in the Metropolitan area, she said she was well aware of all these arguments, and she confirmed that the police rarely hear about batterings from social workers and hospitals. Like every other policeman I met she felt this was unfair, a result of prejudice. 'One argument is always being used, that the police are a punitive organization, which we're *not*: we're merely a law-enforcing agency. It's quite wrong to say that because somebody goes before a court they are automatically punished. If they need help they will get it, and there'll be the power of the law behind them to make sure they not only have that help but that they take advantage of it. They very rarely go to prison, you know—they might get put on probation with the condition they have six months' residence and treatment at a mental hospital, for instance. It's often the only way to see that they do get treatment. . . . They take much more notice than when a psychiatrist or a social worker hints at the same thing.'

All this may be true, but the fact remains that as long as baby battering comes under the Offences Against the Person Act (grievous bodily harm) it is a CID matter and in cases of serious injury an ordinary CID officer has no choice but to arrest and charge a parent. The only way out of this is for a high-ranking officer to be involved who is willing to take upon himself the responsibility of delaying police action while all the people involved including the police conduct their investigations and decide on the best way to treat the case. Even this method is denied by some forces, who insist that no one, however high ranking, has any choice but to make an arrest in such an instance. One police force which does not take this viewpoint is the Northamptonshire Police.

The Northampton scheme evolved through a process of trial and error, the result of friendly co-operation between doctors, the CID and the local NSPCC officer. By 1971 the scheme was working sufficiently well for one of the originators of the scheme, Dr H. de la Haye Davies, Northampton's principal police surgeon, to write a report on it which was published in the *Police Journal*, presumably being seen by most police forces in the country. The scheme is now well-established and has the full support of most local doctors, though even in this area it is still rare for social workers to report cases direct to the police. . . . Because it has successfully overcome most of the hostility between the police and the other professions involved, I feel it is well worth setting out in some detail just how the scheme works.

The basic team consists of a consultant paediatrician, a senior police surgeon, a senior CID officer and a senior inspector of the NSPCC. It is of great importance in the formation of these teams that all the different professions are represented by senior men and women, as only someone of high rank can risk taking responsibility for the kind of decisions which occasionally have to be made. This is particularly important in the case of the police representative, who, when he reports back to his Chief Constable, will naturally find his judgment more highly valued, and more likely to be acted upon, if he is a senior; normally in Northampton either the Detective Superintendent or the Assistant Chief Constable is the officer involved. Members of the team contact each other informally, in the early stages great care being taken to see that nothing is committed to paper which might set in train certain actions which no one wants to take. Without mutual trust such a course would not be possible, and it says much for the tact of the main intermediary, in this case Dr Davies, and the willingness of Detective Superintendent Roy (the police officer most frequently involved) that the team has remained successfully viable for so long. . . .

The police surgeon, the second member of the team, is the liaison man between the medical profession and the law. He is in the advantageous position of having a foot in both camps and is able to appreciate both viewpoints. Within twenty-four hours of the child being admitted to hospital he will have seen and discussed the case with the consultant paediatrician, his forensic expertise being particularly useful in cases which are difficult to diagnose. . . . Clever lawyers can sometimes make mincemeat of men and women who are normally more than capable of holding their own, with the result that a number of children are returned to their families in spite of the expressed fears of the doctors or social workers who have been looking after them. Obviously this is less likely to happen when an experienced police surgeon is presenting the evidence. . . .

The third member of the team must be a senior police officer, and since battering is considered a criminal assault it will normally be the CID who will perform this function. As Dr Davies writes in his report, a CID officer with definite proof that someone has assaulted a child must 'put the evidence before those responsible for deciding whether a prosecution should be instituted, but in our experience, the latter person or persons invariably follow a humane and proper course, and if it is in the best interests of the child that a prosecution should be avoided, then this line is usually taken'. Behind these official phrases lies the fact that the Chief Constable does in fact listen and listen hard.

When the case has been talked about and looked at from every point of view a decision is arrived at, and this will be communicated back to police headquarters. From then on, every case is different, but whatever the final outcome, the team keeps in touch, informally by phone or by occasional meetings.

In a comparatively small county like Northampton it is difficult to produce sufficient statistical evidence to prove how successful or otherwise a scheme has been. Those involved in it can only say they have no doubts about its success and as the years go by they are more than ever convinced that such co-operation is vital in the treatment of battering families. Certainly the police there seem to be far more satisfied with the information they receive from their medical colleagues than others I met in less co-operative areas. Since the rate of battering does not seem to have gone up as a result of police lenience, perhaps other areas might be encouraged to follow suit.

In 1970 the Home Office sent out a directive to all Medical Officers of Health and Chief Constables, asking for meetings of social workers, police and doctors in which questions of co-operation could be discussed. By all accounts some of these meetings were not very successful. As one doctor put it, 'The social workers sat on one side of the hall, the police on the other, and we doctors sat in the middle between them. It was like throwing the fox to the hounds—they yapped at each other over our heads and neither side was prepared to give an inch. Whenever we opened our mouths it seemed to set off one side or the other, so in the end we just shut up and let them get on with it.'

The Home Office soon became aware of the poor co-operation between the police and the rest. A 1972 circular of theirs stated, 'The Department of Health and Social Security hopes that [this] report will stimulate further thoughts on the importance of co-operation between all the professionals involved and they have been careful to focus attention on the problem of defining the role of the police and on the police concern to be involved at the earliest possible moment.' But many feel that it is up to the Home Office to do something more positive than merely quote the hopeful sentiments of the Department of Health. I heard complaints that the Home Office does not give any clear guidance on this tricky problem, especially from doctors who say that quite often individual police officers admit they would prefer not to prosecute but that they have no choice in the matter. No doubt some officers hide behind this excuse and are in fact perfectly content to bring a prosecution, but there are certainly many others who would like not to but feel they dare not take a risk.

The same thing applies to police representation on hospital case committees: several doctors told me they have assured the local police they would welcome them provided they would agree to take no action except in severe cases, but nearly always the police reply that they would like to come but if they heard of anything they thought might be a crime, however confidentially they were told it, they would have to investigate—with the consequence that they are rarely asked on to these committees.

The same circular states: 'A battered baby case is by definition one in which there is at least a suspicion that a serious offence has been committed. *When a case comes to the notice of the police they are bound to investigate it* although a prosecution will not necessarily follow. Once the facts are known to them the police have to decide whether to prosecute . . .' (my italics). On the other hand they admit: 'Police representation at the case committees level is reported in very few areas and this is a reflection of a reluctance of doctors and social workers to involve the police before they have been able to assess the social consequence of such action in situations which are so often complex.' But instead of drawing the obvious conclusion from these two facts, they finish up with a first-rate piece of officialese saying precisely nothing: 'This is one important area where greater flexibility may be needed and where attention should be focused on the possibility of improving co-operation between the police, doctors, nurses and social workers. It would be wrong to assume that the measure of co-operation necessary can be easily achieved but the encouragement of a continuing dialogue between all those concerned might hold out the best hope for the future.'

If a policeman sincerely believes he has no choice but to investigate and possibly prosecute on hearing of certain events, then the first statement above will reassure him he is correct in his belief. The last paragraph will in no way encourage him to co-operate since the first paragraph has just told him he must not. Let us be quite clear about this: to everybody except the police, police investigation at any level is not 'co-operation' unless it has been requested. Thus the second paragraph—'police representation at the case committee level is reported in very few areas'—will continue to be true until the Home Office does something far more concrete than issue a few woolly statements to the effect they expect that it will probably all work out in the end. The Home Office is the only body who can make it work out, and they can only do so by issuing unequivocal directives which everybody can clearly understand. For example, where a paediatrician suspects a battering but does not consider the child's life to be at present endangered then the police should be informed so that they may know what is happening. The police in their turn should undertake to keep right out of the picture as far as the parents are concerned until a case committee (on which they would be presented) has decided what action ought to be taken. Where a case committee cannot come to an agreement then the argument will have to be taken to a further high-level committee, on which all professionals are represented, for arbitration. If, as at present, a doctor knows that the final decision will be made by a policeman, then he will not pass on information, and however many pious hopes the Home Office may express in future circulars, they will be doomed to remain unfulfilled.

It would be unfair to the Home Office, however, to leave the impression that its influence has been entirely negative. The various communications sent out over the past few years have certainly brought the existence of baby battering to the attention of many who might otherwise have preferred to ignore it. The first action was taken in 1970 when the Home Office asked for inter-professional discussions on a local basis.

In a memorandum entitled *The Battered Baby* (February 1970) the syndrome was described in some detail. It was a fair summing-up owing much to the NSPCC's research, though its tone was not always that used by the NSPCC's Research Department (for example, hospital casualty officers are instructed when talking to battering parents that, 'throughout, the parents must be told repeatedly that the first concern of the doctor is to make their child better and secondly, "to make sure that it does not happen again" '). In May 1972 they sent out the circular ... which ... was a broad-based review of what was being done all over the country, and contained various suggestions for improvement. From the analysis it appears that in the majority of counties police were included in the review committees, but these were merely general committees which were supposed to discuss what could be done locally to deal with baby battering in principle; although some meetings no doubt proved valuable, others resulted in the kind of polite squabble described a few pages back. The Home Office analysis suggests that these committees should meet regularly, and that their function should be to 'ensure that research, education and training programmes are carried out', also that they should co-operate with review committees in other areas to 'ensure that management procedures are either uniform or the differences clearly known and understood'. . . .

The second type of committee which local authorities were encouraged to set up was the case committee, designed to deal with individual cases; basically this works on the Northampton pattern, where the police co-operate wholeheartedly. Unfortunately, the Home Office analysis proved that in most areas the police are very rarely invited to these case committees, for the reasons already explained. Again and again in the report the importance of what we might call the three 'c's is stressed—co-ordination, communication and co-operation. But pious hopes are not enough: the Home Office knows what needs to be done—they themselves have made it clear in their own circular—so when will they accept that progress on the vexed question of police co-operation must originate from them? . . . We do not want a police force that can change or adapt the rules as they see fit: the dangers are too great. Therefore it is essential they are given a clear lead where issues such as baby battering confuse the normal process of the law.

Not all policemen will agree with the concept of special rules for baby batterers, and some will object strongly.

... If they are to restore the image of the friendly neighbourhood policeman (and that is how most of those I have talked to seem in essence to see themselves) then they must do more than make protesting noises when they are attacked. They will have to be seen making positive gestures of goodwill as a body, even if it involves them in some sacrifice of their own independence.... Modern social welfare is part of such a complicated structure that it can only function successfully if the interests of the people who are being helped are put before departmental ambitions. The police are no exception and should not be treated as such unless they wish to remain quite apart from other professions and be seen purely as a detecting, punitive force. The choice has to be made, and the sooner it is made the better.

Part Six Therapeutic approaches and long-term effects

In various ways the authors of the papers in this section discuss the long-term effects of child abuse reported from different parts of the world. MacKeith draws attention to morbidity arising from maltreatment. Friedman and Morse report on a five year follow-up of early case finding and Kempe and Helfer describe how 'parent aides' assist professional workers in long-term therapy.

Although untypical the case study of severe deprivation in twins demonstrates the possibility of rehabilitation even in the most unlikely cases.

26 Speculations on some possible long-term effects
Ronald MacKeith

In all countries, children sustain non-accidental injury (NAI). Among the various injuries, head injury is not infrequent. Sometimes it is severe enough to cause death. It is probable that less severe cerebral injuries also occur which are survived. Many of these will recover fully. But it seems likely that between the NAI head injuries which kill and those followed by complete recovery, there are others which lead to lasting brain injury sufficient to produce deficits of cerebral function. It is therefore possible that sometimes cerebral palsy and mental deficiency are late sequelae of cerebral injury by NAI, although there is as yet no adequate long-term follow up to prove it. The justification for exploring this possibility by examining the available data is that no sufficient explanation can be found in half the children with cerebral palsy.

The head injuries sustained from non-accidental injury

Writing of the necropsy findings in children dead of child abuse with no previous history, Weston (1968) says that 'The most commonly encountered pathological finding was that of subdural haemorrhage. This was acute . . . and in most instances was associated with . . . underlying contusion of the cerebral cortex identified by light pink-purple discoloration, slight softening, and sharply outlined dark red-purple/petechial haemorrhages. In the children thrown or hurled against the wall or to the floor, there was evidence, not only of a primary contusion adjacent to the scalp lesions but also of a contrecoup injury, reflected by contralateral subarachnoid haemorrhage and cerebral contusions. . . . Among the 23 children who expired as a result of injuries superimposed on previous injuries, the internal injuries were essentially the same . . . but of considerably greater magnitude'.

Among 42 children admitted to hospital for NAI, Birrell and Birrell (1968) found intracranial haemorrhage in 9 (21 per cent) and skull fracture in 12.

MACKEITH, R. (1975) 'Speculations on some possible long-term effects', in White Franklin, A. (ed.) *Concerning Child Abuse*, Edinburgh, Churchill Livingstone, pp. 63–8.

The possible late effect of shaking a baby

Caffey (1972) has suggested that shaking a baby may damage its brain. The greatest risk is said to be in the first six months, when shaking gives a whip-lash effect that bumps the brain against the side of the skull and causes pinpoint haemorrhages and damage to blood vessels. Follow-up studies of two small groups of 'shaken' children uncovered a surprisingly high prevalence of mental retardation. He suggested that cumulative damage occurs and that some, perhaps many, of the cerebrovascular injuries attributed to pre-natal infections, congenital malformation, birth injuries and genetic metabolic diseases are really caused by undetected whip-lash shakings during the first weeks or months of life.

The sequelae of subdural haematoma

I have not located the two follow-up studies of 'shaken' babies. There is, however, an oblique way of approaching the main problem. Cerebral contusion is potentially much more likely to give fatal or lasting cerebral deficit than is subdural haematoma. While it may be difficult to confirm the existence of a cerebral contusion it is easier to establish the presence of a subdural haematoma which, as Weston's work showed, usually implies the presence of a cerebral contusion. By studying the sequelae of subdural haematoma in fact we shall be discovering the effects of the common combination of cerebral contusion plus subdural haematoma. This view finds confirmation from the conviction of neurosurgeons that NAI is a major, though not the only, cause of subdural haematoma (9 of 21 cases, Köttgen, 1967).

In a follow up of 76 children with subdural haematoma, Till (1968) found that 5 per cent were dead, 8 per cent were ineducable and 12 per cent were educationally subnormal.

In a follow up of 65 children with subdural haematoma, Aicardi et al. (1971, 1973) found that 6 per cent were lost, 10 per cent were dead, 25 per cent were severely incapacitated and 25 per cent were moderately incapacitated.

Of 14 who had status epilepticus at the onset, 12 were severely incapacitated. Of 16 whose coma continued for more than 12 hours after the haematoma was tapped, 11 were severely or moderately incapacitated. The duration of the effusion did not affect the prognosis.

These two series taken together suggest that for every child dead with a subdural haematoma, there may be two or three who survive to be severely incapacitated and another two or three who survive to be moderately incapacitated, notably in intelligence. A tentative conclusion is that for every death from NAI, there may be four children with incapacitating chronic neurological sequelae.

Deaths from non-accidental injury

In 1962 Kempe reported on a sample of 749 cases and said that 10.4 per cent of the children had died. The UK Department of Health pamphlet (1970) calculated that 2 per cent of deaths of infants between 4 weeks and 1 year are due to wilful violence. In 1967 there were 679 such deaths in the UK. On this estimate about 13 infants under 1 year of age die every year as the result of wilful violence. This suggests that there are at least 50 new cases a year of chronic neurological handicap resulting from NAI. In West Germany, Trube-Becker (1971), reporting on 1,385 necropsies, found that 6.4 per cent of children under 6 years of age died of neglect or maltreatment.

Incidence of non-accidental injury in childhood

The incidence of NAI is believed by Kempe (1971) to be 6 per 1,000 live births. For the USA with a population of 225,000,000, he calculated that there are 40,000 cases a year. We should remember that the number of reported cases in the USA in 1967 was 6,000 (Gil, 1969).

For the UK with a quarter of the population of the USA the *Lancet* (1971) gave 3,000 cases each year of NAI. Kempe (1971) also suggested 3,000 cases a year in the UK, a figure derived from the assumption of only 500,000 births a year, instead of 800,000, so that Kempe's estimate should be revised to at least 4,500.

Mortality rate of NAI in children

The mortality rate for battered children has been varyingly reported at:

4 per cent	(Kempe et al. 1962)
1.4 per cent	(California Pilot Survey; Gill 1968)
1.3 per cent	(Skinner and Castle 1969)
3 per cent	(Gregg and Elmer 1969)
6 to 14 per cent	(Moszer and Bach 1969)
13 per cent	(Barnmishandel 1969)
10 per cent	(Cooper 1972)

Two comments may be made on these figures. One is that they suggest that over the last ten years doctors are revising their ideas on the mortality rate of NAI in an upward direction. The other is that these mortality figures are largely based on children who have been seen in hospital and hence on children who have suffered more severe injuries.

At a guess for the UK the case mortality is at least 3 per cent, though it may be several times that figure. The lower estimate of 3,000 cases in the UK each year suggests 90 deaths a year, a figure three times the amount the *Lancet* estimated (1971) and seven times the 13 based on necropsy studies.

Bierman (1969) states that in the German Federal Republic with a population of 50 million, about 1,000 children die every year of NAI and that the number is increasing.

If for every child dead of NAI, four children have a lasting incapacity, and if the estimate of 90 deaths a year in the UK is correct there should be 400 new cases a year of lasting incapacity due to NAI.

Incidence of lasting neurological disorder after NAI

Another estimate could be based on the reports published of the proportion of children suffering NAI who are left with permanent neurological disorder. From a sample of 749 cases Kempe (1962) estimated that 15 per cent were left with 'permanent brain damage'; motor disorder was not differentiated from the mental handicap which might result from accompanying deprivation. Gil (1969) reported 'permanent damage' in 5 per cent of NAI not specifically of the brain. Kempe (1971) stated that 'half' of the NAI children will be significantly injured, but not necessarily in the CNS nor permanently.

Martin (1972) reported that when 42 abused children were re-examined three years after the abuse, 43 per cent were impaired neurologically and 33 per cent were mentally retarded. 'They were a pathetic lot and had little capacity for enjoyment and spent time mothering adults around them and a minority had given up relating normally to other people.' Martin, Beezley, Conway and Kempe (1974) tried to follow up 159 children but only 58 could be persuaded to co-operate. The injuries they had had were relatively mild. Fifty-three per cent had a poorly functioning nervous system, including 31 per cent with serious neurological deficits.

Aicardi et al. (1971, 1973) reported that of children who had had subdural haematoma, 25 per cent were severely incapacitated and 25 per cent were moderately incapacitated. Of 40 children admitted for NAI at the Park Hospital, Oxford, 17.5 per cent had subdural haematoma. If from 8 to 25 per cent of children with subdural haematoma are liable to be left with severe neurological handicap, the Park Hospital figures suggest that 1.5 to 4 per cent of NAI children have lasting neurological handicap.

These papers provide data from which firm conclusions cannot be drawn. Yet if 3 per cent of NAI children develop cerebral palsy, visual defect and so on, then on the lower assumption of 3,000 cases of NAI annually in the UK, NAI will be responsible for 90 new cases of neurological deficit every year. This compares with the estimated 1,600 new cases a year of cerebral palsy in half of which no cause is found. So perhaps NAI may be responsible for 6 per cent of the current new cases of cerebral palsy in the UK.

Incidence of mental handicap after NAI

There are rather more definite data about the later educational difficulties of some of the children who have had NAI.

According to Gil (1969) 3 per cent of children of school age had never attended school and 13 per cent were in grades below those expected of their age. The figures given by Morse et al. (1970) are 2 of 25 children severely retarded and 6 of the 25 were retarded, 5 were disturbed, 8 normal, and 4 were lost.

Gregg and Elmer (1969) studied a group of 30 who had had NAI and found that 24 per cent more children were retarded in development than in a control group of non-abused children.

Martin's re-examination (1972) of 42 children three years after being abused revealed that 33 per cent were mentally retarded.

These reports may be compared with those of children who had had subdural haematoma; of these 8 per cent were ineducable (Till 1968), 25 per cent were severely incapacitated (Aicardi et al. 1971, 1973), 12 per cent were educationally subnormal (Till 1968) and 25 per cent were moderately incapacitated (Aicardi et al. 1971, 1973).

If, as seems possible, after NAI only 5 per cent of survivors are severely subnormal and given 3,000 of NAI a year in the UK, this means 150 new children with mental deficiency a year. This is 25 per cent of the known 600 new mentally deficient children each year. It also seems possible that some 20 per cent of those who have suffered NAI in their early years are likely to be mentally handicapped in later life. This would be some 600 new cases a year of moderate mental handicap. The educational handicap of children who have had NAI could originate in actual cerebral injury but it could also result from the emotional and intellectual deprivation which are very much parts of the syndrome as Birrell and Birrell (1968) have emphasized.

When a child is first assessed several years after infancy, deprivation and NAI as possible causes may be less likely to be considered because the parents may have grown and developed into a more reasonable competence.

Maladjustment

Another late effect of the maltreatment syndrome is emotional maladjustment. Depression and psuedo mental retardation were shown by 6 of 106 survivors (Ebbin et al. 1969). 'Only a few of the (20) battered children gave promise of becoming self sufficient adults' (Elmer and Gregg 1967).

Even if battering parents are amenable to treatment—and probably most of them are—they are sick people who treat their children in a sick way. Ninety per cent have serious problems in mothering or fathering their children and this would be expected to affect the child's personality development. It is generally thought that many battering parents were, as little children, themselves maltreated. Hence one late sequel of NAI is that the child who has had NAI is at high risk for injuring his or her own children. This risk is largely the consequence of the deprivation or maltreatment, but any person with brain injury is probably more vulnerable to untoward environmental experiences and hence is liable to break down under stresses with which ordinary individuals can cope. Nau (1968) stated that from large-scale studies in Germany, he was able to note that a large proportion of criminals, killers and murderers come from the group of people who had been maltreated in childhood.

Fortunately, attention is now being directed to prevention. One way is to attempt to recognize at pre-natal clinics the mothers-to-be who are at risk for inflicting NAI and to follow them up, treat them and support them when the baby is born. Another is to step up the measures in lying-in wards which promote good bonding between mothers and their infants.

Conclusion

In one-half of the children with cerebral palsy and half of the mentally deficient children, no adequate cause of their disability can be identified. Speculation on incomplete data suggests the NAI and the associated deprivation may account for 90 new cases of cerebral palsy each year, that is about 6 per cent, for about 150 or about one-quarter of new cases of severe mental handicap each year, and also for a considerable number, perhaps 3,000 a year, of new cases of children with disturbed personality at risk for developing anti-social behaviour and for injuring their own children. An alternative method of calculation yields a figure of 400 new children each year with chronic neurological deficits.

References

AICARDI, J. and GOUTIÈRE, S. F. (1971) 'Les Épanchements Sous-duraux du Nourrisson', *Arch. franc. Pediatr.*, **28**, 233.

AICARDI, J., BARATON, J. and ASKENIAZI, S. (1973) Paper to European Study Group on Child Neurology, Kungalv.

BARNMISHANDEL (1969) *Socialstyrelsens redovisar*, No. 9, Sweden.

BIERMAN, G. (1969) *Kindeszuchtigung und Kindesmisshandlung*, Munchen and Basle, Reinhardt.

BIRRELL, R. G. and BIRRELL, J. H. W. (1968) 'The Maltreatment Syndrome in Children: a Hospital Survey', *Med. J. Austral.*, **2**, 1023.

CAFFEY, J. (1972) *World Medicine*, 28 July 1972.

COOPER, C. (1972) Personal communication.

DEPARTMENT OF HEALTH AND SOCIAL SECURITY (1970) *The Battered Baby*, Memorandum prepared by the Standing Medical Advisory Committee for the Central Health Service Council, 31 July 1970.

EBBIN, A. J., GOLLUB, M. H. et al. (1969) 'Battered Child Syndrome at Los Angeles County General Hospital', *Amer. J. Child.*, **118**, 660.

ELMER, E., and GREGG, G. S. (1967) 'Development Characteristics of Abused Children', *Pediatrics*, **40**, 596.

GIL, D. G. (1968) in Helfer, R. E. and Kempe, C. H. (eds.) (1968) *The Battered Child*, Chicago, University of Chicago Press.

GIL, D. G. (1969) 'Physical Abuse of Children: Findings and Implications of a Nationwide Survey', *Pediatrics*, **44**, 857.

GREGG, G. S. and ELMER, E. (1969) 'Infant Injuries: Accident or Abuse', *Pediatrics*, **44**, 434.

HELFER, R. E. and KEMPE, C. H. (1968) *The Battered Child*, Chicago, University of Chicago Press.

KEMPE, C. H. (1971) 'Paediatric Implications of the Battered Baby Syndrome', *Arch. Dis. Childh.*, **46**, 28.

KEMPE, C. H., SILVERMAN, F. N. et al. (1962) 'The Battered-child Syndrome', *J. Am. med. Ass.*, **181**, 17.

KÖTTGEN, U. (1967) 'Kindesmisshandlung', *Mschr. Kinderheilk.*, **115**, 186.

LANCET (1971) 'Annotation on violent parents', *Lancet*, **2**, 1017.

MARTIN, H. (1972) 'The child and his development' in Kempe, C. H. and Helfer, R. E. (eds.) *Helping the Battered Child and his Family*, Philadelphia, Lippincott.

MARTIN, H. P., BEEZLEY, M. S. W., CONWAY, E. F. and KEMPE, C. H. (1974) 'The Development of Abused Children', *Advances in Pediatrics*, **21**, 25–73.

MORSE, C. W., SAHLER, O. K. Z. et al. (1970) 'A Three Year Follow-up Study of Abused and Neglected Children', *Amer. J. Dis. Child.*, **120**, 439.

MOSZER, M. and BACH, C. (1969) 'Le syndrome des enfants maltraitée', *Progrès Medical*, **97**, 303.

NAU, E. (1968) 'Kindesmisshandlung', *Mschr. Kinderheik.*, **115**, 192.

SKINNER, A. E. and CASTLE, R. L. (1969) *78 Battered Children: a Retrospective Survey*, London, NSPCC.

TILL, K. (1968) 'Subdural haematoma and effusion in infancy', *Brit. med. J.*, **3**, 40.

TRUBE-BECKER, E. (1971) 'Obduktion beim plötzlich gestorbenen Kind', *Medizinische Klinik*, **66**, 58.

WESTON, J. T. (1968) in Helfer, R. E. and Kempe, C. H. (eds.) (1968) *The Battered Child*, Chicago, University of Chicago Press.

27 Child abuse: a five-year follow-up of early case finding in the emergency department

Stanford B. Friedman and Carol W. Morse

[Editorial introduction

One hundred and fifty-six children under 6 years of age seen for injuries in an emergency department had been previously studied and their injuries were judged by the investigators to represent unreported 'suspected abuse', 'gross neglect', or an 'accident'. Five years later, all cases of 'suspected abuse' and 'neglect', and a random sample of 'accidents', were included in a study involving interview of parents and a survey of medical facilities for subsequent contact with these children. Seventy-five per cent (41 of 54) of this sample were located and available for study. At the time of follow-up, it was found that children judged to have experienced 'accidents' had a lower incidence of subsequent injuries, their siblings had fewer injuries, their relationship to their mother was judged to be better, and there were fewer emotional and social problems in their families. These differences did not reach statistical significance except in a single instance, though by all of these measurements the children from the 'suspected abuse' and 'gross neglect' groups did not do as well as the children judged to have experienced 'accidents'.]

Behavioral and developmental characteristics

In trying to account for differences among the groups in frequency of subsequent injuries, the authors examined behavioral and developmental characteristics of the children and general family stability. A number of areas of child behavior were explored with the mothers at the time of the follow-up interview; specifically, physical activity, temperament, sibling and peer relationships, obedience, specific bedtime and mealtime problems, school performance and punishment. There were no notable differences among the groups in these areas. However, it is of interest that the vast majority of parents in all groups relied on physical punishment for disobedience as opposed to removal of privileges or restriction of activity.

FRIEDMAN, S. B. and MORSE, C. W. (1974) 'Child abuse: a five-year follow-up of early case finding in the emergency department', *Pediatrics*, vol. 54, no. 4, pp. 404, 408–10.

Generally, they believed this method to be effective. Also, mothers were asked during the follow-up interview these two questions: 'Which child in the family is hurt most often?' and 'How often is the child in question hurt in comparison to other children?' In no group did a majority of the parents believe that the child in the study was hurt most often in the family or more than other children.

From previous studies (Morse 1970, Court 1969) the abused child has been singled out as being somehow different. These vulnerable children are described as being seen as sickly, spoiled, bad, or problem children. Therefore, an assessment was made at the time of the follow-up interview of the mother–child relationship. As might be expected, more children in the 'accident' group (66%) exhibited good relationships with their mothers than in the 'suspected abuse' (43%) and 'suspected neglect' (29%) groups. Only one child in the 'accident' group (6%) was considered to have a poor mother–child relationship as contrasted with four children (28%) in the 'suspected abuse' group and one child in the 'suspected neglect' category (14%). These differences did not reach significance by χ^2 analysis.

Expanding on the mother–child relationship, the authors also made observations and assessments of the general emotional and behavioral status of other family members. Sixty-seven per cent of the children in the 'suspected abuse' category came from families with notable behavioral and/or emotional problems, as compared to 28 per cent and 33 per cent of the 'suspected neglect' and 'accident' categories, respectively. These differences are not statistically significant. It should be understood that these impressions reflect only those problems which were noted at the time of follow-up interview and are undoubtedly conservative as the questionnaire focused primarily on the previously injured child.

The most prevalent problems were in the realm of child rearing, with parents not setting and maintaining effective and consistent limits for their children's behavior. Some of the parents themselves suffered from emotional problems, with no single diagnosis prevailing. Depression, 'nervousness', marked overprotection of children, chronic medical problems, and mental retardation were among the problems noted.

Discussion

In their original paper on case findings in the emergency department setting, Holter and Friedman concluded: '. . . placing a child in the suspected abuse category is a clinical judgment, and only long-term follow-up will define the accuracy of these judgments.' The current study was basically an attempt to see if the original judgments were predictive of relative subsequent risk to the child and his siblings. The findings of the study would appear to indicate that young children identified as having experienced abuse or gross neglect are more vulnerable to further injuries, as are their siblings. However, the results are far from definitive, and though in the expected direction, do not reach statistical significance.

In this study, the investigator not previously involved in the case finding survey agreed in 85 per cent of the cases with the original judgment of 'suspected abuse', 'suspected neglect', or 'accident'. This degree of agreement is not surprising in that the same criteria for inclusion in any of these three categories were used; and though the judgments were made independently, both studies reflect the same research orientation. However, a significant degree of disagreement would invalidate all other findings in this follow-up study in that the reliability of the judgments themselves would be very much in question.

The fact that over 70 per cent of the children from the 'suspected abuse' and 'suspected neglect' groups had injuries requiring medical attention during the five-year follow-up period would appear higher than what would be expected in a sample of children from the general population. However, these authors were unable to find a satisfactory comparison group, and unfortunately we did not include in our study children who were seen in the same emergency department setting for reasons other than injuries. Finding that seven out of every ten children might be anticipated to have a subsequent injury during the five-year period would, nevertheless, appear to identify a high risk group, though such an interpretation is tenuous when such a figure is compared to slightly over 50 per cent of the children in the 'accident' group also sustaining an injury during a comparable period of time. The lack of a significant difference between the suspected 'abuse' and 'neglect' groups and those children judged to have sustained an 'accident' may reflect the fact that accidents themselves are known to recur in certain children at a higher than expected incidence (Husband 1972; Klonoff 1971; Matheny 1971; Martin 1970; Baltimore 1969; Wight 1969; Manheimer 1967; Meyer 1963; Haggerty 1959; Fuller 1948). Childhood injuries may, therefore, be viewed as occurring on an accident child abuse continuum. It also may be that if our sample had been larger, even the relatively minor differences among groups might have reached significance. The siblings of the children judged to have experienced 'abuse' or 'neglect' had a significantly higher number of injuries requiring medical attention.

The number of children thought to have experienced abuse during the follow-up period was too limited for statistical analysis. . . . In an assessment of the mother–child relationship, more children in the 'accident' group were judged to exhibit good relationships with their mothers than in the 'abuse' and 'neglect' groups. Also, there was a tendency for the families of children judged to have been abused to have a higher frequency of emotional and behavioral problems. However, none of these differences reached statistical significance.

193

I

In the original case finding study (Holter 1968), there was an empirical association between the type of injury and whether that injury was judged to reflect 'abuse', 'neglect', or an 'accident'. Specifically, with one exception, lacerations and ingestions had all been judged to represent 'accidents', and bruises and abrasions, fractures, dislocations, burns, and head injuries judged to represent 'abuse' and 'neglect' cases. In examining the injuries occurring in the five-year follow-up period in a similar manner, the same association was noted but a sharp distinction of a 'high-risk' and 'low-risk' group of children definable by the type of injury sustained was not confirmed. However, the relative infrequency of lacerations and ingestions in cases of abuse also has been noted by others (McRae 1973).

In summary, young children previously judged to have experienced 'abuse' or 'gross neglect' did tend to experience a greater number of injuries needing medical attention than those children judged to have experienced an 'accident'. However, this incidence of approximately 70 per cent was not significantly greater than the 50 per cent rate of repeat injury for the 'accident' group. There was a higher incidence of injuries of the siblings of the combined 'abuse' and 'neglect' groups than in the 'accident' group. Though again statistical significance was not reached, except in one instance, there did appear to be a greater number of behavioral problems and poor mother–child relationships in the combined 'abuse' and 'neglect' groups than in children judged to have sustained 'accidents'. Two cases of abuse were identified in the follow-up period and in both instances these children came from the group originally categorized as 'suspected abuse'; each also had a sibling judged to have suffered from abuse during this same follow-up period.

References

BALTIMORE, C. and MEYER, R. J. (1969) 'A Study of Storage, Child Behavioral Traits and Mother's Knowledge of Toxicology in 52 Poisoned Families and 52 Comparison Families', *Pediatrics*, **44**, 816.

COURT, J. (1969) 'The Battered Child: I. Historical and Diagnostic Reflections', *Med. Soc. Work*, **22**, 11.

FULLER, E. M. (1948) 'Injury-prone Children', *Amer. J. Orthopsychiat.*, **18**, 708.

HAGGERTY, R. J. (1959) 'Home Accidents in Childhood', *New Eng. J. Med.*, **260**, 1322.

HOLTER, J. C. and FRIEDMAN, S. B. (1968) 'Child Abuse: Early Case Finding in the Emergency Department', *Pediatrics*, **42**, 128.

HUSBAND, P. and HUNTON, P. E. (1972) 'Families of Children with Repeated Accidents', *Arch. Dis. Child.*, **47**, 396.

KLONOFF, H. (1971) Head Injuries in Children: Predisposing Factors, Accident Conditions, Accident Proneness and Sequelae', *Amer. J. Public Health*, **61**, 2405.

MCRAE, K. N., FERGUSON, C. A. and LEDERMAN, R. S. (1973) 'The Battered Child Syndrome', *Canad. Med. Assoc. J.*, **108**, 859.

MANHEIMER, D. I. and MELLINGER, G. D. (1967) 'Personality Characteristics of the Child Accident Repeater', *Child Develop.*, **38**, 491.

MARTIN, H. L. (1970) 'Antecedents of Burns and Scalds in Children', *Brit. J. Med. Psychol.*, **43**, 39.

MATHENY, A. P., BROWN, A. M. and WILSON, R. S. 'Behavioural Antecedents of Accidental Injuries in Early Childhood: A Study of Twins', *J. Pediat.*, **79**, 122.

MEYER, R. J., ROELOFS, H. A., BLUESTONE, J. and REDMOND, S. (1963) 'Accidental Injury to the Preschool Child', *J. Pediatr.*, **63**, 95.

MORSE, C. W., SAHLER, O. J. Z. and FRIEDMAN, S. B. (1970) 'A Three Year Follow-up Study of Abused and Neglected Children', *Amer. J. Dis. Child.*, **120**, 439.

WIGHT, B. W. 'The Control of Child-Environment Interaction: A Conceptual Approach to Accident Occurrence', *Pediatrics*, **44**, 799.

28 Innovative therapeutic approaches
C. Henry Kempe and Ray E. Helfer

The obvious limitation in availability of skilled psychiatrists and social workers demands that other therapeutic approaches must be sought if we hope to help the battered child and his family. Our experience has been that in the great majority of cases, the problem of 'insufficient mothering' can be handled by someone other than a highly skilled professional therapist.

Extensive experience has shown that it is absolutely essential to have a highly skilled and accurate evaluation of the psychopathology within the family structure when the battered child syndrome is first suspected or diagnosed. In less than 10 per cent of the cases, the diagnosis is that one of the parents is suffering from a major psychosis or the attacking parent may be an aggressive psychopath. In these cases it is unrealistic to expect a therapist other than a skilled psychiatrist, psychologist or psychiatric social worker to be involved. Clearly, such mentally ill parents deserve excellent psychiatric care.

If, after the initial psychiatric evaluation, the diagnosis of the family pathology is that of 'insufficient mothering'* then, in our experience, an individual with considerably less training can also be most effective. Fortunately, the great majority of parents who abuse small children are not paranoid or psychopaths and can benefit significantly from an intense relationship with a nonprofessional therapist.

Although excellent results can be obtained in most families by having the therapist be a psychiatrist, psychologist, social worker, general physician, pediatrician, or public health nurse, the qualities that a therapeutic person must possess are not necessarily related to a particular professional identification, course work or training. We have had excellent results with lay workers (Parent Aides) who receive their training 'on the job'. The ideal therapist is one who is prepared to become meaningfully involved over a period of eight to 12 months in the lives of these very deprived parents in a very major way. This is accomplished through weekly or

---

* The term 'insufficient mothering' is used in general terms to describe the problem seen in the large majority of families who come to our attention'

KEMPE, C. H. and HELFER, R. E. (1972) 'Innovative therapeutic approaches', in Kempe, C. H. and Helfer, R. E. (eds) *Helping the Battered Child and his Family*, Philadelphia, Lippincott, pp. 41–54.

twice-weekly visits, often in the parents' home. This relationship is characterized by a listening, approving and noncritical point of view. A great deal of dependency is encouraged early, and the therapist often shows special affection and concern with a birthday card or small present. He or she must be available, often by telephone, in the evenings and on weekends, and a substitute made available when this is not feasible. In other words, a lifeline or rescue operation is firmly established for moments of crises.

The goals of therapy by the Parent Aides are limited since it is not realistic to expect a substantive maturation to occur which will undo the severe deprivation experience by these parents. They are:

1. That the child eventually be returned to his home.
2. That the child not be reinjured.
3. That the child is seen as an individual and somewhat enjoyed.
4. That the family is now well enough to recognize impending crises.
5. That the parents reach out to others in the community for help and friendship and are able to give as well as receive.
6. That they can mature and gradually relinquish their marked dependency on the primary therapist.

Foster grandparents (parent aides)

For the past four years the Pediatric Service at Colorado General Hospital has utilized the services of a group of 'foster grandparents' whose job is simply to cuddle hospitalized children. They are paid a modest wage to supplement their pension. Each 'grandparent' is assigned one child for the duration of his hospitalization if the mother is not able to remain for long periods of time. The foster grandparents are all over 65 years of age because of rules of the funding agency.

In the early course of this work a few of the foster grandparents were assigned battered children. Some were totally unable to form any relationship with the parents of these children because of their understandable great anger. Approximately one third uniquely began to fill the mothering needs of some of these parents. This relationship occasionally was extended beyond the hospital with good results. It seemed quite feasible that a larger lay treatment program, therapeutically directed toward the parents, could be developed that would utilize these elderly men and women as Parent Aides.

The program was begun on a small scale, using a group of lay therapists in a similar therapeutic role and in the absence of any formal training. These men and women come from all walks of life and social classes. They are paid a small hourly wage. To date, our Parent Aides, whose age range is from 24 to 60 (use of individuals over 65 also would be most advantageous), have had the good fortune of being raised by loving mothers and fathers. They themselves are parents and are quite ready to take on the care of a deprived adult.

The selection of therapeutic foster grandparents or Parent Aides was done with some care. We try to match up our therapists and patients by social and economic class. It is often important to have a working class therapist for a working class family. Flexibility, patience and compassion, a willingness to listen and be nondirective and noncritical, are the basic requirements for a successful Parent Aide. The qualities are those of a mild and loving individual who is not easily upset by an ungrateful, suspicious and often initially unwilling client.

We introduce the lay therapists to the parents by saying that we would like to have someone visit who is interested in them and their problems. We urge our therapists to ask for a cup of coffee or tea and sit in the kitchen, to pay little attention to the children and to listen with interest to the problems of the *parents*. Sometimes they see both parents together and other times the mother alone. They must be available in moments of crisis; their phone number and that of an alternate lay therapist is in the client's hands.

Every two weeks a group therapy session of the Parent Aides is held with a pediatrician, psychiatrist and/or social worker. The lay therapists are allowed, indeed encouraged, to ventilate some of their frustrations, anxieties and anger at their clients. They often require encouragement because progress is slow; they may be feeling that they are wasting time and money. Ongoing supervision by a highly skilled social worker is also extremely important. One social worker can work with several Parent Aides in addition to having a small caseload of her own.

Provided the goals are limited and an initially correct diagnosis is made of the family pathology as being deficient mothering, clinical results have been outstandingly good at a fraction of the cost of employing psychiatrists or social workers as therapists. By and large the training of these lay therapists is not difficult. Essentially they already have had the basic course—the experience of having been raised by a good mother or father themselves. With the shortage of skilled psychiatrists and other professional mental health workers, it is clear to us that a broad part of therapy must involve what amounts to substitution of intense therapy for the parents who are in need of mothering by those in the population who have the interest, time and talent to provide such help.

The emotional wear and tear on the therapists precludes their having more than two or three families on a part-time basis, with one or two visits each per week. Parent Aides are encouraged to take the clients out for tea or a meal, and to begin to function as a mature and reliable friend. Much more needs to be learned about the selection of these lay workers, but one must not be afraid to try someone who looks promising and then discontinue after a trial period if necessary. Simply the desire to help or the feeling of compassion for battered *children* is not enough to be a successful Parent Aide. The focus is on the *parents* and not the children. Our premise is that if the parents are all right, the children will be protected.

The job would seem clearly to require a kind of empathy, gentleness and patience which comes with time to all those who have the basic capacity to love and mother other adults in need. Those who have had some of the difficult experiences which come with marriage and parenthood, who have a few 'scars of battle', are most successful. To date we have found that many very pretty, young unmarried girls who have all the desired qualities to be successful therapists, somehow have considerable difficulty getting started. To the abusive mother these girls represent everything she has herself failed to achieve. It is important to regard the therapist as something other than ladies bountiful. They should, if possible, be well matched in terms of educational achievements as well as economics, class and race.

Since Parent Aides need ongoing careful supervision it seems best if they are hired by an agency or hospital that has these backup professionals available. Any group, be it state or private, wishing to provide help to abusive parents could well use the services of the skilled and motivated lay worker.

The visiting nurses

By training and experience public health nurses are comfortable in calling on clients in their homes, having coffee in the kitchen and providing many needed health services. Such nurses are often readily admitted to family homes and they are a potential resource for advice in many aspects of health care. Some, but not all, public health nurses have great talents in caring for parents who batter their children. As described above, a helpful person is one who is not critical or judgmental and who is prepared to use himself or herself as a therapeutic agent.

This very deep involvement with the life of another person does not come readily to everyone. The very crisp and efficient nurse, or one who is critical of a slovenly home or an inadequate mother, simply becomes another condemning figure to the abusive mother, reminding her of her serious experience with her own critical mother. Nurses are often trained to give 'how-to' advice and to direct attention toward the child. In her role as a therapeutic person, the public health nurse must not give very much advice. She does a great deal more sympathetic listening than talking. She is patient, takes time and does not obviously seem to teach. When possible, a weekly or twice-weekly visit to the home in an informal friendly way, with ready willingness to listen, is often an acceptable way to provide treatment. In parts of the country where highly trained social workers, psychologists or psychiatrists are not readily available, or where the patient is only willing to deal with a nonthreatening health professional, the visiting nurse becomes an invaluable person.

It must be stressed that the job of the visiting nurse is *not* that of an 'inspector' and is *not* to provide 'supervision'. Treatment of the battering family involves an experience in 'mothering', the development of trust of another adult and the gradual improvement of the parents' self-image. Helping these parents to obtain a reasonable understanding of their child and to enjoy his presence are two very important goals. Many public health nurses function in such a role quite spontaneously and with considerable success. One has to be certain, however, that they do not discontinue their visiting too soon. The plan should be to continue a relationship on a regular basis, first twice a week and then weekly for approximately a year, but never less than eight or nine months. In time, spacing between visits can be increased but it must not be discontinued and contacts should be maintained essentially until the child is clearly no longer at risk. This decision must be made jointly by the nurse, physician and social worker, if one is involved.

Homemaker services

Many mothers simply do not have the strength to cope with all the demands of several children. In some situations a part-time homemaker may be an essential part of treatment and support in order to keep the family together or to return the child to the family at an early date. Clearly the homemaker who is too brisk or efficient would simply make the mother feel worse, more inadequate; but one who is willing to work along in a gentle way, by actually helping in the house and with the children, and also providing some of the support which we have described above, can be most helpful. The homemaker is also a part of the therapeutic team. She must not be considered either as *the* therapist or the spy within the household who checks up on the childrens' welfare. She will have problems in dealing with her anger at the mother. This must be recognized. Often the homemaker needs to be part of the group therapy which is established for the Parent Aides. An urgent need for the development of these special homemaker services in communities will, if met, undoubtedly benefit such families who can then be kept together at a much less cost to the community.

One word of caution must be interjected. When a homemaker is sent into a home that clearly does not need the services of someone to cook, clean, help with the children, buy groceries, etc., then the roles of the homemaker and the mother become confused. The very tidy woman who keeps an immaculate home with one or two children does not need a homemaker in the usual sense of the word. She may, on the other hand, be in great need of a Parent Aide or foster grandparent.

Crisis nurseries

While it is readily possible to park a car for a modest fee in all parts of the United States, it is extremely difficult to have, without much explanation or preparation, a place where a mother might leave her child for a few hours, in moments of great stress. This service should be available either on an intermittent or even regular basis each day. We have known many mothers who would be quite able to cope with their two or three children if they had some relief, even if it were only for two or three hours a day. At some economic levels this is readily arranged for by employment of babysitters or by the mothers seeking employment outside the home on a part-time basis. This is often done not for the financial reward but, in fact, to get away from their child and thereby prevent battering. At the other end of the economic scale, and particularly when mothers have no special working skills, it becomes very difficult to find a place where a child can be safely placed for no other reason than that the mother wants relief.

The attitude of many welfare agencies appears to be, 'you have had your fun now take care of it'. The fear expressed by many departments is that once the word got around that a child could be placed for a time, the welfare departments would be confronted with thousands of children, many of whom would never be picked up again. In our modest experience thus far, it would seem clear that when given a free choice mothers do not abuse this kind of liberal facility. Clearly, in housing developments or by arrangements between groups of mothers and under the supervision of welfare departments or the schools, it should be possible to provide drop-in nurseries. Justification for use of this service is a positive rather than a negative action on the part of the parents who have come to recognize their limitations and are willing to contribute as much as they can for this type of relief.

Mother's anonymous

Mother's Anonymous is one of the brighter lights that has recently appeared upon the horizon of therapeutic innovations for parents who abuse or may abuse their children. This self-help group was founded by a striking, dynamic woman whose enormous energies were, for 29 of her 30 years, directed toward the destruction of herself and the 'little slut I brought into this world'. This woman's educational experiences and preparation for motherhood included approximately 100 foster homes, 32 institutions, rape at age 11 (which she enjoyed, for this was the first time she had personally 'meant anything' to an adult), exotic dancing, prostitution, five years of grade school, a disastrous first and second marriage, and innumerable negative experiences with men in general. Her background, coupled with her basic innate intelligence, driving personality, seemingly unlimited stamina and a fortuitous third marriage, provided the leadership for this new and exciting therapeutic adventure.

Her 'credentials' and cries for help turned off at least nine established agency 'professionals' who found it difficult to accept this form of 'field work' as suitable criterion for motherhood, much less leadership. Fortunately for many women and their children, one social worker, who had worked with her for several months, recognized the potential and seized upon the opportunity. The 'conversion' came after one particular harassing session of complaints about the dearth of services available to abusive mothers, when finally the suggestion was made by the social worker that she should 'do something about it'.

Something *was* done about it and, in early 1970, MA was founded. . . . The members are understandably turned off by professionalism. They have been beat on so frequently by our unhelpful social system that no love is lost by the attempts to keep the 'establishment' ties with MA from developing. Some way must be found to maintain this necessary autonomy and yet profit by the guidance and help of certain *special* 'professionals'.

First, the weekly group meetings are such an important and integral part of the MA program that the recognized leader(s) must be guided in developing the skills of running small groups and understanding their dynamics. Second, any MA program would do well to *loosely* but specifically identify themselves with a recognized hospital or community-based child abuse consultation team. The professionals on this team could provide the necessary backup for those mothers and children who occasionally need the special care and treatment that MA cannot provide.

Third, these mothers need and are ready for some ongoing counseling in usual child rearing practices and the normal growth and development pattern of children. Rarely do their individual or collective backgrounds provide enough experience for the MA members to be helpful to each other in this area.

Fourth, an active follow-through program for the 'drop-outs' or 'no shows' is mandatory. The present MA program represents only those mothers (and fathers) who, on their own, could make it to the first or second meeting. The scores of parents who could not get that far are unaccounted for.

Finally, there is the problem of love. 'I don't beat him any more, but I cannot really say I have any feeling or love for him'. MA rightfully has the initial limited goal of decreasing or eliminating the abuse (physical and emotional) of the children. But then there is the next step—'How can I love that little bitch?' Somehow a mothering model must be injected into the MA concept. Possibly this would be the 'graduate' program, the *second step*.

MA is exciting, it is beginning to meet its limited but critically important goals. With the proper support and nurturing, this youthful program could have as significant an impact on child abuse as AA has had on alcoholism.

Summary

Regardless of who is involved in the care of battering parents it seems clear to us that a lifeline must be provided which is available seven days a week, 24 hours a day. All clients should know at least two telephone numbers to call: that of their primary 'friend' (Parent Aide) and a backup number. In time of crisis it is essential that if one therapist is not available some other knowledgeable person is. In the city this can be the pediatric emergency room in a local hospital, assuming the staff is trained and understanding. In time, answering services will have to be provided by all social agencies handling these cases. The use of a telephone lifeline has worked well in the prevention of suicide in the United States and Great Britain. Clearly, the battered child syndrome desires a similar approach for those crises which do not occur between 9.00 a.m. and 5.00 p.m., Monday through Friday. Finally, available therapeutic manpower in the population at large is not limited to the skilled professional therapist in the fields of psychiatry and social work for the specific needs of the battering parents. There is an immense reservoir of capable potential Parent Aides, paid or unpaid, who are ready to be brought into the therapeutic picture provided they are given encouragement and adequate consultation and supervision.

We view this as the next important step in the field of child abuse. The major role of the social worker, psychologist and psychiatrist should probably be limited to making an accurate diagnosis of family pathology early in the treatment program and then to the supervising of the Parent Aides, visiting nurses, therapeutic homemakers and the staff of drop-in nurseries. All of these individuals will be regarded as multipliers of the primary skills of the more highly trained professionals.

29 Severe deprivation in twins

Jarmila Koluchová

Case history

This is a case record of monozygotic twins, two boys P.M. and J.M., born on 4 September 1960. Their mother died shortly after giving birth to them and for eleven months they lived in a children's home. According to the records their physical and mental development was normal at that stage. Their father than applied to take them into the care of his sister, but soon afterwards he remarried and the boys were again placed in a children's home until the new household could be established. This new family included two natural elder sisters of the twins, and two children (a boy and a girl) of the stepmother—six children altogether, the oldest being nine years old. The married couple M. bought a house in the suburbs of a small town where nobody knew them. All the subsequent events concerning the twins could only be reconstructed after their discovery in the autumn of 1967.

For five and a half years the twins lived in this family under most abnormal conditions. Some of the neighbours had no idea of their existence, others guessed there were some little children in the family although they had never seen them. . . . During the trial, however, the people next door testified that they had often heard queer, inhuman shrieks which resembled howling, and which came from a cellar leading to the back court. The father was once seen beating the children with a rubber hose until they lay flat on the ground unable to move. . . .

The central figure in the family . . . was the stepmother. . . . She was a person of average intelligence, but egocentric, remarkably lacking in feeling, possessing psychopathic character traits and a distorted system of values. The father was a person of below average intellect, passive and inarticulate; the stepmother dominated the family. Her own two children (the first of them illegitimate and the second the product of a disturbed marriage which ended in divorce) were reared in early childhood by their maternal grandmother. The stepmother therefore had little experience with small children and showed no interest in them. When the twins joined

KOLUCHOVÁ, J. (1972) 'Severe deprivation in twins: a case study', *Journal of Child Psychology and Psychiatry*, vol. 13, pp. 107–14. Reprinted in Clarke, A. M. and A. D. B. (eds) *Early Experience: Myth and Evidence*, London, Open Books (1976) pp. 45–54.

the family she fed them, but the other aspects of their care were left to their father. This disinterest developed into active hostility towards the twins, and she induced a similar attitude towards them in other members of the family. The other children were forbidden to talk to the twins or to play with them. The father, who worked on the railways, was often away from home and took little interest in the boys. . . . The twins therefore grew up lacking emotional relationships and stimulation, and were totally excluded from the family. Relationships between the other members of the family were also unnaturally cool due to the mother's abnormal personality. . . . She accepted the two stepdaughters into the family though she preferred her own children, but with none of the children did she have a genuine maternal relationship.

The boys grew up in almost total isolation, separated from the outside world; they were never allowed out of the house or into the main living rooms in the flat, which were tidy and well furnished. They lived in a small, unheated closet, and were often locked up for long periods in the cellar. They slept on the floor on a polythene sheet and were cruelly chastised. They used to sit at a small table in an otherwise empty room, with a few building bricks which were their only toys. . . .

The twins also suffered physically from lack of adequate food, fresh air, sunshine and exercise. At the end of August 1967 the father brought one of the boys to a paediatrician, asking for a certificate that his son was unfit to enter primary school. Because the boy looked as if he were three years old rather than six, hardly walked, and was at first sight severely mentally retarded, the doctor agreed to postpone school entry, but insisted that the twins should be placed in a kindergarten,and that the family situation should be investigated by a social worker and a district nurse. . . .

Gradually it became clear that this was a case of criminal neglect. In December 1967 the twins were removed from the family and placed in a home for pre-school children, while legal proceedings were taken against the parents. Several days after their admission to the home it was found that the twins suffered from acute rickets, a disease which has been practically eliminated in modern Czechoslovakia. The children were admitted to an orthopaedic clinic and at the same time examined by a multi-disciplinary team.

Psychological findings

On admission to hospital attempts were made to assess the mental status of the twins. It was clear that the improvement in their living conditions during the three months prior to hospital admission had allowed some progress to take place. For example on admission to the kindergarten the twins did not join in any activities but were timid and mistrustful. They had to be brought to the kindergarten in a wheelchair, because they could barely walk, and when given shoes could not walk at all. During their last three months with the family they were not locked in the cellar and their little room was better equipped, but at the same time the stepmother's negative attitude towards them became even more acute, because she saw in them the cause of the unwelcome interference from outside.

While in hospital, the children were psychologically examined. They were encouraged to become familiar with the testing room and adapted to it very well. At first it was impossible to use a diagnostic tool which required their direct co-operation, and the preliminary step in assessment was the observation of their spontaneous behaviour, and in particular of their free and controlled play. Later it was possible to establish direct contact and to move on to more formal testing in which the author used Gesell's scale and the Terman–Merrill test.

The boys' restricted social experience and very poor general information was most strikingly shown in their reactions of surprise and horror to objects and activities normally very familiar to children of their age— e.g. moving mechanical toys, a TV set, children doing gymnastic exercises, traffic in the street, etc.

However their inquisitiveness gradually prevailed, the reactions of terror disappeared, and they began to explore their environment, although often they were easily distracted. Their shyness with people was reduced during their stay in the children's home, and in the hospital ward they were the centre of interest. They related to adults positively and indiscriminately, in a way that is typical of deprived children. Their relations with other children were at an immature and uncontrolled level for their age.

The spontaneous speech of the boys was extremely poor. In order to communicate with each other they used gestures more characteristic of younger children. They tried to imitate adult speech, but could repeat only two or three words at a time with poor articulation. They could not answer questions, even if it was evident from their reactions that they had understood them. It was obvious that they were not used to speech as a means of communication.

Their spontaneous play was very primitive, and predominantly at first it was only the manipulations of objects, but imitative play soon developed. As they became familiar with the toys and with their surroundings in the clinic their play gradually reached more mature levels, but they continued to need adult intervention to initiate and develop a play activity and were unable to join in the play of other children.

A remarkable finding was that the boys could not understand the meaning or function of the pictures. It was impossible therefore to measure the extent of their vocabulary by means of pictures, because they had never learned to perceive and understand them. We started therefore with pictures which were of the same size and colour as the real objects which they represented. After repeated comparisons of picture and object, understanding of the relationship emerged and extended to a constantly widening range of phenomena.

The author felt that to express the boys' intellectual level in terms of an IQ would be quite inadequate. Their IQs at that stage would have been within the range of imbecility, but qualitative analysis of their responses, their total behaviour, and their considerably accelerated development since they had been taken away from their family, all unambiguously suggested that this was a case not of a primary defect in the sense of oligophrenia, but of severe deprivation. It seemed more appropriate therefore to consider their mental ages, which in December 1967 varied for both boys round the three-year level, with a range of ±1 year for separate component items. At this time their chronological age was seven years and three months.

After the period of hospitalization the children returned to the children's home where they made good progress. They began to participate with the children there; this was made easier for them by the fact that the other children in the home were some two to three years younger. Relationships with adults and children improved and they acquired much of the knowledge and many of the skills appropriate to pre-school children. As their health improved so their motor abilities developed; they learned to walk, to run, to jump, to ride a scooter. Similar progress was also noted in their fine motor co-ordination.

After six months' stay in the children's home the boys were readmitted to the clinic for a short time to enable paediatric, audiological and psychological examinations to be made. Their mental age was by this time approximately four years, with a narrower range of passes on the component items than on the previous examination. There was evidence of considerable progress in habit formation, experience and the development of knowledge.

The forensic problem

During the first period of hospitalization the investigating authorities requested a report from a forensic paediatrician, who in turn asked for a consultant psychologist's report. However, the problem of assessment seemed too complex to be handled on the basis of one or more consulting examinations. We therefore asked the investigating authorities to assign an expert psychologist to the case, who would have both the support of the court and the right of a forensic expert as well. The panel of forensic specialists followed the progress of the boys for a period of six months while they were in the children's home, and undertook careful control examinations during the second period of hospitalization. . . . to assess the total developmental picture presented by the children, and to decide whether their disabilities were likely to have been congenital or acquired. The psychologist, moreover, had also to try to answer the question as to whether the twins were likely to grow up to become mentally and emotionally normal people.

The psychologist's report was of considerable importance in this case. It was necessary to disprove the statement of the defendant that the children had been defective from birth, and to prove that their disabilities were caused by severe neglect and lack of stimulation. . . .

It was more difficult to answer the question about the future development of the twins. . . . We could therefore only outline a probable prognosis and assume that in a good environment the children would develop in every respect, that their developmental deficits would show a tendency to be reduced, but that it was necessary to take into account the possible consequences of such severe deprivation on the development of personality. We pointed out to the judges some of the handicapping effects of this deprivation: entry to school delayed by three years, the probable necessity for the boys to attend a school for mentally retarded children, the effects on employment prospects, and the possibility of other difficulties in their social and intellectual development. We recommended that the children be placed as soon as possible in a compensating foster home, on the grounds that even the best children's home could not be the optimal solution in the long term. . . .

The further development of the children

In the school year 1968/9 the boys remained in the pre-school children's home. Their mental development was better than the original prognosis had suggested. Whereas some experts were doubtful about their educability, a psychologist's assessments showed that the retardation was diminishing and that the boys had reached a level of readiness for school. Because of their retarded speech, and relatively poor fine motor co-ordination and powers of concentration, we thought that a school for mentally retarded children was indicated as an initial step, since there were greater possibilities of individual teaching and a slower pace of learning.

Simultaneously with their starting school we tried to solve the problem of their foster home placement. A number of families were willing to take the children, but we had to assess the motivation of the applicants very carefully, considering the personalities of the potential substitute parents, and existing family structures. Finally in July 1969, the boys were placed with a family who have been able to accept them as natural and loved children. After two years' observation we still consider this to be the optimal placement, although in the conventional sense the family is not a complete family at all. It consists of two unmarried middle-aged sisters, both intelligent, with wide interests, living in a pleasant flat, and capable of forming very good relationships with the children. One of these sisters had already adopted a baby girl some years before, and this child is now an intelligent well-educated thirteen-year-old. The second sister became the foster mother of the twins. Our observation and information from many sources, show that deep emotional bonds have been formed between the children and their foster family, and many of the consequences of deprivation—e.g. a narrow outlook, a small range of emotional expression, etc.—which had remained during their stay in the children's home, are gradually diminishing. The boys have recollections of their original home, and though the foster family tries to avoid reviving the past, the boys themselves will sometimes begin to talk about it; we also have touched on this during our psychological examinations. Until recently the boys did not have sufficient language ability to describe even in outline their life in their original family. If we compare their story now with the facts established during and before the trial, it is evident that their account is reliable. They have a completely negative attitude to their stepmother, and refer to her as 'that lady' or 'that unkind lady'. They remember the names of their brother and sisters, and they recollect how they used to be hungry and thirsty, how they were beaten about the head (their scalps are badly scarred), and how they used to sit at the small table. The stepmother often carried them into the cellar, thrashed them with a wooden kitchen spoon until it broke, and put a feather-bed over their heads so that no one would hear their screaming.

For a long time they had a dread of darkness. They appreciated the physical warmth of their new home, the good food they received, and the fact that they were no longer beaten. During our first visit to them in the foster home we had to reassure them that we would not take them away from their foster mother.

In September 1969 they were admitted to the first class in a school for mentally retarded children. On the basis of our observations of the children in class, the teacher's records, and our further examinations, we found the boys soon adapted themselves to the school environment and began to outstrip their classmates. Their writing, drawing and ability to concentrate improved remarkably in the second term, and it became clear that this type of school would not extend them sufficiently. Accepting that there was a risk involved, we recommended a transfer to the second class of a normal school from the beginning of the next school year. In spite of the difference in curriculum and teaching methods, they proved to be capable of mastering the subject matter of the normal school, and did well enough to suggest that they have the ability to complete successfully the basic

nine-year school course which, however, they would finish at the age of
eighteen instead of the normal age of fifteen. . . .

A summary of the psychological test findings shows that in the fifteen
months from June 1968 to September 1969 the mental age of the twins
increased by three years; this was an immense acceleration of development,
indicating how the change of living conditions provided a rapidly effective
compensation for the consequences of earlier deprivation.

At first the children were assessed using Gesell's Developmental Scale
and later the Terman–Merrill Scale in which their verbal level was markedly
below non-verbal test items. Since the age of eight years and four months
the boys have been examined by means of the Wechsler Intelligence Scale
(WISC). The test scores are presented in Table 1 and indicate the low-level
verbal response initially, especially in the Twin J, and the subsequent
improvement over three years. Both children now seem to be functioning
almost at an average level for their age.

Twin P. I.Q.		Twin J. I.Q.	
8 years 4 months			
verbal	80	verbal	69
performance	83	performance	80
full scale	80	full scale	72
9 years			
verbal	84	verbal	75
performance	83	performance	76
full scale	82	full scale	73
10 years			
verbal	97	verbal	94
performance	85	performance	86
full scale	91	full scale	89
11 years			
verbal	97	verbal	96
performance	93	performance	90
full scale	95	full scale	93

Table 1   Wechsler Intelligence Test Scores (W.I.S.C.)

Conclusions

This is a very exceptional case of deprivation, firstly because of the lengthy
period of isolation, and secondly because of the unusual family situation

which by outward appearances was a relatively normal and orderly one.

The children suffered from a lack of stimulation and opportunity for psycho-motor development. The most severe deprivation, however, was probably their poverty of emotional relationships, and their social isolation. The stepmother did not even partially satisfy their need for maternal nurturance. She was on the contrary, as the dominating person in the family, the instigator of hostile attitudes towards the children and an active agent in their physical and mental torment. The influence of the father was confined to occasional repressive actions. The stimulating influence of brothers and sisters was also lacking. Thus we may speak of a combination of outer and inner causes of deprivation, the inner or psychological ones being primary. . . .

30 A report on the further development of twins after severe and prolonged deprivation
Jarmila Koluchová

This paper follows up a previous study of severe and prolonged deprivation of twin boys born in 1960 (Koluchová 1972). Although their development had been surprisingly good even at the time of the first report, and it was possible to exclude gross damage of their intellect and personality, there remained a number of problems, which could only be solved in a long-term study. . . .

In the school year 1971–2 the twins, now aged between eleven and twelve, attended the third class. Their speech was entirely adequate to their age both in form and content. As the prediction of phoniatricians and paediatricians concerning the development of speech had been rather pessimistic, an attempt will be made to explain the fact that the twins' speech is at a good level and allows full social integration.

Until the eleventh month of their life the children had lived in an infants' home, then—for a shorter period of time—in a family of their relatives and later, in a home for toddlers. According to the available records of the infants' home, the children had been developing adequately for their age. It is possible to presume that at that time, which is usually regarded as a preparatory period of speech, and during which a mainly passive knowledge of a language is developed, the children had mastered actively several words and had comprehended the communicative function of speech. They had probably retained those abilities during the whole period of deprivation, mostly in a latent form only, because the small amount of speech they had been used to hearing between eighteen months and seven years had not had a communicative character for them. The basic prerequisite for the development of speech had also been missing, i.e. the individual contact of an adult with a child and the resulting positive stimulating relationship. But, although the period until their third year, which is usually considered the terminal limit for generating the ability to speak, had been missed, the twins' speech started to develop in spite of the fact that they had scarcely spoken at all until the age of seven. The development was quickest after their ninth year when they came to their foster family, which provided them with all the prerequisites both for the

KOLUCHOVÁ, J. (1976) 'A report on the further development of twins after severe and prolonged deprivation', in Clarke, A. M. and A. D. B. (eds.) *Early Experience: Myth and Evidence*, London, Open Books, pp. 55–66.

development of speech and the whole personality. At school and in a collective of children, the boys were agile, cheerful and popular; there were no signs of eccentricity or troubles in the social sphere. Until the fourth class of their school attendance their results were very good—they used to have a grade two only in the Czech language (mother tongue). They were the best pupils of the class in arithmetic (grade one), which arose, first, by a quick compensation of the retardation in the sphere of intellectual functions, and second, by their being two to three years older then their fellow pupils.

Gradually they began to feel older in comparison with their schoolmates and began to be aware of their late start at school, both these being due to the acceleration of their growth and a rather delayed commencement of pre-puberty. Both the teachers and the foster mother supported their natural ambition to master, during the fourth class, also the subject matter of the fifth class. They succeeded in their effort and after the holidays passed the examinations of the fifth class; then they were moved up from the fourth, direct to the sixth class. Thus they found themselves among children of more approximate age and their self-confidence was reinforced. Their results fell to the average, but the situation has been gradually improving hitherto. Both of them like attending school. . . . They love reading, ride bicycles, can swim and ski, they play the piano well and they have both creative and technical talent. It is interesting that musical ability started to develop only at about the age of ten, but it is now at a good level. In the present school year (1974/75) the boys attend the seventh class; their schoolmates are on the average one and a half years younger. As their adolescence began about a year late in comparison with the average of our population, the whole status of their development and interests now corresponds approximately with the standard of their present schoolmates. After finishing basic education (nine classes) they would like to study at a secondary vocational school, for which they show sufficient aptitudes.

The development of the twins' intellectual level has been observed continually by means of several methods; to compare previous scores with more recent findings the author presents in Table 1 the boys' IQs obtained by means of the WISC.

It will be recalled that shortly after their discovery, IQs were probably in the 40s but later, on the WISC Test, it was evident that their development was quickest between the ninth and tenth years, namely the first year of their stay in the foster family and the first year of their school attendance. According to the past trend it is possible to anticipate that their intelligence scores may be raised a little. In the non-verbal scale of the WISC and in Raven's Matrices Test the achieved scores are a little higher than in the verbal, which may be explained by the fact that the verbal score is to a certain extent dependent on education, which is still

213

retarded according to their age. In spite of initial differences in the intellectual level of the boys, and distinctive differences in their development, their general standard has now come to be equal; however some features of their character have continued to differ. J is a little slower in comparison

Age	Twin P. I.Q.	Twin J. I.Q.
8	80	72
9	82	73
10	91	89
11	95	93
12	95	104
13	98	100
14	100	101

Table 1   Wechsler Intelligence Test Scores (W.I.S.C.)

with his brother, but he is in general of calmer disposition. P perceives more quickly, he reacts more promptly, but his attention is rather labile, he is a little preoccupied and shows symptoms of autonomic lability.

In the development and forming of the personalities of the boys no psychopathological symptoms or eccentricities appear at present. It is possible to say that there are no consequences of the deprivation remaining which would cause retardation or damage to their development. It does not mean, however, that five years of hardship and ill-treatment by their cruel stepmother have not left any traces at all. The dread of darkness, which outlasted for a long time, has already faded, but under oppressive or unusual conditions the boys sometimes show the feeling of fear and their reaction is neurotic. For example, once they happened to come to a cellar similar to the one in which they had often been imprisoned. This frightened and upset them, and again revived the recollection of past suffering. In the cheerful environment of their new family, and with the help of their foster mother, who is always ready to understand, the boys will calm down quite easily and revert to their normal mood.

The twins hate recalling the conditions of their deprivation, and are even unlikely to speak about it with one another. However, by occasional remarks and the reactions mentioned above, it is evident that some recollections have remained and will probably be retained for ever. The boys' foster mother mentions that they will tell her something about their cheerless childhood now and then, but always each of them separately in an intimate talk. Comparing their previous and present recollections, it is apparent that there is no tendency to distort or exaggerate their experiences; their evidence conforms with the data stated in the judicial trial of their step-mother. The boys' recollections of the past are no longer associated with fear of possible recurrence of such living conditions and of losing their new family.

The awareness of the relations with the family is really profound and makes the boys feel safe and assured. Natural emotional bonds with all members of the family have arisen; apparently the relation with their foster mother, who is in a dominant position in the family, is emotionally deepest. Her sister is an aunt for them. As mentioned in the 1972 paper, the latter had adopted a girl—now sixteen years old—and besides her there is another ten-year-old girl (staying with the family during the last four years). . . . Thus, there are two foster mothers and their four children, who have very nice brother and sister relations with one another, although they of course know they are not consanguineous relatives. There is a happy atmosphere in the whole family, full of mutual understanding. Undoubtedly, it is possible to object to such a family without a father, whom the boys would need just at present in the period of their puberty. The boys' foster mother is aware of this and is trying to compensate for the lack of a man in the process of bringing up the boys by their frequent meeting with her brother and other relatives and friends, who have close relations with the boys.

The fact that has intensified their awareness of firm relationships in this family and has helped to establish the feeling of safety and assurance, was the agreed change of surname to that of their foster mother. . . .

As the most important factor in the conditions of deprivation of the twins from eighteen months until seven years of age was almost total social isolation and hostile relations of the members of that family, especially with their stepmother, a question arises—how has it been reflected in their social relations and behaviour?

In the 1972 report, the relations of the twins to one another, to other children and also to adults were described. The situation has been developing as follows: immediately after they had been removed from the family and placed in the children's home, a strong emotional bond with one another was evident. Apparently it had developed because it had been the only positive emotion that could have been built up and, moreover, it had helped them to bear the difficult living conditions. The outer demonstration of their relations, however, corresponded with a much lower age: they used to make themselves understood like toddlers, using mostly mimicry and gestures. Their original shyness with people and reactions of terror had disappeared rather quickly and the children related both to adults and children positively in a way that is more characteristic of younger children. Mainly they showed a lesser differentiation of emotional relations and a prevailing interest in adults.

The children's gradual socialization was facilitated by the fact they they had lived for a longer period of time among children approximately three years younger, which corresponded with their developmental deficit. Starting to attend a school for mentally retarded children at the age of nine, they were for the first time with a larger well-organized group of children, which they joined in successfully; undoubtedly the individual attention of their teacher, who had been informed of their history, helped a lot. There were no striking features in their social contacts, they did not show any symptoms of timidity, shyness or some other kind of abnormality and they never behaved aggressively either at the school for mentally retarded children or at the normal school later on. The boys have always had close relations with one another—an emotional bond much firmer than is usual with brothers of their age. But common teasing or petty conflicts are present of course as is usual with children in normal families.

Making the boys acquainted with their suffering during the early and pre-school age appears to be a relatively difficult educational and psychotherapeutic problem. They can remember that period of time only in fragments without being able to comprehend the essentials of the whole event, its circumstances and causes. We consider it advisable to make them acquainted with the main facts concerning their parentage, family, the trial, and further events until their coming to this family, from the point of view of realization of the continuity of their personalities, self-evaluation and also as a precaution against possible trauma caused by an incidental information or experience in later life. It is necessary to respect the long-standing aversion to reverting to the past, but at the same time their pubescent inquisitiveness and their efforts to know and to evaluate themselves should be employed. The foster mother is aware of the gravity of this task and she is thought to manage it well. The author wants to focus her attention on those problems too, in her talks with the twins within the framework of their psychological observation, naturally in close co-operation with their foster mother.

Appreciating the children's general development as highly successful—in contradiction with the original prediction of doctors—it is also necessary to evaluate the therapeutic factors that have contributed to this. As already stated in the 1972 report the children had been treated at an orthopaedic and paediatric clinic after their withdrawal from the family and after their rickets had been overcome. At the same time they had been examined at some other clinics—psychiatric, optic and in a phoniatric ward. Their somatic condition having improved, they were then placed in a children's home. Also, there, exceptional individual care was bestowed upon them and their future was discussed and planned carefully. The most important factor for solving that problem was a good prediction consequent to psychological examinations. The present foster family was selected from several families interested. Having been placed in this family the children started to attend speech training and they were also practising their pronunciation intensively at home. Consequently they managed to inhibit their nasal speech and in general to modify their poor articulation. The children have also been carefully looked after by a district paediatrician, who knows everything about the family and about the children themselves. Another important curative factor is the attitude of their teachers, which is individual and full of sympathy, although they expect the boys to meet reasonable scholastic claims without any preference or special tolerance.

Continuing care, carried out during the whole period by the same psychologist (the author), has proved to be fortunate. Besides the experimental direction, she also acts as an adviser and passes psychological reports to school and other institutions. In the author's opinion the main advantage of such a procedure lies in her detailed knowledge of the whole history, including court reports. Moreover the twins trust her, which has enabled her to observe the dynamism of their development over seven years.

Even if all the above mentioned curative factors are by no means significant, it is necessary to emphasize that the most effective and integrative curative factor is their foster mother and the whole environment of their family. Although the lady is employed, she devotes all her leisure time to the children with a lot of self-sacrifice; her solicitude for them is the content and purpose of her life, without spoiling the children or adopting uncritical attitudes.

The specialists, who had not believed in any possibility of remedying the severe deprivation damage in the twins, later referred to their quick development as an exception to the rule which states that severe deprivational damage at an early age is irremediable. According to the author's experience, however, there is a number of similar cases, but they are not usually correctly diagnosed, professionally observed and described. . . .

We have recorded more cases similar to the twins . . . but their detailed history has not yet been obtained and they have been observed only for a shorter period. The author could often confirm, in her work as a clinical psychologist, that children who suffered severe and prolonged deprivation, coming either from inadequate families, often chastised and socially isolated, or living for a long time in a children's home environment, are misdiagnosed as mentally subnormal both by paediatricians, paedopsychiatrists and psychologists. The clinical picture of severe deprivation and mental subnormality is similar in certain symptoms, which can lead to a confusion of the two diagnoses. . . . Both the cases are typical of general retardation of development and speech, social immaturity and a lowered ability to learn. Especially the development of children up to the third year of age may be so profoundly affected as a consequence of all the external and internal conditions of a children's home environment lacking stimulation, that it is rather difficult to differentiate such cases from mental subnormality.

As these children are usually socially forlorn—i.e. their parents cannot or do not want to look after them—it is necessary to solve the problems of their future and therefore a correct diagnosis is of immense value. The author thinks that, in understanding the difficult task of differential diagnosis, particular attention should be paid to psychological findings. Only psychological examination can reveal subtle differences between severely deprived and mentally subnormal children. However, cursory, non-residential examination will not do; it is absolutely necessary to carry out a detailed repeated examination by means of both test and non-test methods, aimed at the structure and dynamics of their development deficit. Such an examination enables a skilled psychologist to differentiate deprivation from subnormality and to determine the prognosis for its development. Here the psychological diagnosis is not only a theoretical problem, but above all a basis for educational, juridical and therapeutic actions.

In cases of severe deprivation, originating at an early age, the therapeutic prognosis has usually been considered poor. But the above-mentioned cases of deprived children, together with others that are still being observed, prove that even gross damage, previously considered to be irreversible, can be remedied. Our experience with the development of speech, too, contradicts the traditional view concerning the critical period for the development of speech. In the twins, as well as other cases, a successful development of speech was observed three to six years after their passing to a stimulating environment, sometimes even later. Thus, the prediction for the retarded development of speech in deprived children seems to be more optimistic if the defect is not organically or genetically conditioned, and when the child is given sufficient professional care and, above all, placed in a kind-hearted family environment.

The view that the effects of severe deprivation were irreparable arose from the fact that severely deprived children usually could not be found a new family. According to our experience the environment of a family, stimulating and full of understanding, giving them a feeling of safety and a firm relationship, is the only effective therapy, very exacting and time-consuming. This conclusion, together with the fact that the family is considered to be the most important educational factor, led to several arrangements for the care of children living outside their own families in our country, which are designed to prevent deprivation or remedy existing deprivation. There has been a general effort to assimilate a children's-home environment to a family environment, e.g. to integrate a number of children of different ages into so-called 'family groups' with unchanging tutors.

Besides the standard children's homes there have arisen new forms of substitute family care—so-called 'children's villages' in which foster mothers with eight to ten children live in separate houses; then, there are so-called 'big families', where a married couple looks after a similar number of children. These 'big families' are not concentrated in 'villages', but they live in normal houses, both in towns and in the country. 'The father' is employed somewhere like the father of a normal family and 'the mother' looks after the children and is paid by the state on the same basis as 'mothers' in 'children's villages'. There are also cases of paid foster parentage in natural families. Both such families and the people interested in the work either in 'children's villages' or in 'big families' are carefully selected, including by psychological examination; all the forms of substitute family care are paid and methodically guided by the State authorities and advisory boards, in which psychologists also work. A special advisory service has also been established with psychologists and paediatricians, and, if necessary, other experts can be summoned, for example, paedopsychiatrists.

Several years' experience with these forms of care indicate the great therapeutic prospects offered by a stimulating family environment. To observe and evaluate them is a task for long-term studies which might be a valuable contribution to the diagnosis and remediation of deprivation.

31 Concluding thoughts on continuing problems

It is difficult to know who are the battered and who the most at risk. Is it the newspaper reader who is battered each morning by a succession of headlines—'Baby hit by Mother went Blind', 'Starve my Child said Devil Woman'? Is it the reader of the medical journals, at risk of boredom from a surfeit of articles ranging from 'the neurological sequelae of non-accidental injury' to 'the marital status of the parents of battered children'? Is it the paediatrician, battered by too many case conferences and at risk of neglecting other needy families and ill children because this week he has cancelled Tuesday morning outpatients to attend a case conference, has cancelled his visit to the special-care baby unit on Wednesday afternoon because of a case conference, and has cancelled his Friday afternoon spina-bifida clinic in order to attend yet another case conference? The Friday case conference, like the others, was attended by eight highly paid, highly trained professionals who sat solemnly around a table discussing a robust healthy child with a bruise on his bottom. (The paediatrician, that afternoon, felt uneasy because his own son had rather more bruises on his bottom, incurred as a result of damaging the clematis in the front garden the previous weekend.)

Non-accidental injury is an important and serious problem. The British Paediatric Association has performed an important service, and the Department of Health and Social Security an important duty, in alerting medical and social workers to the prevalence of battering and in preparing guidelines for management of the problem. Multidisciplinary case conferences emerge as a vital part of the early management, but probably few people realize how much time they take from the lives of busy people with many other commitments. It will be important for area review committees and all associations concerned with non-accidental injury to keep a close check on the effectiveness of their case conferences and of the service that they have set up. It was easy to justify concentration of resources on battered children when statistics suggested that 10 per cent died and that 30 per cent had permanent brain damage, but now the level of detection has risen to such an extent that it must be only a tiny fraction of reported cases who are at risk of death [or] permanent handicap. Some of the teams concerned with non-accidental injury and some of the case

---

ANONYMOUS (1975) 'The battered . . .', *The Lancet*, May 31, pp. 1228–9.

committees are finding an increasing proportion of their time spent with trivial and doubtful cases. The time has come when some must be finding themselves dealing with 'false-positive' cases. Other workers must sometimes feel that they could be more usefully employed on other problems concerned with children and families in trouble.

This does not mean that the problem of child abuse is solved. A great many problems remain, particularly on the legal side. There are medical problems too. Whilst the level of notification of suspected battering from paediatric departments, from casualty departments, from social workers, and from NSPCC staff is extremely high, the notification-rate from general practitioners in many areas is extremely low (are they still unaware of the problem, are they unobservant, or is it that they have things in the right perspective?). Physical abuse of children is now recognized quickly in most areas of the country—some might say too quickly. However, whilst machinery exists for dealing with it, the machinery for reporting and dealing with other types of abuse is abysmal. A two-year-old child who has a happy relationship with his parents and a decent home, who incurs a scald on his wrist, may find himself the subject of a case conference with a team of professionals rushing in to identify the problem and try to help. A similar child without a scald or bruise, who is emotionally neglected or mentally abused, is left to suffer and fail. To some extent we have all been battered in our time, some physically, some emotionally, and some by circumstances. We must hope that, in the elaborate and expensive organization set up in most parts of the UK for dealing with physical abuse, self-scrutiny will not be neglected. The areas have an important job reviewing the work of their case conferences and evaluating their effectiveness. The Department of Health and Social Security must audit the national situation and must bear in mind the problems of other disadvantaged and abused children and assess its priorities in the use of staff and resources.

221

Part Seven Appendices

These are under two main sections; the first contains a complete list of government circulars relating to non-accidental injury published since the reorganization of the National Health Service. The extracts from reports of official inquiries were chosen with particular reference to Child Abuse: a study text.

The second section contains a short introduction to normal child development and a selection of charts.

32 Government and local authority papers

i Circulars concerning non-accidental injury, sponsored or co-sponsored by the Department of Health and Social Security since reorganization of the National Health Service

LASSL (74)13 CMO(74)8	Memorandum on non-accidental injury to children. [See 32ii.]
LASSL (74)25	'Maria Colwell' issued with copies of Report of Committee of Inquiry.
LASSL (74)27	Non-accidental injury to children: questionnaire relating to setting up of Area Review Committees.
LASSL (75)4 CMO(75)6	Non-accidental injury to children: model instructions for accident and emergency departments.
LASSL (75)29	Circular enclosing articles from the *Police Surgeon* journal.
LASSL (75)30	Proceedings of a conference on non-accidental injury to children held by DHSS. Issued with the proceedings.
LASSL (75)37	Committee of Inquiry into the services provided to the family of John George Auckland. Issued with the report.
LAC (75)3 Welsh Office Circular 52/75	Prisoners convicted of offences against children in the home, when released on parole (concerned with liaison between prison authorities and SSDs).
LAC (75)18	Children and Young Persons Act 1969: Section 1(2)(b) (draws attention to a Court of Appeal ruling that evidence of earlier ill-treatment or neglect of a child who is, or was, a member of the household may be considered by a court hearing on application for a care order for another child).

LAC (75)21

Children Act 1975: Main provisions and arrangements for implementation (paragraphs relevant to non-accidental injury to children are given in the summary of non-criminal legislation).

LASSL (76)2 CMO(76)2
CNO(76)3

Non-accidental injury to children: Area Review Committees (feeds back information from questionnaire and provides additional guidance). [See 32ii].

HN (76)4

Health visitors and home nurses and the legal problems of their clients.

LASSL (76)25
Revised January 1977

Names and addresses of ARC Chairmen.

LASSL (76)26 HC(76)50
HO(179/76)

Non-accidental injury to children. The police and case conferences.

Annex to
LASSL (76)26
HC (76)50
HO Circular 179/76

Roles of the organizations chiefly concerned in cases of non-accidental injury to children.

Department of Health and Social Security Northern Ireland

HSS (Gen 1)1/75
Ref. A1507/73

Non-accidental injury to children.

Scottish Home and Health Department

NHS Circular No. 1975 (Gen)23   Non-accidental injury to children.

J

ii   Local authority social services letters

LASSL (74)13, CMO (74)8   Memorandum on non-accidental injury to children

Introduction

1.   There is an urgent need to check and strengthen measures to prevent, diagnose and manage cases of non-accidental injury to children. Recent cases have underlined the need for regular joint reviews of these measures by all the agencies concerned (see para. 13 below). This circular is designed to assist by consolidating and supplementing earlier guidance.[1] It is in three sections, concerned with:

a.   diagnosis, care, management and rehabilitation; [not included in this extract]

b.   local organization including review committees;

c.   prevention and training [not included in this extract] . . .

Local Organization

Area Review Committees

12.   The formation of area review committees as policy making bodies for the management of these cases is strongly recommended. Where such committees do not already exist urgent joint action should be taken by the local authority and area health authority to establish one for their area. Regular meetings should be held three or four times a year with more frequent meetings as needed. The committee should:

---

[1] 'The Battered Baby' DHSS June 1970. 'An analysis of Reports' DHSS May 1972. 'Report of Tunbridge Wells Study Group' issued by DHSS October 1973. 'Non-Accidental Injury to Children. A Guide on Management' BMJ 15 December 1973 (656–660).

DHSS (Department of Health and Social Security) (1974) 'Government Circular LASSL (74)13 CMO(74)8', pp. 1–5 para. 1, paras. 12–17.

a. advise on the formulation of local practice and procedures to be followed in the detailed management of cases;

b. approve written instructions defining the duties of all personnel concerned with any aspect of these cases;

c. review the work of case conferences in the area;

d. provide education and training programmes to heighten awareness of the problem;

e. collect information about the work being done in the area;

f. collaborate with adjacent area review committees;

g. advise on the need for inquiries into cases which appear to have gone wrong and from which lessons could be learned;

h. provide a forum for consultation between all involved in the management of the problem;

i. draw up procedures for ensuring continuity of care when the family moves to another area;

j. consider ways of making it known to the general public that e.g. health visitors, teachers, social workers, the NSPCC and police may be informed about children thought to be ill-treated.

13. The committee should be at a senior level and should include representatives of:

Local authority: Chief Executive
Director of Education
Director of Housing
Director of Social Services

Health services: Area Medical Officer
Specialist in Community Medicine
(Child Health)
District Community Physician
Consultants in Paediatrics, Surgery, Obstetrics, Orthopaedics, Accident and Emergency and Psychiatry
General Practitioners
Dental Surgeon
Area Nursing Officer
Nursing Officer (Area) Child Health
District Nursing Officer from each of the Districts within the Area.

Other agencies: Senior Police Officer
Chief Probation Officer
Senior Inspector NSPCC.

Case Conference

14. A case conference is recommended for every case involving suspected non-accidental injury to a child. In this way unilateral action will be minimized and all those who can provide information about the child and his family, have statutory responsibility for the safety of the child, or are responsible for providing services, will be brought together to reach a collective decision which takes into account the age of the child, nature of injuries and a medico-social assessment of the family and its circumstances.

15. A case conference should meet to consider a case as soon as possible and one person should always be made responsible for co-ordinating the agreed treatment. The co-ordinator should ensure that every member of a particular case conference is informed when a child leaves hospital, which should only occur after consultation with the Director of Social Services concerned. The case conference should retain overall concern for the management of the case and should be prepared to reconvene at each successive development in it or when any professional worker is particularly worried about the family.

16. A case conference should normally include:

   a.   persons having statutory responsibilities for the continuing care of the child, e.g. the appropriate senior member of the social services department, the consultant in charge of the patient's medical care;

   b.   persons concerned with the provision of services likely to be relevant to the case, e.g. area social worker, voluntary agency representatives, family doctor and health visitor, psychiatrist treating child or parents, day nursery matron;

   c.   persons with information regarding the child and his family, e.g. family doctor and health visitor (if not included under (b)), social workers including probation officers in previous and present contact, paediatrician and members of medical and nursing staff.

   Others who may also be invited when appropriate include police surgeons, police officers, teachers and education welfare officers, representatives of housing departments, local authority legal staff, and any voluntary organization working with the family (NSPCC, Family Welfare Association, National Council for One Parent Families, Family Service Units, etc).

Registers

17. A central record of information in each area is essential to good communication between the many disciplines involved in the management of these cases. Area review committees should give urgent consideration to setting up within existing resources an adequate system in their area for this purpose. Authorities might wish to contact the NSPCC who have carried out a study of suspected child abuse in which they considered the question of registers. . . .

LASSL (76)2 CMO (76)2, CNO (76)3   Non-accidental injury to children: Reports from area review committees

Membership of Area Review Committees

3. In general membership of ARCs has reflected the recommendations in the April 1974 memorandum of guidance (LASSL (74)13/CMO (74)8). Most Committees have a varied and balanced membership with the professions and agencies most closely concerned with non-accidental injury well represented. The need to have clinical representatives of both primary health and specialist care teams, as well as of nursing and medical administration, tends to result in the Area Health Authority providing the most members of the Committee, and, exceptionally, in a few areas Social Services representation is confined to the Director. There was wide variation in the professions from which Chairmen were chosen. . . .

4. All ARCs contain police and probation representatives. Only 11 do not include a general practitioner, and we hope that this omission will be remedied. Only one Committee has no representative from education; those on other Committees may include education welfare officers, head teachers or officers of the local education authority. The majority have representatives from Housing Departments, and a number of Committees include magistrates or justices' clerks in their membership. Most contain a representative from the NSPCC. Other professions or agencies represented on some Committees include police surgeons, Family Service Units, Community Relations

DHSS (Department of Health and Social Security) (1974) 'Government Circular LASSL (76) 2 CMO (76) 2, CNO (76) 3', pp. 1–5, paras. 3–31.

Officers and the Legal or Administrative Departments of local authorities. One ARC contains an Army paediatrician, reflecting the large number of service families in the area.

5. *We accept that the membership of ARCs is for the responsible authorities to determine in the light of local circumstances and needs. Some reports suggested that membership of Committees is so large as to make them unwieldly. It must however be borne in mind that Review Committees, as the main local policy-making bodies, need to be fully representative of the professions involved with non-accidental injury, and that specific subjects that can best be tackled initially by a smaller body may be delegated to sub-committees or working parties. It is important that there should be adequate representation of social services departments, who have statutory duties relating to non-accidental injury, and it is therefore desirable that the Director should not be the sole representative. In addition to the membership suggested in the Memorandum of Guidance (Para. 13) representation of Legal and Administrative Departments of local authorities, and of appropriate voluntary bodies seems well justified.*

Terms of reference

6. The majority of ARCs have taken as their terms of reference the recommendation about their scope made in paragraphs 12a–k of the Memorandum of Guidance, and those which have drawn up shorter and more generalized terms have taken those recommendations into consideration. A number of Committees also include in their remit the making of reports to DHSS and the drawing of DHSS' attention to problems which can only be solved at national level.

Sub-committees

7. A number of ARCs had established District Review Committees usually based on health districts), from which they received regular reports. In some areas health districts and social services districts share boundaries, but difficulties can occur where they do not do so. There is a special problem in Greater London, since local authority areas frequently do not coincide with those covered by ARCs, there being more than one borough to each AHA. Various solutions to this difficulty have been found, and most London Boroughs have their own ARC, with the Area Health Authority represented on each Committee with which it might be concerned. Some have the

main ARC based on the Area Health Authority, with or without district committees at borough level, while others have a joint steering committee to co-ordinate procedures throughout the health authority area. *Whatever arrangements are adopted it is important that all health and local authorities involved are adequately represented.*

8. Other sub-committees, or working parties, are set up by ARCs to consider particular subjects such as professional education and training, or central registers, or to review the work of case conferences. Some may be Standing Committees while others are established on an ad hoc basis with a particular remit.

9. *Membership of sub-committees and working parties will necessarily depend to a large extent on their function. Wherever possible (and always in the case of District Review Committees) the composition of such Committees should reflect the same multi-disciplinary approach to non-accidental injury as ARCs do.*

10. *Most ARCs, recognizing the importance of reconciling procedural differences between areas have discussed collaboration with their neighbouring Committees, and this should be a primary task for those who have not yet done so. It is particularly important where boundaries do not coincide that each Area and District Review Committee should keep in touch with adjacent Committees and should be familiar with their current practices and procedures.*

Frequency of Meeting

11. Most ARCs meet every three months, although some meet only once a year and others, by contrast, monthly or even more frequently.

12. *It is for each ARC to decide when it should meet but Committees may find that it is impossible (even if many of their functions are delegated to smaller bodies) to play an effective part in forming local policy, provide adequate guidance and monitor progress if they meet only every 12 months. At the other extreme, meeting once a month or more often is likely to place too heavy a burden on members of the Committee. We recommend quarterly meetings.*

Subjects Discussed

13. Most of the subjects mentioned in the questionnaire (LASSL

(74)27) had been discussed by ARCs, although both collection of information about work going on in the area and collaboration with adjacent Committees had been omitted by a significant number of Committees. Other topics which had been discussed by many ARCs included the Maria Colwell Report, the role of the Police, confidentiality and research.

14. *The ARCs multi-disciplinary structure offers a valuable medium through which information about the management of non-accidental injury both nationally and locally may be shared among the appropriate professions. The continued development of effective channels of communication with the various authorities in the field is an essential part of the ARCs role in co-ordination and evolving policy. . . .*

Register systems

16. All but two ARCs have discussed register systems. When Directors reported, some 60 ARCs had established central registers. By July 1975, 83 ARCs had done so; a further eight had taken the decision to do so and were going fully into methods and procedures while others had the matter under active consideration. In a few areas, separate registers are kept by the Area Health Authority and the Social Services Department. *Where such arrangements exist we recommend the early amalgamation of the separate registers to prevent fragmentation of effort and guarantee a uniform channel of information.*

17. *All areas which have not yet established a central register should now do so. We expect that ARC members will ensure that all staff in relevant disciplines are familiar with the existence of the register and procedures for its use.*

18. Of those established at the time the reports were submitted, in the majority of cases (45) the register was kept, or was to be kept, under lock and key by a senior designated officer in the Social Services Department. In 19 cases it was similarly kept by the Area Health Authority (both figures include those where duplicate sets are kept by each authority). In nine areas the local NSPCC special unit for the battered child was, or would be, responsible for maintaining registers. A number of authorities near the special units continued to keep their own registers but tied them in with the NSPCC ones.

19. The registers vary greatly in comprehensiveness of records, access to those outside the holding agency and criteria for inclusion on the

register. At one end of the scale there were registers which simply contained the bare details—name, age, address, sex and the appropriate agency to contact for further information. Those seeking information from a register of this type would learn that a child was already considered to be at risk and which agency had the immediate responsibility for the welfare of the family concerned. At the other end were such registers as those kept by the NSPCC which included very detailed information. A number of ARCs had taken or were taking steps to standardize procedures for notification of suspected cases to the register and to inform all welfare agencies believed to be in contact with the family of these procedures; others continued to use procedures already in operation. Many provided printed cards on which to make the initial report. . . .

20. A senior officer of the Social Services Department or the Area Health Authority or both is normally designated to receive referrals, keep the register and give genuine enquirers, with valid reasons for requesting it, information about cases on the register, which is usually kept in conditions of strict confidentiality. Most registers only provide information for senior staff of named agencies (usually those participating in the ARC itself), and a call-back system is often operated to establish bona fides. In some cases to satisfy concern about confidentiality, information is only released after consent has been obtained from the originator of the report. The NSPCC registers are among those operating a call-back system: they also undertake to provide a 24 hour phone service. In a few authorities the police are automatically informed if a child is put on a register: others consider that what information is passed to the police should be for the case conference to decide. Once children are placed on the register they are usually kept in some kind of category listing according to the degree of risk, for speed of reference.

21. Some authorities never remove children from the register because a significant number of 'genuine' accidents can build up a picture of a child at risk. Others destroy records if an injury is proved to be accidental. A number of registers incorporate a procedure for regular reviews through the case conference system or a reviewing committee. These ensure that the case is followed up by the appropriate staff, and provide checks that the child has been placed in the right risk category and that where appropriate the record card is either removed from the register or categorized as inactive.

22. *It is of the utmost importance to safeguard the confidentiality of registers. For this reason all registers should be kept in conditions of the strictest*

*security and maintained by designated officers of the appropriate author-
ity who will receive referrals. While there should be ready access to the
register for all the caring professions relevantly concerned the bona
fides of enquirers must be established by the operation of a 'call-
back' system (see also paragraphs on Confidentiality in general).*

23. *Whilst the case for register systems which are geared to particular
local needs is acknowledged, it is nevertheless desirable to establish
some minimum requirements that should be satisfied by all register
systems. The considerable problem of forming a reliable estimate of
the incidence of non-accidental injury cannot be overcome by register
systems alone (for instance, criteria for inclusion are themselves a
problem), but it is aggravated by the absence of any common core of
information. The following conditions are therefore recommended:*

i. *Registers should include details of injured children up to the age
of 16. In deciding on criteria for the inclusion of 'at risk' cases,
authorities should consider how to ensure that the children
believed to be in greatest danger will be recorded without
entailing an unrealistic workload in the review of cases.*

ii. *Registers should be kept on an area basis (the area being that
covered by the ARC) to facilitate the transfer of information
when families move and the identification of children who may
be presented at a number of different hospitals. Where an ARC
spans more than one local authority area, there is much to
commend the maintenance of duplicate registers, covering the
whole ARC area, by each participating authority.*

iii. *All register entries should include at least the following details:*
a. *Child's full name, sex, date and place of birth.*
b. *Full names, address, known aliases, date of birth and
occupation of parents, caretakers and other adult members
of household (other than siblings) together with information on the relationship of the child to others—e.g. stepfather, co-habitee, lodger—in the house.*
c. *Full names, occupation if relevant, date of birth of siblings.
(Separate cards are unnecessary, unless the sibling is
also injured).*
d. *GPs name, address, telephone number.*
e. *Child's school, if any.*
f. *Nature of injury/reason for referral.*
g. *Date and time of referral.*
h. *Name of referrer and agency to which he/she belongs.*
i. *Agencies involved.*
j. *Action taken.*

iv. *There should be a built-in procedure to ensure the regular review of cases on the register which should take account of the presence of siblings in the household and the likelihood of other children being born into it.*

v. *Entries relating to children who are known to have been injured should be clearly distinguished from those entries which concern the children who for whatever reason (e.g. neglect; failure to thrive) are believed to be at risk but where non-accidental injury has not been proved.*

Confidentiality

24. The question of confidentiality and the disclosure of information about children and adults concerned with their care was mentioned as a problem by many ARCs and is closely linked with register systems; it extends further, however, to case conferences and other situations calling for the release of information which may have been obtained as a result of a professional relationship.

25. *The safety of the child must in all circumstances be of paramount importance and must override all other considerations. It is nonetheless undeniable that there will be occasions when the need to protect a child will conflict with the wish to preserve a relationship of trust with another party, and that the problems posed by confidentiality admit of no easy solution, although it is important to work towards solving them. Any decision about the release of information is normally one for professional judgement but the factors which ought to be taken into account in reaching such a decision are the 'need to know' and the consequent restriction of information to those directly concerned with the family and who have the duty legitimately to perform a service on its behalf; and the importance of taking action in a child's best interests in the light of all relevant facts. It would be helpful if the passing of information between the caring professions were regarded and treated as analogous to that passed in confidence within a single discipline. Whenever possible however an adult's agreement should be sought to the sharing of information about him with professionals from a different discipline.*

Case Conferences

26. The case conference is recognized in all areas as a vital process in handling cases of children injured, neglected or at risk. Arrangements

for convening case conferences vary from area to area, but the responsibility most often rests with a senior member of the social services staff at area level. In some cases the hospital social worker or a senior member of the hospital staff convenes the conference if the child is a patient in hospital. A few areas provide for a senior member of the hospital/nursing/Community Physician/social work staff each to be able to convene a case conference, while others define the convenor less sharply.

27. *In reporting on their arrangements, some ARCs made reference to 'standing case conferences'. The issue may simply be one of definition, but it is important to distinguish between the function of the case conference and that of the case review committee, which some ARCs have established to review the decisions made by case conferences. The case conference normally comprises those who have a direct concern with the family under discussion, while the membership of case review committees will ordinarily be drawn at a senior level from those professions who are most regularly involved with non-accidental injury: where cases closely involving other professions come under review, representatives of those professions should for that meeting be co-opted to the case review committee.*

28. *Attention was frequently drawn to the difficulty faced by general practitioners in finding time to attend case conferences. Where a system of health visitor attachment to a general practice is in operation, the problem is often overcome by the health visitor and doctor sharing information on a case and standing in for each other at case conferences. It is important to involve the family practitioner to the full in discussions affecting his patients, and where he is unable to attend a case conference, steps should be taken to ensure that he is informed of the discussion and any decision taken.*

29. *We recommend the practice of nominating one of the participants in a case conference as the 'key worker'. The professional most closely concerned with the case and responsible for the actual management of it is identified as the focal point through whom information is channelled, and is made responsible for ensuring that it reaches all the other participants. This arrangement does not relieve the other professionals of their own responsibilities, but facilitates the swift and ready exchange of information between those concerned. Any member of a case conference should be able to convene a further meeting of all participants at any stage if there continues to be serious cause for concern or if there seems to be a need for action to be reviewed. In all cases where it is proposed to vary the action decided upon or where new*

factors become apparent, the case conference should be reconvened. The main points of case conference discussions and decisions should be recorded and circulated in strict confidence to members unable to attend.

30. *It is acknowledged that the decision of a case conference cannot be binding on the representatives of bodies with statutory powers and duties in relation to children and that, where a consensus view cannot be reached, any participant may, after consultation with senior officers, find himself constrained to take action contrary to that recommended by other members of a case conference. Where this occurs, we urge that the other members be notified of the proposed action and the reasons for disagreement, before such action is taken, unless an emergency demands otherwise.*

31. Many ARCs mentioned liaison with the police, and in particular the question of whether or not police should be invited to participate in case conferences, as one of the problems which they had encountered. In some areas there are established liaison schemes and the police are invited to case conferences as a matter of course: in others the police's investigative and prosecuting powers in cases where assaults had occurred were regarded as inhibiting case conference discussion. A number of areas reported that police co-operation in case conferences had led them and the other professions involved to a better understanding of their roles. *Urgent consideration is being given by DHSS and Home Office to ways in which the respective roles of the police and other professions who may participate in case conferences might be clarified. . . .*

iii   Child abuse: professional guide on detection and treatment

Introduction

This code of practice has been designed to provide a rapid point of reference for professional people handling problems of child abuse. The procedures have been deliberately condensed in order to clarify the steps to be taken. The NSPCC Special Unit (in a few areas only) . . . provides a central point for the registration of cases and convening of case conferences. The Unit's staff are available at all times . . . for advice and consultation on procedures and the case management of families.

A child abuse referral

Professional people have a responsibility to assist in the detection of child abuse in the city. Incidents of child abuse may come to light in a wide variety of different ways, for example by direct referral or through the course of on-going supervision. In all instances it is important that the essential details are recorded. Care must also be taken to ensure that there is no unnecessary duplication of the investigation procedures in a case prior to a case conference.

Child abuse case conferences

The conference provides an opportunity for all professional people involved with a family, where child abuse is thought to have occurred, to meet and pool their information and opinions. From a conference come recommendations for a treatment plan. The agency which initiates the case conference is normally expected to provide a written or verbal report which should include any known previous history, the problems apparent at the time of referral and the methods used so far for attempting to resolve these problems. A report should also be provided by the agency involved if an application has been made for a Place of Safety Order. If

COVENTRY AREA HEALTH AUTHORITY (1976) *A Professional Guide on the Detection and Treatment of Child Abuse*, pp. 1–3, 7–8, 17–18.

the members of the case conference decide that the information available is insufficient on which to make recommendations a professional person will be elected to pursue enquiries and present a further report at a future case conference.

Degree of injury or neglect a child has received

The instructions in this guide have been divided into three categories for each professional group. The categories are determined by the type of child abuse problem and the action taken varies with each category.

Emergency
This section is concerned with children who are seen to be in serious danger and who cannot be left unattended. This will include children who have been severely attacked by their parents or ill-treated in some other way. In these cases the first step is always to secure the physical safety of the child and to ensure that medical treatment is given. This is usually effected by the admission of the child to . . . hospital. If, however, parental consent is withheld, a Place of Safety Order can be obtained by a social worker in the Social Services Department, the NSPCC Inspector or the police. It should be noted that the police, under their discretionary powers, are able to remove a child from a dangerous situation more speedily than any other agency.

The NSPCC Special Unit should be requested by telephone to register each case in this section and convene a case conference by inviting all the professional people involved with the family.

High suspicion
This section concerns cases where children may have been injured or ill-treated by their parents but are apparently in no immediate danger. The evidence may suggest that the child has been abused but further investigation is needed before recommendations, for a removal of the child to a place of safety, can be made. Consideration should be given to whether the child needs medical attention or examination and arrangements made accordingly. This should be followed by the registration of the case with the NSPCC Special Unit who will convene an immediate case conference, normally within 24 hours.

Low suspicion
This section discusses the procedures to be followed when parental behaviour towards their children arouses suspicion, but where there is no clear evidence of physical ill-treatment or neglect.

239

Aspects of detection of child abuse

1. The diagnosis and case management of non-accidentally injured children are joint processes involving the social work, health visiting, medical and allied professions.
2. Children of all ages are the victims of non-accidental injury but clearly the youngest children are at greatest risk of the severest injuries and of the most serious long-term consequences of injuries.
3. Abuse covers not only acts of commissions of violence but also acts of omissions on the part of parents or caretakers. Children who 'fail to thrive' or who are seriously neglected may be the subjects of abuse and consideration should also be given when an accident is reported whether the child was deliberately or consciously put in the way of danger.
4. Careful consideration must be given to every injury and explanation. A check needs to be made on whether the injuries and explanations are compatible under the headings of:
   extent of injury; spread of injury; timing and history; age and mobility of child.
5. Each separate injury, however trivial it may appear, should be accounted for and suspicions should be aroused if inadequate, discrepant, or excessively plausible explanations are offered for different injuries. Explanations given by parents to different people, e.g. hospital staff, doctor, social worker, health visitor, should be compared and any discrepancies should be high-lighted and suspected.
6. Presentation at hospital with a delay, or only under pressure, or admissions and presentations of the child at different hospitals at different times, are often symptomatic.
7. The accepted rebattering rate of a child and/or battering of siblings is recognized to be quite high. Professional bodies should therefore be aware of previous injuries to children in the family.
8. The family functioning and parental reaction must be carefully assessed when a child is considered to be at risk of abuse. Abnormal or inappropriate responses of the parents to an injury may arouse suspicion in conjunction with precipitating stress factors.

Health visitors/school nurses

Emergency

1. Take the child, with the parents' consent, to the . . . hospital, either to the Paediatric outpatient clinic . . . or the Accident Department. Ensure that the medical and nursing staff are aware that the injuries may be non-accidental so that emergency attention is given.

2. If the family refuses to co-operate contact:
   a. the police in a dire emergency, or
   b. the appropriate District Manager of the Social Services Department or out of hours phone ... the Social Work Emergency Service, or
   c. NSPCC Inspector ...
3. Consult the NSPCC Special Unit. ...
4. Discuss the case with the Nursing Officer/Health Visiting.

High suspicion
1. When medical attention or examination is required:
   a. take the parent and child to see GP during surgery hours, or
   b. phone the appropriate Area Health Office (Community) for an immediate appointment with a Clinical Medical Officer in a Child Health Clinic ... , or
   c. take the parent and child to the Accident Department of the ... hospital.
2. Consult with NSPCC Special Unit ... for registration and immediate case conference.
3. Discuss with Nursing Officer/Health Visiting.

Low suspicion
1. Liaise with the social worker, school, GP or other professional people involved with the family.
2. Discuss with Nursing Officer/Health Visiting.
3. Consult NSPCC Special Unit ... for information or registration and case conference.

General practitioners

Emergency
1. Arrange for the child and parent to be escorted to ... hospital Paediatric out-patient clinic or for urgent admission to a Children's Ward, phoning the information to the appropriate hospital department beforehand.
2. If the parent refuses to co-operate and/or a responsible escort is not available contact:
   a. the police in a dire emergency, or
   b. the appropriate District Manager of the Social Services Department or out of hours telephone ... the Social Work Emergency Service, or
   c. NSPCC Inspector. ...

3. Inform the Health Visitor involved with the family and the District Manager of the Social Services Department.
4. Consult the NSPCC Special Unit available at all times. . . .

High suspicion
1. Where treatment is necessary the child should be sent with the parents as an urgent case to the . . . hospital, either to the Paediatric out-patient clinic, . . . or to the Accident Department, phoning to ensure the nursing and medical staff know that the injuries may be non-accidental.
2. Discuss straight away with the Health Visitor and social worker involved with the family, or inform the relevant Area Health Office and Social Services district office immediately.
3. Inform the NSPCC Special Unit for registration and urgent case conference. . . .

Low suspicion
1. Discuss with Health Visitor and social worker involved with the family, or contact relevant Area Health Office and Social Services District Office.
2. Inform the NSPCC Special Unit for checking with register and arranging case conference if necessary.

The statutory powers of the police

Section 28, Children and Young Persons Act 1969 Detention of child or young person in place of custody

Under Section 28(2) a police constable has the power to remove a child or young person to a place of safety without a court order, if he has reasonable cause to believe that the conditions set out in Section 1 (2)(a) to (d) of this Act are satisfied (i.e. in need of care).

Under Section 28 (4) a police officer not below the rank of Inspector or the police officer in charge of a police station shall as soon as practicable enquire into the case. After enquiries the child or children may be released or received into voluntary care. If he decides that the child or children should be detained under Section 28 (5) the period of detention is for no more than eight days beginning with the day of detention.

Parents must be informed of the action taken and of their right to apply to a Magistrate for the release of the child Section 28 (3) and Section 28 (5).

This is a discretionary power given only to the police, if a senior officer is satisfied that the situation warrants this action.

This power should only be used in an emergency situation and not at a time when it is possible to obtain a Magistrate's 28 day Place of Safety Order under Section 28 (1) which authorizes any person who has reasonable cause to believe that these conditions are satisfied in respect of a child or young person, to apply to a Magistrate. Section 28 does not give anyone power to remove a child or young person by force.

Section 40, Children and Young Persons Act 1933 Warrant to search for and remove a child or young person

Under Section 40 (1) any person acting in the interests of a child or young person may apply to a Magistrate's Court, by information on oath, for a warrant to search for and remove a child or young person. If it appears to the Magistrate that there is reasonable cause to suspect that the child or young person has been or is being assaulted, ill-treated or neglected or is the victim of any offence mentioned in the 1st schedule of the 1933 Act, the Magistrate may issue a warrant authorising any constable named therein to search for the child or young person and if it is found that any of the above conditions are satisfied he may take him and detain him in a place of safety until he can be brought before a Juvenile Court, or authorising any constable to remove him with or without search to a place of safety and detain him there until he can be brought before a Juvenile Court.

Under Section 40 (2) a Magistrate issuing a warrant under this section may by the same warrant cause any person accused of any offence in respect of the child or young person to be arrested and brought before a Magistrate's Court.

Under Section 40 (3) any constable authorised by warrant under this section to search for any child or young person, or to remove any child or young person with or without search, may enter (if need by force) any house, building or other place specified in the warrant and remove the child or young person.

Under Section 40 (4) every warrant issued under this section shall be addressed to and executed by a constable who shall be accompanied by the person laying the information, if that person so desires, unless the Magistrate otherwise directs and may also if the Magistrate so directs be accompanied by a duly qualified medical practitioner.

Section 40 (5) states that in any information or warrant under this section it is not necessary to name the child or young person.

iv   Extracts from reports of official inquiries

Maria Colwell

[Maria Colwell was born in March 1965, the fifth child of her mother's first marriage. Her parents separated within weeks of her birth, her father left home, and a few weeks later he died. At four months Maria was voluntarily placed by her mother in the care of her late husband's sister and later in the same year the other children were committed to the care of the local authority who placed them with foster parents. Ten months later Mrs Colwell, on the point of making a home with her future husband William Kepple, removed Maria from her sister-in-law's care but within a week placed her in the care of another, highly unsatisfactory, home from which she was removed under a place of safety order. Maria was returned 'temporarily' by the Children's Committee to her aunt and uncle where she was later officially fostered under a care order. She formed a close bond with her foster parents and remained with them until she was six and a half when her mother, who now had three children by Mr Kepple, regained possession of Maria on application to the court and the care order was revoked in favour of a supervision order. During the fourteen months that followed evidence began to accumulate, largely from neighbourhood sources, that Maria was unhappy, exploited, underfed and frequently subjected to imprisonment and violent treatment, but no effective action was taken to protect her. In January 1973, within eleven weeks of her eighth birthday, Maria died of multiple injuries. Her stepfather William Kepple was found guilty of her murder, a verdict later reduced to manslaughter by the Court of Appeal which sentenced him to eight years imprisonment.

The Committee of Inquiry found evidence of professional misjudgement and of many failures in communication both within and between the various agencies responsible for Maria's welfare. To understand the complexity of the case with its background of family feuding and complicated inter-agency relationships it is necessary to read the full report including the minority report by Olive Stevenson.]

DHSS (Department of Health and Social Security) (1974) *Report of the Committee of Inquiry into the Care and Supervision provided in relation to Maria Colwell*, London, HMSO, pp. 61–71, paras. 149–87.

Communications. An introductory comment

149. In the course of analysing the many failures of communication in the Colwell case, we have considered, as our terms of reference required, the part played by a number of agencies who were involved in more or less degree with the Social Services departments of East Sussex and Brighton, upon whom, of course, the primary responsibility for Maria's welfare lay. Other cases would no doubt have thrown up other agencies. But in Maria's case, the most relevant of these appear to have been the schools (and their own educational welfare and health services), the NSPCC, the housing department of Brighton Corporation and the Brighton police.

150. The adage 'too many cooks spoil the broth' may come into the mind of the outside observer. It is inevitable that a considerable number of different agencies and persons will be involved in such cases. What is important is that their respective roles should be clearly defined and that they should not overlap unnecessarily. It is salutory to note how little the recommendations of the Seebohm Committee and subsequent legislation* altered the situation in Maria's case. It is possible that had the Committee's proposal that the Educational Welfare Service should join the Social Services Department been accepted one of the more conspicuous difficulties in communication in Maria's case would have been lessened but, as we shall comment later, this was strongly opposed by the senior officials of the Brighton Education Department.

151. It was represented to us that a general practitioner cannot be construed as coming within our terms of reference as 'another agency'. We do not wish to dispute this as, in any case, the part played by the GP in this particular case cannot be regarded as central. Nonetheless we would point out that we have received evidence† that the GP's are key people in the detection of children at physical risk and we would not wish to refrain from general (as distinct from particular) comments on their part in the network of communications. In 1972, it was common practice to link the health visitors, employed

---

* Report of the Committee on Local Authority and Allied Personal Social Services 1968, Cmnd 3703. Local Authority Social Services Act 1970.

† D40 The Tunbridge Wells Study Group on Non-accidental Injury to Children—1973.

by local authorities, to general practice and this brought this area of the medical services into even closer relationships with the social services than previously. With the re-organization of the National Health Service the structural link has changed.

152. Whilst we entirely accept that a heavy responsibility for passing on and eliciting information to these 'other agencies' rests on social services departments, we must nonetheless stress that this should not be a one way process and that the social workers may reasonably expect that matters of concern about individual families or children will be passed on to them by these agencies whether or not they have already indicated their interest to them. The problem of communication is a complex one, resting as it does on a combination of formal and informal arrangements, of administrative systems and direct personal contact. But in view of the fact that Maria, despite an elaborate system of 'welfare provisions', fell through the net primarily because of communications failures, we feel it helpful to discuss in some detail the implications for 'the other agencies' of the points at which, in our view, serious flaws in the information flow *to* the social services departments occurred. It was emphasized frequently in the course of the inquiry, ... that there were many times when the social workers concerned with Maria simply did not know who else was involved and the nature of their involvement.

Recording: case notes and messages

153. It will be apparent from the preceding narrative that certain inaccuracies and deficiencies in the recording of visits and telephone messages played a part in the tragedy. In saying this, we fully recognize the difficulties under which social workers and other busy professionals such as teachers and general practitioners are frequently labouring and which affect the quality of recording. This is not simply a problem of overwork, in consequence of which recording may be given a low priority. It is also clear that in some agencies the necessary secretarial and mechanical aids were deficient. We heard in evidence from the Hove Area Director of East Sussex Social Services Department of the difficulties which the telephone engineers experienced in devising a switchboard system to cope with the flood of incoming calls, sometimes numbering 120 calls an hour. We cite this as an example of the pressures under which many professionals are labouring. It is therefore not surprising, if, for example, an intended 'phone call is not made or a message goes astray. Nor is it surprising if case notes are at times inadequate.

154. It was not within our competence to probe deeply into such administrative procedures but their importance should not be underestimated in considering breakdowns in communication. We consider that investment in secretarial resources and mechanical aids to communication would pay heavy dividends in efficiency and could release professional staff for their proper task.

155. So far as East Sussex Social Services Department is concerned, it is fair to say that the overall standard of case recording and recording of telephone messages was high and such criticisms as we make should be taken in that context. Indeed, the very fact that we were able to pinpoint certain specific deficiencies bears witness to the fact that their records of the Colwell case (numbering some 631 pages) were, in general, more than adequate throughout Maria's life.

156. There are four matters which in our view deserve criticism and which we commend to the attention of all those who train and supervise social workers in the field. The first concerns the importance of recording the actual dates of visits, even if, on occasions, pressure of work demands a summary of those visits rather than a running record. This is for the protection of the social workers as well as in the interests of accuracy per se. In our opinion, this is as important in relation to children visited in their own homes, whether voluntarily or statutorily, as it is for children in foster homes. There was a noticeable difference within the East Sussex records in this respect. It would seem that the Boarding Out Regulations give an impetus to social workers to note the actual dates of each visit.

157. Secondly, we would stress the importance of distinguishing in recording between fact and impression, both of which are, of course, essential to good records. A minor example, the statement 'has gained weight' (as distinct from 'appearing to have done so') should not be made unless this is proven.

158. Thirdly, when impressions or messages are recorded, it is very important to make clear the source of the information, whether, for example, it comes direct from a doctor or teacher or via a foster mother, parent or child. It appears that sometimes this was confused in recording and it is important for those with whom the field social worker is in consultation to have the distinction clear.

159. Fourthly, there are occasions, especially those when allegations of ill-treatment of children have been made and are being investigated, when the detail of the alleged incidents and how it is suggested they

have come about must be recorded minutely and accurately, having been probed with sufficient thoroughness, as was discussed above. For example, we feel that neither East Sussex nor the NSPCC paid sufficient attention in their records to the minutiae of the April incident, although the NSPCC recording of the general situation and impression in the Kepple household at that time was quite full. When children are at physical risk, or in any other comparable 'life and death' situation, the style and content of their recording may well have to be more detailed and precise than on those more frequent occasions when they seek to record general impressions of intimate conversations. It is also important that communications, formal and informal, between administrators and professionals within their own Department should be effective, which implies an understanding of each other's procedures.

160. We have referred in the narrative to the fact that the NSPCC admitted deficiencies in the recording and passing on of telephone messages by duty officers working from home and that since this case new procedures have been instituted. It must be said that some of our difficulties in analysing the events after Maria's return home stemmed from uncertainty as to what had reached the NSPCC of the complaints alleged to have been made by the neighbours. We heard in evidence of the extremely low costs of the NSPCC administration. We must of course make clear that we recognize that a voluntary charitable body can only cut its coat according to its cloth but we think a true balance between expenditure on administration and fieldwork is essential. Admirable as it may be to keep administrative costs low it may be that skimping on such servicing is not in the long run conducive to efficiency and is thus counter-productive to the Society's aim of protecting children from abuse. We refer in particular to office accommodation and secretarial facilities. We understand that many NSPCC officers still work from home and must of necessity depend on their relations to take 'phone messages for them on occasions.

161. It would be unfair, however, to suggest that the responsibility for efficient recording lies solely within the social services departments concerned or a comparable organization such as the NSPCC. The method of recording and transmitting information by the Brighton education welfare officers to the school itself, to the School Services Section of the Education Department and, thus, eventually to the Social Services Department seemed to fall well below what one would expect from a competent administrative or professional service. There appeared to be no machinery by which concern about

the welfare of school children automatically reached the Social Services Department. Thus it must be noted that not until December 8 did the education welfare officer, at the request of her superior, make a full written report of a situation which had been causing her increasing concern for nearly the whole of the autumn term.

162. Furthermore a method of recording on handwritten slips, of which no copies were kept, matters of welfare relating to the children and the manner in which these slips passed between the teachers and the education welfare officers seemed to us somewhat amateurish. In our view it would not usually be necessary or desirable for an education welfare officer to take notes whilst actually in the house or at the doorstep. We hope that the standards of recording produced to us are not typical of education welfare as a whole. It is possibly a matter to which inservice training programmes could profitably devote some attention. Similarly the heads or deputy heads of schools who have responsibility for the welfare of children at risk would be well advised to keep brief records of conversations concerning such children. No doubt many of them do so.

163. It is unprofitable to labour the point by referring in detail to each agency involved. We would, however, emphasize that not only social workers and other professionals are involved in the recording of messages. Clerical staff are often crucial in the system. Their training and instructions, especially concerning telephone communications, are vital elements in the protection of children at risk; in this we would, of course, include doctors' receptionists.

Communication within and between schools

164. Maria attended three schools, [X] Infants, [Y] Infants and [Y] Junior, the last two after she returned to her mother in November 1971. We heard in evidence of the communications, both formal and informal, between and within the schools. This was for Maria an important link in the 'welfare chain' and one which was on occasions weak. We hope it will be of some general value for the welfare of other school children at emotional or physical risk to analyse this matter in some detail.

165. First, as to formal communications: these were maintained by the use of record cards, of which there are two independent systems, one compiled by teachers or the school secretaries, the other by the school doctor or nurse. The school record card contains 'boxes' in

which information concerning anything of note about a child's welfare, including home circumstances, may be recorded. We have noted that Miss L. [social worker] visited [X] School in June 1971 to discuss Maria with her headmaster and class teacher. There was no entry in her school record card, completed at the end of the summer term, 1971, to indicate her unusual home circumstances. We heard in evidence from Maria's class teacher that, in the autumn term of 1971, the period immediately before her return home, she had been told by the foster-mother of Mrs Kepple's wish to have Maria home and that a court order existed. She also said that she had met a social worker from Hove who had told her of plans to return Maria, of trial weekends and of the care order. None of this was recorded on the card.

166. When Maria moved to [Y] Infants, some of the information given by Miss L. to the headmaster was recorded on the school record card by the class teacher, Miss D. Under 'special home circumstances' she wrote 'has returned home to natural mother'. 'Has four younger brothers and sisters under school age'. Under 'report on general development' she wrote 'needs to be noticed and (? given) affection'. It is to be noted that this record card at no time showed that there was or had been a care order, although both the [X] and [Y] staff knew of it. (They did not, however, know of the existence of the supervision order made in November 1971, when the care order was revoked.)

167. When Maria moved up to [Y] Junior School, the school secretary there, Mrs C., copied the old school record card. In evidence, we learnt that in the Junior School the cards were kept in the school secretary's office. They were not looked at as a matter of routine by the headmaster or deputy. Class teachers were expected to look at them and to tell the head, deputy or school secretary, anything of importance. The Education Welfare Officer called frequently at the secretary's office but the cards would not be seen by her as a matter of routine and only if something was specifically drawn to her attention.

168. It is reasonable to infer from the above that the staff of the Brighton schools did not regard the school record cards as an important part of their communications system and preferred to rely in great measure on exchange of information informally. No administrative system can ever substitute for such informal exchange but if a routine exists for the transmission of factual information, it is obviously desirable either that it should be followed or else abolished.

Otherwise there is a kind of false security. Since it is inevitable that teachers come and go, it would seem that there is a case for keeping careful, if brief, records. For instance, we know in Maria's case that the class teacher at [Y] Junior was told by Miss D. something of Maria's history. But that teacher had left, and Mrs T. had taken over by the time Maria arrived in September and only some of what was known had been recorded. Above all, the crucial information that East Sussex Social Services Department had a particular interest in Maria was not on the card.

169. The school medical cards were, perhaps, more peripheral to the matter, although they, as the main school cards, did contain boxes for 'family history' and 'significant home conditions'. We learnt that the former was more concerned with medical than social matters. Neither box on Maria's card contained any entry. In any case, the opportunities for the school staff to learn anything from them were very restricted, since they were regarded as confidential to the medical staff and kept for most of the time at the main school clinic. These cards were updated by checking with parents at the time of the examination, not by consultation with the school. We learnt that when there were medical matters about which it was necessary for the school to know, this was imparted in a confidential letter to the headmaster, which listed 'defects'. Clearly, therefore, this independent system was primarily focused on matters of physical health, rather than the social and emotional background. This may be quite appropriate but the inter-connection between the two, especially in the case of young children like Maria, is obvious.

170. Whilst acknowledging the importance of medical confidentiality, we hope that Maria's case will prompt a new look at the connections which it is reasonable to make between these two systems of recording.

171. There is one other aspect of formal communications to note, namely that of the 'slips' which passed between teachers and education welfare officers. We comment later on the weaknesses of this and other recording. At this point, we would simply stress that in our view the mechanics of this system need close scrutiny. The referral 'slips', we learnt, were made out by teachers or secretaries and passed to the education welfare officer for action, usually regarding lateness or absence from school. The education welfare officer noted her action on the slip and it was passed back to the school. Copies were not kept by the school, or the education welfare officer, and the arrangements for keeping, or disposing of, the slips seemed somewhat uncertain. These records are potentially a source of important

information about children in trouble or at risk, even more than the school record cards which, of course, cover all children. Maria's case illustrates vividly the confusions which can arise. One important example concerned a slip raised in February 1972 which recorded that 'A Child Care Officer from Hove had rung. . . .' Maria's last class teacher had not known of East Sussex involvement with Maria. On the other hand, the school secretary said she had passed this slip on to Mrs T. with the school record card. Be that as it may, the education welfare service knew from that slip of East Sussex's concern. But because no copies were kept by the school services section, this information reposed in the school and did not apparently come to the knowledge of the education welfare officer, Mrs D., who was increasingly concerned about Maria in the autumn term of 1972.

172. The minutiae of these matters may become tedious. But we explore them in an attempt to illustrate that, if formal systems for communication are devised, and in our view this is inevitable when one is dealing with large numbers of children and staff, close examination of their day-to-day working is needed. Too often, in the course of the inquiry, we heard of 'fool-proof systems', which in the event proved faulty. We accept that there will always be an element of human error whatever is devised. But we formed the general impression that the staff in the Brighton schools which Maria attended may not have been much convinced of the importance of routine communications. If this is the case, the administrative system is bound to fail, however efficient it looks in the abstract. One then has to look at the best ways of ensuring co-operation from staff over such matters.

173. So much for formal communications. However important, they are secondary to the flow of information about individual children which must pass within and between schools by word of mouth. There are four groups of people crucial in this process, namely, the heads or their deputies, the class teachers, the school secretaries and the education welfare officers.

174. It was strongly argued by the Chief Education Officer for Brighton that the responsibility for welfare of individual children, and therefore the contact with outside agencies, must rest with the head or his deputy. We gathered that this was the usual practice in Brighton and elsewhere. It is obvious that the ultimate responsibility must rest with the headmaster. The only question at issue is whether this responsibility may on occasions be delegated to the class teacher, provided that the head knows what is happening. It was put to us

that there was a risk in such delegations, in that class teachers might not always refer appropriately or sensibly. Clearly, this is a matter upon which the head would have to use his discretion although we imagine that many class teachers would be well able to exercise discrimination in such referrals. What seems to us essential is that the class teacher is always involved, preferably through direct contact with the social worker concerned. We were impressed by the sincerity and perceptiveness of Maria which all three of her class teachers showed. We feel that it is possible that anxieties about Maria's situation might have been conveyed with greater accuracy and urgency if her last class teacher, Mrs T., had herself spoken to Miss L. in the autumn term of 1972. It will also always be important for information reaching the school to be fed back to the class teacher, if they are to retain an informed interest in their children's welfare. (Mrs T. said she did not hear of the outcome of her referral to the deputy headmaster in November 1972 although we now know that he took appropriate action at that stage.)

175. The position of the school secretary, who is sometimes also referred to as a 'welfare assistant' is of importance in considering the links within the schools. In both [Y] Infants and Junior Schools, although especially the latter, the secretaries were involved in Maria's case. It seemed that in the Junior School, the secretary, Mrs C., was often the channel of communication between the class teacher and the education welfare officer and, according to the gravity of the situation, between the class teacher and the head or deputy. Furthermore, if, as at [Y] Junior, the secretary has some responsibilities in supervision of school dinners, she has an opportunity to observe children directly. For Maria, we know that this was important since she was seen by Mrs T. and Mrs C. to eat 'ravenously'. It seems that Mrs C. heard a good deal from Mrs T. of her anxieties about Maria, some of which resulted in referral to the education welfare service. But, as we have remarked elsewhere, the information which the two earlier schools had of the East Sussex Social Service Department's concern somehow did not get picked up at [Y] Junior. We are not sure why. We simply point to the fact that there is some division of responsibility for the noting and referring of such matters between the teachers and the school secretaries. We wonder if the significance of the latter's position as a 'go between' is always fully appreciated and acknowledged, in terms of the status accorded to the job and (possibly) certain basic training for it, if the role in fact goes beyond the purely clerical, as was the case here.

176. It will be apparent from the narrative and the preceding comment

that we were much concerned about the liaison between the education welfare service and the Social Services Department in Maria's case. But this is inseparable from the position of the education welfare officer, Mrs D., within the schools which she served. We cannot, of course, generalize from the particular instance but, in the light of comments made by the Plowden Committee,* brought to our attention, we think it is possible that this particular situation may not be uncommon. It seemed to us that, although the notion of 'education welfare' as something going beyond simply ensuring school attendance, was accepted in principle, the role and status of the education welfare officer within the school was uncertain. We noted with surprise that Mrs. D. had not met Mrs. T., despite the latter's mounting anxiety about Maria and frequent referrals, including the important matter of Maria's alleged shopping expeditions. We learnt that there was no reason why the two should not have met and that Mrs D. was welcome to join the staff in the common room. We are not sure how often she did so and whether there were any 'invisible barriers'. We also noted that, when Mrs T.'s anxieties caused the deputy headmaster, Mr M., to take action, it was to Mrs P., Mrs D.'s senior, that he spoke about Maria, although by this time Mrs D. was as worried as Mrs T.

177. We heard that it was accepted that the education welfare officers should receive training comparable to, or the same as, other social workers. This will assist them in taking their place as full and respected members of the education team with a defined role which is clear to all concerned and a close liaison with other social workers. But the issue of effective communication within and between schools, and in turn, the relationship between schools and 'welfare agencies' cannot be solved by improvements in the training of education welfare officers, desirable as that may be.

Communications between schools and social services departments

178. This is a complex issue, partly because there are a number of people within the schools with whom a social worker in the social services department may be in communication. This immediately

---

*Department of Education and Science, 1967. *Children and their Primary Schools: Report of the Central Advisory Council for Education (England)*. London, HMSO.

raises the important issue of communications within schools, which we have already considered. We now focus our attention upon the external relationship of the school staff with the social worker in the social services department. We discuss this in some detail because we regard it as a crucial factor in the liaison between agencies which we were asked in our terms of reference to consider. Whilst acknowledging that certain weaknesses in this chain of communication may have been exacerbated because responsibility was divided between the authorities of East Sussex and Brighton, we do not think this is itself a sufficient explanation. We wonder whether there were problems which are not simply administrative, which reflect a lack of confidence in, and understanding of, respective roles and responsibilities between the professions. We heard in evidence from three of Maria's class teachers, before and after her return home, and we were impressed by their sincerity and perceptiveness of Maria as an individual.

179. Yet we were unable to make a finding of fact upon the evidence, which conflicted at several points, presented to us by those teachers who had direct contact with Miss L. and that of Miss L. herself. Since we have no doubt of the veracity of all concerned, we are left pondering how it comes about that responsible professional people do not substantially agree in their recollections of conversations which were of crucial importance concerning plans for Maria's future and her subsequent situation. Perhaps the social workers do not always explain carefully enough to the teachers the legal aspects of the situation, for example, the implications of care or supervision orders or of court hearings for revocation. They may assume that matters with which they are very familiar will be readily understood by the teachers. It is also obvious that the bustle of a crowded school may not be the easiest place for social workers to communicate effectively, whether in person or by telephone, to class or head teacher.

180. Our difficulties in determining what teachers and social workers said to each other about Maria were compounded by the deficiencies in recording, upon which we comment later; Miss L.'s recording of such encounters were variable, those of the teachers almost non-existent. Given the pressures under which both professions operate and the inevitability of staff changes, recording becomes of particular importance if misunderstanding or simple forgetfulness is to be avoided.

181. The evidence suggests, although it had not been fully recorded on

either side, that the head and class teacher of Maria's first school, [X] Infants, were put in the picture about Maria quite fully by Miss L. There were, however, discrepancies in the interpretation of the situation between the class teacher, Mrs L., and Miss L. which we were unable to resolve.

182. When Maria moved to [Y] Infants, Miss C., the headmistress, learnt something about Maria from Miss L. and from her previous headmaster. Miss C. recorded Miss L.'s name and telephone number in her diary but it is not clear from these notes what information Miss L. did impart. Miss C. told us in evidence, however, that she knew Maria had been fostered, was going back to her mother and had been in care. She also knew of Miss L.'s continuing interest, since she 'phoned again in November 1971 and February 1972 and on one occasion at Miss C.'s suggestion spoke to Maria's class teacher, Miss D. It is, therefore, rather strange that the school did not contact Miss L. in May of that year when, as we have described, the class teacher observed Maria with a bruised face and took her to the head and the school secretary. All three doubted Maria's explanation of the bruise.

183. We have referred to the fact that Miss L. was never in touch with Maria's last school, [Y] Junior, and have explained that she was unaware that the Infants and Junior schools were quite separate, although on the same campus. This has implications for communications between schools, but it also illustrates lack of familiarity, which we suspect may be quite common, on the part of social workers about the structure and organization of the schools which children under their supervision attend.

184. In the 'welfare links' between the schools and social services the role of the education welfare officer is of considerable importance in many cases, as it was with Maria. We have already described the part played by Mrs D., the Brighton education welfare officer, who was attached to [Y] Junior School. In the course of the inquiry, we heard that the Seebohm Committee had recommended that the education welfare service should be incorporated into the Social Services Departments. Senior officials who gave evidence from the Brighton Corporation were strongly opposed to the proposal that education welfare officers should be responsible to Social Services Departments rather than to Education Departments. It is clear and somewhat disturbing that, in Maria's case, the division between the education welfare service and the Social Services Department made it more difficult for Mrs D.'s concern about Maria to reach the

proper person, Miss L., with sufficient urgency and promptness. It is true that other factors may have entered into this, for example, the division between the two local authorities, to which we have already referred. But, nonetheless, we cannot but note with regret that at no time were Miss L. and Mrs D. in direct contact. Apparently, Mrs D. did not know of Miss L.'s interest in Maria until November or December 1972, by which time she (Mrs D.) had paid frequent visits to the Kepple household. There was insufficient evidence to determine whether Miss L. ever knew before Maria died, of Mrs D.'s involvement on the case. It is inconceivable that this contact would not have been established had they both been social workers within Social Services Departments.

185. It seems likely that such difficulties are by no means unique to Brighton and East Sussex. If these workers are to remain administratively separated, we hope that every effort will be made to ensure direct and frequent communication between the social workers in the Social Services Department and the education welfare officers. We learnt that the Brighton Education Department considered the task of the education welfare officer should go beyond concern for regular school attendance and extend to more general issues of welfare. We understand this is generally accepted. If this is so, then, at the least, liaison and co-ordination between workers with substantial areas of mutual interest is indispensable.

Social Services Departments and the NSPCC

186. As has been indicated in the narrative, we consider that serious flaws in communication arose between Miss L. and Mrs K. [NSPCC] because of the blurring of roles and inadequate clarification in April 1972 of the part each was to play in looking after Maria thereafter.

187. So far as Miss L. was concerned it may be that Mrs K. became involved almost by accident because Mrs R.'s complaint came to the NSPCC and that Mrs K. (who did not know Miss L. beforehand) might not have been involved if this had not happened. However, there is every reason to suppose that, largely for historical reasons, complaints commonly reach the NSPCC rather than the Social Services Department. Therefore the difficulties which arose in this case may be of some general application. We heard from witness upon witness that it is to the NSPCC that they naturally turn when they wish to complain about children at physical risk; they are known, we learnt, as 'the cruelty people'.

Auckland family

Introduction

1. Mr John George Auckland killed his fifteen-month-old daughter Susan on the night of 11 July 1974. He was convicted of manslaughter on 29 November 1974 at Sheffield Crown Court and is now serving a sentence of five years' imprisonment. At the end of the trial it was stated that he had also killed his nine-week-old daughter Marianne in June 1968, and in October of that year had been convicted of manslaughter on the grounds of diminished responsibility.

2. At the trial in November 1974 there was no reliance upon the defence of diminished responsibility. The trial judge, Mr Justice Lawson, said he was greatly concerned that a man who had already been convicted of manslaughter of one of his children, should have been allowed to take sole charge of three others. He wrote to the Secretary of State for Social Services, Mrs Barbara Castle, putting his view that this tragedy was a matter of public concern.

3. On 23 April 1975 the Secretary of State appointed us as a Committee to inquire into and report upon the provision and co-ordination of services to the family of John George Auckland by the relevant local authorities and health services and by any other persons or agencies.

4. The Inquiry was announced publicly and we asked anyone who wished to give evidence to contact the Secretary to the Committee.

5. We decided that we should sit in public because our task was to investigate services provided by the community for members of the community. The community was therefore, in our view, entitled to hear the evidence as well as our conclusions. In reaching that decision we recognized the risk that witnesses might be deterred from giving evidence, or might be less frank because of the possibility of adverse publicity, but in the event we have no reason to think that sitting in public had any harmful effect. We even venture to hope that those

---

DHSS (Department of Health and Social Security) (1975) *Report of the Committee of Inquiry into the Provision and Co-ordination of Services to the Family of John George Auckland*, London, HMSO, pp. 11–12, paras. 1–11; pp. 85–92, paras. 250–76; Appendices A, B, C, D and E.

who followed the proceedings will have been able to see for themselves that a full and fair investigation did take place, and that our conclusions as set out in this report can be supported by the evidence which we heard.

6.   After a preliminary hearing in London on 30 May 1975, the Inquiry was held in Sheffield on eighteen days between 30 June and 23 July 1975. We heard oral evidence from 50 witnesses and received written evidence from a further 34 witnesses.[1] We also considered a number of documents[2] amounting to some 1,000 pages which were submitted to us as exhibits, and we visited the areas with which our Inquiry was concerned.

7.   We had the assistance of several members of the Treasury Solicitor's Department who, under the leadership of Mr Duncan Watson, collected relevant documentary evidence for us and interviewed and took statements from witnesses. They also instructed counsel, Mr D. Herrod QC and Mr J. Deby, to appear on behalf of the Committee. We are indebted to both Mr Duncan Watson and his staff and to those they instructed for the efficient and helpful way in which the relevant material was collected and presented to us.

8.   Various persons and bodies asked to be represented at the Inquiry, and the right of representation was granted to all who asked for it. However, we were anxious to ensure that no party should be put to unnecessary expense and we therefore suggested to those representing the medical profession, the South Yorkshire Probation and After-Care Service, Mr John Auckland, and Mrs Barbara Auckland that their representation be limited to attendance at the Inquiry when the matters being covered were of direct interest to them. In the cases of Mr and Mrs John Auckland the limitation was made a term of the grant of representation as it was clear from the outset that the costs of their representation would be likely to fall on public funds. Details of the parties and those representing them are given at Appendix A, and we would like to express our gratitude to all those who appeared before us.

9.   As to procedure, witnesses were examined-in-chief by counsel to the Committee or by their own counsel if they were represented. It was open to all counsel to cross-examine any witness if they wished to

---

[1] See Appendix B, p. 271.

[2] See Appendix C, p. 273.

do so. At the beginning and end of the Inquiry we were addressed by counsel to the Committee, and by counsel representing other parties.

10. The structure of our report is that in Chapter 2 we deal briefly in turn with the persons or agencies supplying services to the family of Mr John Auckland, comment on some pertinent features and indicate, in some instances, how, in our view the service should be carried out. Chapters 3–18 deal chronologically with the period from 1944, the year of Mr John Auckland's birth, up to the death of Susan Auckland in July 1974; each chapter is divided into two parts, the first of which contains a narrative for the period covered and the second our findings as to the services provided in that period. Finally in Chapter 19 we summarize our findings and list our main conclusions. Among the various appendices are charts showing the organizational structures of the health visiting and social services, and a table which can be extended whilst the report is being read[1] which shows who was supplying services at various points in time.

11. Although the preparation and presentation of material was the responsibility of the Treasury Solicitor's Department and those whom they instructed, all of the other arrangements for the holding of the Inquiry and for the preparation of this report were the responsibility of our Secretary, Mr G. E. Grimstone, his assistant, Miss Hackworth, and the other members of his staff. They carried out their duties to perfection and we thank them all, especially Mr Grimstone whose efforts have been tireless and who has done everything possible to ease our task.

Summary and conclusions

250. During the years from 1965 to 1974 the Auckland family received much help from many persons and many agencies. For most of the time the people and the agencies who helped the family did all that could possibly be expected of them, but ... there were occasions when in our view the service given to the family faltered. It may be that if there had been fewer faults the life of one child could have been saved, but no one fault, or combination of faults, can be said to have been of paramount importance, and many of the faults were

---

[1] See Appendix E, p. 277.

peculiar to one individual or one set of circumstances, so nothing of any value would be achieved by simply listing again here what we think went wrong. However it is our view that certain lessons can be learnt from the matters which we have been asked to investigate which might help to improve the quality of the service given by various agencies to other families in the future. Some of the suggestions we make may be novel, but many of them are well known principles of the various disciplines to which they apply,[1] and are only worth re-stating because our Inquiry has shown that on occasions they are overlooked. There is no order of priority to be found in what follows, but the points are made under sub-headings which in most cases indicate the agency or service to which they particularly apply.

On discharge from prison

251. Where a prisoner is discharged who has been serving a sentence for an offence against a child we would like to see more information passed to agencies outside the prison so that they may be aware of any potential risk and take steps to guard against it. At present there is a better passage of information when a prisoner is discharged on licence or is to receive voluntary after-care, but we would like to see information passing in every case. Subject to further investigation by those more intimately involved, we suggest:

From the prison welfare service

i. The probation service in the area where the discharged prisoner is expected to reside should be sent a full report containing enough information to allow the relevant social services department to assess any risk to a child that might arise. If there has been any information passed from the prison medical service to the general practitioner that fact could also be stated, and the general practitioner could be identified, but to respect medical confidentiality there need be no indication of the nature of the information given.

---

[1] For example so far as the social services are concerned, the British Association of Social Workers (BASW) has published in the 4 September 1975 issue of *BASW News*, a code of practice covering children at risk cases in which many sound and existing principles may be found.

ii.   A brief intimation to the social services department in the relevant
      area that the prisoner is about to be discharged into their area and
      that a report has been made to the probation service.

From the prison medical service

The general practitioner who is expected to have charge of the prisoner
after discharge should be sent:

i.   a copy of any substantial medical report upon the prisoner
      which has been prepared or obtained whilst he has been in
      custody;

ii.   details of any major events in the prisoner's medical history
      whilst in custody . . .

We understand that at present there is normally only contact between the
prison medical service and the general practitioner if the prisoner is ill
when discharged or if there is a course of treatment to be continued after
discharge.

Hospital medical staff

Contact with general practitioners

252. We consider that when a patient is referred to a consultant by a
      general practitioner or another consultant it should be the duty of
      the consultant to whom the patient is referred to notify the general
      practitioner, either directly or via the referring consultant, if he loses
      contact with the patient, and he should have adequate secretarial
      help to enable him to do so.

253. When a consultant to whom a patient has been referred reports back
      to a general practitioner we consider that he should do so in terms
      which the general practitioner can reasonably be expected to
      understand. . . .

Contact with social services

254. We consider that doctors working in hospitals, especially those in
      maternity, paediatric and accident units, should be able to recognize
      evidence of a situation where a child not at present injured may be
      at risk, and when they see such evidence should at once notify the
      social services, probably through the medical social worker. We
      make this comment because in early 1971, when John Roy Auckland
      was born, the social services were not notified by the hospital, by the

medical officer of health or by the health visiting service although the health visitor did know what had happened to the previous child of the family and passed on her knowledge in a report to the paediatrician. The paediatrician concerned, and other professional witnesses who appeared before us, told us they would feel free to pass on information necessary to safeguard a child, so we are satisfied that in this case the duty of confidentiality was sensibly interpreted and did not give rise to any problem.

General practitioners

Records

255. We consider that a general practitioner should keep a proper record in relation to each patient, noting when the patient is seen at the surgery or at home, and adding to the record any other information which may be relevant to future diagnosis or treatment (e.g. that a particular patient has killed his child). With the record should be kept all documents which may be relevant in the future (e.g. reports from hospital consultants or the Regional Medical Service), so that if another doctor has to treat the patient he can, by referring to the record and its ancillary documents, obtain all the information about the patient which he needs to know.

256. Furthermore we consider that when a general practitioner sees a patient, who is registered with one of the members of the practice in which the practitioner is operating, the record of the patient and the ancillary documents should normally be available for consultation. A doctor who has not previously encountered a particular patient should not normally act in relation to that patient without reference to the records. We appreciate that records can easily be made available where a practice operates only from one surgery, or where it operates an appointments system; but we have been told[1] that in many practices records are kept centrally, there are branch surgeries, and there is no appointments system, so it is not practical for the doctor to refer to the records of a patient who attends at a branch surgery. If this situation is widespread then it seems to us that reform is urgently needed, because records are only of value if they are available for consultation. To quote one example given to

---

[1] By the Medical Protection Society and the Medical Defence Union.

us, there can be little point in recording that a patient has a violent reaction if treated with penicillin, and then not having the record available when the possibility of treating him with penicillin recurs.

Patients incapable of work

257. Unless a general practitioner is satisfied that his patient is incapable of work we consider that he should not go on issuing certificates to that effect. We appreciate that if a general practitioner refuses to certify that a patient is incapable of work that may provoke a semi-public argument with a patient, and waste time when other patients are waiting to be seen, but it is easy for a general practitioner to pass to someone else the burden of saying that a certificate shall not be issued by making his doubts about the patient known to the Department of Health and Social Security's Divisional Medical Officer; for further information about a patient's clinical condition the general practitioner can refer the patient to a consultant. If a patient claims to be receiving treatment as an out-patient at hospital, and the general practitioner receives no communication from the hospital for a considerable period of time he should contact the hospital to find out what is going on.

258. When a general practitioner receives an enquiry from a Divisional Medical Officer as to his patient's present condition and fitness to undergo a medical examination he should respond fully to the enquiry, and should if necessary consult the patient's record before doing so. If a Regional Medical Service examination takes place, the general practitioner should consider carefully any information he receives from the examining medical officer of the Regional Medical Service so as to check the information given to the officer by the patient, and also so as to increase his own knowledge of the patient and his condition. The examining officer may have been able to obtain information of which the general practitioner was unaware, and may have made some diagnosis or recommendation which merits consideration.

Liaison with other agencies

259. We consider that there should be close contact between the general practitioner and any health visitor working in the practice area.[1] In

---

[1] We appreciate that the vast majority (79%) of health visitors are now attached to general practices and we welcome this.

addition a general practitioner should be aware of the existence and responsibilities of other agencies, such as the social services, the probation service, and the NSPCC.[1] We consider that a general practitioner should be able to recognize evidence of a situation where a child might be at risk, and should not hesitate to notify either a health visitor, or the social services, or both, if he finds evidence of that kind.

Regional medical service

260. At present examining officers of the Department of Health and Social Security's Regional Medical Service complete an examination form which they send to the Divisional Medical Officer, and write (on another form) to the general practitioner. We consider that it would assist the general practitioner if he were to receive a copy of the document which goes to the Divisional Medical Officer. The general practitioner would then know what his patient was recorded as saying, everything found upon examination, and the examiner's conclusions. This would enable a conscientious general practitioner to increase his own knowledge of the patient and his condition, and it would also enable him to advise the Regional Medical Service if at some point the examining officer was misled. If the examining officer wishes to pass certain information to the Divisional Medical Officer and not to the general practitioner, that information could be written only on the copy of the document sent to the Divisional Medical Officer (perhaps in a space provided for that purpose) or in a separate document.

Social services

Procedure on opening a case file

261. We consider that if a social services department is notified of a family where a child may be at risk the matter should be considered initially at a level not below that of a senior social worker who is a team leader. A check should be made to see if the social services

---

[1] The general practitioner's terms of service require him to refer patients as necessary to other services provided under the Health Service Acts and to give advice to his patients to enable them to take advantage of local authority social services.

have any file in relation to the family in any area where the family is known to have resided, and the social worker to whom the matter is assigned should at once look for and establish contact with other sources of relevant information (e.g. the probation service if it has been involved, the health visiting service, the general practitioner, etc.). Once contact is established it should be maintained and the social worker should regard it as a duty to give information as well as to receive it. She[1] should also be constantly alert to new sources of information (e.g. temporary foster mothers). Care should be taken to ensure that no error creeps into information being received or transmitted (e.g. the suggestion that Mrs Barbara Auckland was partially responsible for the death of Marianne). An error which becomes a part of the record can have a far-reaching effect on future attitudes to a family's problems.

262. So far as possible a social worker with responsibility for supporting a family where a child may be at risk should be qualified and experienced in that work ... and should have a case load which permits frequent visiting. She should be alive to the danger of being over-impressed by good housekeeping or a glib tongue. She should not over identify with one member of a family or one faction in a family. She should be constantly looking for signs of violent behaviour ... such as drunken brawls or bruised children. The violence of Mr John Auckland to his family in October 1972 seems to have passed almost unnoticed, and even after a second child died a social worker failed to observe obvious bruising on the face of a child who survived.

Records

263. We consider that once a file has been opened everything done in relation to a family should be recorded legibly on the file (e.g. all contacts or attempted contacts with the family, all contacts by whichever means with other agencies even if the contact is fruitless, all case reviews, and all decisions taken in relation to the family or any member of it). If information is received in relation to the family it should be passed to the social worker in contact with the family and should then go on to the file .... As a result the file should constitute a full record available to any social worker required to take over the case, and no part of it should be lost. ...

---

[1] We use 'she' for convenience to refer to social workers of either sex both here and later.

Supervision

264. At regular intervals, the case file of a family where a child may be at risk should be read by a senior social worker, who should then discuss the case with the social worker responsible and initial the file. On each occasion the social worker and the senior social worker should be considering the problems and needs of the family; the work to be undertaken by the social worker; the frequency of visits; and, of paramount importance, if there is any cause for anxiety about the safety of the child, they should consider the possibility of initiating care proceedings. In the context of this case there should have been recognized as causes for anxiety matters such as the birth of a child into a family whose only previous child had been killed by one of the parents, the serious scalding of a young child in such a family, any display of violence by a parent known to have been violent previously to a child, and any situation where such a parent was in sole charge of a child. In deciding whether or not to initiate care proceedings where there is cause for anxiety and where the child is in the care of one parent only, the social worker and the senior social worker should normally seek the views of both parents, and should not normally withhold information from either parent except for good reason. They should also seek the views of other agencies involved with the family, such as the health visiting service, and should not rely upon any other agency doing anything for the family without first obtaining an assurance from the agency that it will do what is expected of it (c.f. the false assumption that the Auckland family would be visited regularly by a health visitor which was said to be relied upon when it was decided to discharge Susan from care). Once there is a cause for anxiety a social worker should immediately inform her senior social worker, and no decision about care proceedings should be taken below senior social worker or even perhaps area officer level.

When a family moves

265. If a family moves out of a social services area, the social worker responsible for the family should make an accurate summary of the case ... and the file should then be transferred at senior social worker level, with an entry upon it recording the transfer and the persons involved. The recipient should then read the file before assigning it to a new social worker. Where other agencies are involved with the family those agencies should be informed of the move.

Closing a file

266. We consider that the decision to close a file or to render it inactive should not be taken by anyone below the level of senior social worker, and the decision and the reasons for it should be recorded on the file.

Health visiting service

Assignment

267. We consider that a health visitor responsible for a family where a child may be at risk must so organize her work as to give that family a considerable degree of priority. If necessary it must have attention at the expense of others, but there does come a point when the burden of work upon a health visitor is so heavy that little if any of her work is likely to be done properly, and we were very troubled to hear of the case-load which . . . a newly qualified health visitor, was expected to carry.[1] It seems to us that somehow the burden should be eased,[2] either by providing others to help or by relieving health visitors of some of their present duties.

268. A health visitor to whom a family with problems is assigned must be properly briefed in relation to that family. She must know the problem and what is expected of her in terms of visiting and reporting beyond the care she is expected to give to every young child. . . .

Records at field level

269. A health visitor should record every contact or attempted contact with each child on that child's card, and, if the child moves out of the health visitor's area, every effort should be made to find out where the child has gone, so that as soon as possible the record card and all other relevant documents can be officially transferred to a health visitor in the new area. If the child cannot be traced, the appropriate Nursing Officer should be told.

---

[1] Miss E covered a population of 10,000: DHSS circular 13/72 states that a ratio of one health visitor to 3,000 population may be desirable in certain areas in contrast to the Jameson Report in 1956 recommending a ratio of one to 4,300.

[2] The team work now developing in primary health care may help in this respect; teams often comprise health visitors, Registered Nurses, and State Enrolled Nurses, and may also include social workers.

Liaison with other agencies

270. It is the health visitor's duty to seek the assistance of the social services or the general practitioner or both if she sees a situation in which this is necessary. And once a social worker or a doctor does become involved we consider that there should be an effective liaison established, involving a ready exchange of information and if possible a plan of visiting.

Supervision

271. The monthly reporting system initiated by Miss M. in relation to families with problems did provide a useful way of checking that those families were being effectively supervised, and we consider that some such check is desirable.

272. We are also of the opinion that the quality of a health visitor's service is likely to be improved if she is in regular personal contact with her immediate superior and her colleagues, and is not left to operate entirely on her own.

General

Care proceedings

273. A social worker who considers that care proceedings should be initiated must first satisfy herself that a court is likely to make the order which she seeks, because if it does not do so her relationship with the family can be jeopardized. She must therefore know precisely what the court will be looking for when deciding whether or not to make an order, and she will not find that easy to discover by looking at the Children and Young Persons Act 1969. Furthermore, we consider that the relevant section of the Act is so worded that the matters upon which the court will be focusing its attention will not always be those which appear material to a responsible social worker who has to consider whether, in relation to a particular case, an order is desirable. We would like to see this situation changed.

Funds for training wives

274. Despite a positive recommendation from a High Court Judge that Mrs Barbara Auckland should receive some training in household management, and despite the existence of suitable training facilities,

she only received training because a conscientious probation officer managed, by dogged persistence and with local help, to raise some funds for her. In general we avoid suggestions which involve additional public expenditure, but in this limited field it seems to us desirable that something should be done to make funds more readily available, especially where one child has already died and other children in the future may benefit from any training that is received.

Manpower

275. Our Inquiry demonstrates that in more than one service in the relevant geographical area there was a shortage of suitably qualified and experienced staff. Some staff had to carry excessive case loads, but a more serious problem was that some staff were required to undertake work beyond their competence. This disturbing situation seems to have arisen largely as a result of the responsibilities of the various services being increased by the passing of legislation and by the arousal of public expectations without adequate regard being paid to local and national manpower resources.

Re-organization

276. We recognise that those who advocate drastic re-organizations in public services often foresee great benefits, and sometimes great benefits do result. But there is also nearly always great disruption, which careful planning may reduce but cannot eliminate. The disruption, although well-known, is rarely emphasized, but in this case it almost certainly contributed to depriving a child of supervision and support that were literally vital.

Appendix A

Representation of Parties

Parties	*Representatives*
The Committee	Mr D. Herrod, Q.C. and Mr J. Deby instructed by the Treasury Solicitor.
Barnsley Metropolitan District Council	Mr P. M. Baker, Q.C. and Mr A. Goldsack instructed by Mr D. P. Clephan.
Medical Defence Union on behalf of the general practice	Mr M. Baker instructed by Messrs Hempsons.

South Yorkshire Probation and After-Care Service

Mr M. Adam.

Trent Regional Health Authority and Barnsley Area Health Authority and those health visitors concerned with the Auckland family before 1 April 1974

Mr R. Maxwell instructed by Mr Griggs.

Mr John Auckland

Mr H. Hanbury-Sparrow instructed by Messrs Mills, Kemp and Brown.

Mrs Barbara Auckland

Mr T. Hartley instructed by Messrs Dib and Clegg.

Appendix B

A. Witnesses examined before the committee

Social Services
Mrs Angela Baines
Mr Carel Carlson
Mr James Cole
Mr Douglas Drane
Mr Geoffrey Dunn
Miss Joan Ebo
Mr Geoffrey Hall
Mr David Hart
Mr Philip Hudson
Mr Philip Hughes

Mr Timothy Jones
Mr Martin Nurcombe
Mr David Parkin
Mrs Carol Phillips
Miss Mary Prout
Miss Mary Ryan
Mrs Judith Sewell
Mr George Simpson
Miss Lilian Wood

Family
Mrs Barbara Auckland
Mr George Auckland
Miss Jennifer Auckland
Mr John Auckland

Mrs Mary Auckland
Mr Michael Beaumont
Mrs Doreen Nunn
Mrs Eileen Wilson

Foster Parents
Mrs Anne Brown

Mrs Doreen Harper

Neighbours
Mr Peter Dunhill

Miss Fay Williamson

Probation and After-Care Service
Mr Raymond Tindall

Health Visiting Service
Mrs Nancy Cookson
Miss Rosemary Eagland
Mrs Kathleen Hemsworth
Miss Doris Marsh
Dr Clifford Oddy
Miss Margaret Pilling

Miss Marjorie Sorby
Mrs Jane Sweetnam
Miss Marjorie Thompson
Dr John Walters
Mrs Cynthia Wilson

Medical Services
Dr Michael Beasley
Dr Kenneth Blyth
Dr Ajmal Khan
Dr Harold Lee

Dr Eileen O'Neill
Dr James Orr
Dr Herbert Murray Park

B. Statements read before the committee

The Family
Mrs Anne Beaumont

Mrs Helen Marsden

Neighbours
The Reverend Myles Bebbington
Mrs Betty Broadhead
Mrs Nora Brook
Mrs Christine Dunhill
Mrs Lilly Fowell

Mrs Doreen Greenfield
Mrs Ethel Wilmott
Mr James Wilmott
Mrs Ruth Wilmott

Probation and After-Care Service
Mrs Hilda Horbury

Department of Health and Social Security
Mr Reginald Hill

Mr Peter Wells

Social Services
Mr Jack Armitage
Mrs June Bedford
Mrs Hilary Clarke (née Hilton)

Mr Gerald Parkin
Mr Stanley Wheater

Health Visiting Service
Miss Shirley Abbott
Dr Peter Brewin
Miss Mary Gooddy
Mrs Alice Harston

Mr Alexander Mitchell
Mrs Joyce Rose
Mrs Kathleen Rowe
Miss Ann Senior

Medical Services
Dr Martin Fiddian   Dr Alan Usher
Dr Edward Lyons

Miscellaneous
The British Association of Social   Mr Lawrence Whitfield (NCB)
    Workers (2 Memoranda)   Mr William Elliott (NSPCC)
Police Inspector Mary Thomas

Appendix C

Documents considered by the committee

The documents listed below relate to either Mr John Auckland or his family unless otherwise indicated.

Barnsley District General Hospital: case papers

Barnsley Juvenile Court: miscellaneous papers

Barnsley Metropolitan District Council Social Services Department: case papers

Barnsley Metropolitan District Council Social Services Department: miscellaneous papers including guides to standard practice

Barnsley Magistrates' Court: miscellaneous papers

Barnsley Police: extracts from files

British Association of Social Workers: code of practice

Cawthorne Building Services Limited: work record

Council for Education and Training of Health Visitors: miscellaneous papers

Crown Court Leeds: certificate of conviction

Crown Court Sheffield: miscellaneous papers

Department of Health and Social Security: circulars and guidance

Department of Health and Social Security: Divisional Medical Officer's papers

Department of Health and Social Security: medical certificates

Department of Health and Social Security: social security case papers and correspondence

General practice: medical records

Health visiting service: case papers

Health visiting service: recommended procedures and miscellaneous papers

HM Prison Durham: miscellaneous papers including medical records

HM Prison Leeds: miscellaneous papers including medical records

Home Office: circulars and guidance

Kendray Hospital, Barnsley: case papers

London Borough of Hounslow Social Services Department: miscellaneous papers

National Coal Board: work record

Probation and After-Care Service: miscellaneous correspondence

Probation and After-Care Service: records of supervision and contact

Statutes: relevant Acts and Statutory Instruments

West Riding County Council Social Services Department: Barnsley Division case papers

West Riding County Council Social Services Department: Pontefract Division case papers

West Riding County Council Social Services Department: miscellaneous papers including guides to standard practice

West Riding County Fire Service: record of fire dated 30 March 1974.

Appendix D

Note on relevant statute law relating to care proceedings

As far as our immediate interests are concerned, relevant sections of statute law relating to care proceedings are as follows:

Children and Young Persons Act 1963

S2(1) A child or young person is in need of care, protection or control within the meaning of this Act if—
    a.   any of the conditions mentioned in subsection (2) of this section is satisfied with respect to him, and he is not receiving such care, protection and guidance as a good parent may reasonably be expected to give

(2) The conditions referred to in subsection (1)(*a*) of this section are that—

   a.   the lack of care, protection or guidance is likely to cause him unnecessary suffering or seriously to affect his health or proper development, or

   b.   any of the offences mentioned in Schedule 1 to the principal Act has been committed in respect of him or in respect of a child or young person who is a member of the same household, or

   c.   he is a member of the same household as a person who has been convicted of such an offence in respect of a child or young person.

The principal Act referred to in the above subsections is the Children and Young Persons Act 1933 and Schedule 1 to that Act in its list of offences against children or young persons includes the murder or manslaughter of a child or young person.

As from 1 January 1971 the above section of the 1963 Act was repealed and there was substituted:

Children and Young Persons Act 1969

S1(1) Any local authority, constable, or authorized person who reasonably believes that there are grounds for making an order under this section in respect of a child or young person may . . . bring him before a juvenile court.

(2) If the court before which a child or young person is brought under this section is of opinion that any of the following conditions is satisfied with respect to him, that is to say—

   a.   his proper development is being avoidably prevented or neglected or his health is being avoidably impaired or neglected or he is being ill-treated; or

   b.   it is probable that the condition set out in the preceding paragraph will be satisfied in his case having regard to the fact that the Court or another court has found that that condition is or was satisfied in the case of another child or young person who is or was a member of the household to which he belongs and also that he is in need of care or control which he is unlikely to receive unless the court makes an order under this section in respect of him then . . . the court may if it thinks fit make such an order.

(orders that can possibly be made include a supervision order or a care order.)

In the case of *Surrey County Council v. S and others*, both the Divisional Court ((1973) 2WLR 649) on 2 February 1973 and the Court of Appeal ((1973) 3 All ER 1074) on 30 July 1973 have considered S.1(2)(b) of the 1969 Act, and it has been decided that the Juvenile Court before which care proceedings are brought is itself competent to make a finding that a previous child suffered as in S.1(2)(a) whether or not a previous court has found likewise.

Appendix E

Individuals providing services

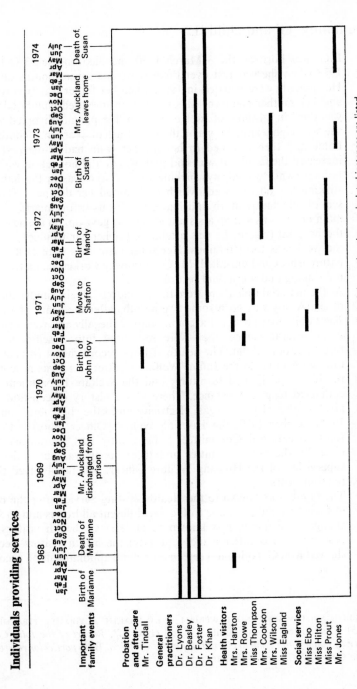

Note Supervisory staff are not shown and only those supplying services over a period of time rather than on isolated instances are listed.

277

The family 'G' and child 'L'

5.   L.G. was born on the 3 March 1970 and died on the 23 October 1973 when she was just over three years and seven months old.

6.   Her parents were married in 1967, when her father was twenty-one and her mother eighteen. Mrs G. had an unsettled childhood: she was third in a family of twelve children, her parents divorced when she was eight, and she spent three and a half years in a children's home and then returned to her mother, who had re-married and increased the family. It was said that Mrs G. did not get on with her mother, who 'was always picking on her' and was in the habit of striking her on the head, which had caused her deafness. She left school reluctantly at 16 and had several jobs before marriage: the main one was as a shop assistant which she gave up, on the advice of the hospital (where she was attending for her ear trouble) because the work was too strenuous. Her subsequent jobs were of a casual nature, short and unskilled. Mr G., a railway worker, had a troubled upbringing and a criminal record.

7.   At the material time there were three children, all girls under the age of six. A boy was born some five months after the death of L.

8.   The family first occupied accommodation illegally and were evicted. After several moves, they were re-housed into a self-contained three-bedroomed flat. The health visitors' record shows visits at this time by Mrs G. to the Infant Welfare Centre; there was no cot for the baby and limited furniture; and the Welfare Department was contacted to give assistance. There was a history of constant rent arrears, also of unpaid gas, electricity and other bills until, on the 19 November 1970, the Housing Welfare Officer reported to the Rent Arrears Sub-Committee. Subsequently rent guarantees were given by the Sub-Committee and the tenancy was put under the supervision of the Housing Welfare Officer. The family lived there for four years.

9.   The family was known to the Health Visiting Service after the birth of their first child but due to the five different addresses and to staff changes, the family was known to at least six health visitors. In November 1969 (after a move in July) the health visitors' record showed Mrs G. failing to keep an ante-natal appointment on account

LAMBETH, SOUTHWARK AND LEWISHAM AREA HEALTH AUTHORITY (TEACHING) (1975) 'Case history of the family 'G' and child 'L''. *Report of the Joint Committee of Inquiry into Non-Accidental Injury to Children. With particular reference to the Case of L.G.*, pp. 4–12, paras. 5–71.

of illness and the first visit made to Mrs G. on the 16 March 1970, following the birth of L. on the 3 March. After the birth of L., marital difficulties were noted; Mrs G. suspected her husband of infidelity and there were frequent quarrels. Mrs G. left home with the two children, to live with her sister, although Mr G. maintained her voluntarily until September 1970, after which she obtained a separation order (with maintenance) in November 1970. In the meantime, Mr G. had left home and was staying with friends and Mrs G. and the two children moved back into the home. At Christmas 1970 the G.'s were reconciled and Mr G. moved back into the home. During his absence, Mrs G. had been supported by payments from the Department of Health and Social Security. After his return to the home, there was a heavy accumulation of debts and, because of substantial arrears of rent, notice to quit had been given.

10. With her husband's apparent connivance, Mrs G. failed to notify the Department of his return and of his regular employment and in a joint effort to clear outstanding debts (which by December 1971 they had succeeded in doing) continued to draw the social security benefit. It was for this offence that Mrs G. was prosecuted and placed on probation on the 31 July 1972. (See paragraph 14.)

11. Both Mr and Mrs G. had seen the Family Practitioner 'for nerves'. Mrs G. was again pregnant. The eldest child's name had been entered for a playgroup. L., who had been seen by the Health Visitor in October 1970, had a history of bronchitis and was recorded as 'still being rather chesty'. The Housing Welfare Officer was now visiting regularly, supervising because of the rent arrears.

12. By April 1971, the rent arrears which had accumulated during Mr G.'s absence had been reported to the Social Services Directorate, who notified the Health Visiting Service. By the 9 September 1971 the rent was being paid and the arrears were being paid off; Mr G. had left home and returned again; and on the 18 September the youngest girl was born.

13. In November 1971, bad relations existed with their neighbours and Court proceedings for assault ensued. These problems continued and in February 1973 further assaults were reported and the Probation Service was involved with both families. Complaints were made about dampness in the walls of the house to the Health Visitor who referred the question of a transfer to the Housing Directorate. The Family Practitioner had recommended that Mrs G. should live on the ground floor and the family were in the top priority housing list. This was the G. family situation when Mrs G. became the responsibility of the Inner London Probation and After-Care Service.

14. Mrs G. had appeared before a London Magistrates' Court on the 3 July 1972, charged with an offence of defrauding the Department

of Health and Social Security by continuing to draw benefit to which she was not entitled after her husband had returned to the home while in regular employment and she was remanded on bail for a social inquiry report. When Mrs G. reappeared in Court on 31 July she was placed on probation for two years.

15. A probation officer was assigned to the case and Mrs G. reported to her for the first time on the 16 August 1972, when it was agreed that she should report on a fortnightly basis.

16. On the 1 September 1972, the Probation Officer telephoned the Welfare Centre, informed the Health Visitor of the probation order, and discussed accommodation, child minding and L. with the Health Visitor, who said she would visit the home. The health visitor's record mentions an application for a free playgroup place and contact being made with the Housing Welfare Officer regarding the possibility of a transfer.

17. In October 1972, Mrs G. told the Probation Officer about problems with the neighbours and that Mr G. was involved in assault proceedings. By the 28 October the two older children had been given places in a playgroup and Mrs G. had heard from the Council that the family would be rehoused, possibly just after Christmas.

18. In early November the Health Visitor recorded that the Playgroup Leader had noticed the children had bruising occasionally but on the 17 November, when the Health Visitor visited the home, no bruising was seen. The matter, however, was reported to the Area Nursing Officer, and the case was discussed with the Area Co-ordinator of the Social Services Directorate.

19. On the 8 November Mrs G. told the Probation Officer about an injury to L.'s head which she said had arisen from a fall and that she was going to see the doctor about it. At this time Mrs G. was very depressed about a number of things: the Court case concerning neighbours, the urgent wish to be rehoused, the pressure from Social Security to repay the benefit wrongfully claimed and fears about her own health for which she was attending hospital as an outpatient. The Probation Officer expressed concern about these problems. In December the hospital discharged Mrs G. as nothing abnormal was found. She and her husband had turned down an offer by the Council of alternative accommodation as unsuitable and, as this was the second refusal, she thought they would have to wait a long time.

20. On the 11 December 1972, L. was admitted to hospital suffering from a cyst on the bladder. She was operated on and discharged on Christmas Eve.

21. On the 10 January 1973, the Outpatients' Clinic at the same hospital recorded an attendance by L. when a further appointment three months hence was given. Not until October 1973 was it disclosed to the

Social Services Directorate that, in the previous January, bruising of the pelvic area had been observed.

22. On the 16 January 1973, the Probation Officer visited the home. Mrs G. said she felt guilty at smacking L. for wetting when she was ill. The child seemed to have regressed since the operation and was wetting and soiling herself; and Mrs G. asked the Probation Officer about the possibility of a holiday for her. The Family Practitioner was recommending that they should be given ground floor accommodation. Later on this day (stated in the health visitors' record to be the 17 January), when the Probation Officer telephoned the Infant Welfare Centre and spoke to the duty Health Visitor, the Probation Officer expressed her concern about Mrs G.'s health although a hospital had, a month earlier, found nothing wrong and had discharged her.

23. The duty Health Visitor was recorded by the Probation Officer as saying, after referring to the file, that the health visitors were seriously concerned as the two children were coming to the Playgroup bearing bruises; and that a watch was being kept on them as the Service was conscious of the needs of parents with 'battered babies'. The duty Health Visitor suggested that, on the following Monday, the Probation Officer should speak to the regular Health Visitor who knew the case.

24. The health visitors' record of the 17 January 1973 noted a message from the Probation Officer regarding Mrs G.'s concern about L.'s stumbling (which had also been observed by the staff at the Playgroup) with the suggestion by the Probation Officer for a recuperative holiday. It was recorded that the information had been passed to the Social Services Directorate.

25. On the same day the duty officer of the Social Services Directorate recorded a telephone call from the Probation Officer saying that the family might be in need of help as there was a history of bruising amongst the children and that the Health Visitor and Probation Officer were in touch with the family and were arranging a recuperative holiday. The family was known to the Housing Welfare Section as a rent arrears case. The case was then passed to an Area team of the Social Services Directorate for further investigation.

26. The 17 January was also significant to the Probation Officer in the way she used her relationship with Mrs G. who, in the course of a long conversation which included reference to the relationship with her own mother, disclosed her feelings about L. and how she felt the child provoked her to lose her temper and to hit her. This had on occasion caused trouble with her husband.

27. On the 22 January the Probation Officer spoke to the regular Health Visitor who confirmed that they had been concerned for some time

about Mrs G., that the Social Services were also involved because of the state of the children and that there were rent arrears. On the 26 January there was contact with the family by the Health Visitor who noted that the child had been unsteady on her feet on discharge from the hospital but was improving.

28. On this day also and on the following day, there were contacts between the Probation Officer and staff of the Social Services Directorate, who referred the Probation Officer to the Housing Directorate (which she followed up) and to the Medical Officer of Health regarding the recuperative holiday. From these contacts the Probation Officer learned that Mrs G. was being allocated to a Social Services caseworker, as yet unnamed. The Probation Officer discussed this with her Senior who agreed that she should make known her own situation with regard to casework for Mrs G. and that the Probation Officer should increase her contact with this mother to at least once weekly.

29. By the 30 January, from her records, the Probation Officer appeared not to be accepting at face value all Mrs G. was saying about a big improvement in the children. On the 31 January the Probation Officer discussed the suggested holiday for Mrs G. and the children with the local authority officer concerned with recuperative holidays, referring to Mrs G.'s hope that the children alone could be sent. On being told that this would mean the children being received into care, the Probation Officer said she would discuss it further with Mrs G.

30. On the 1 February Mrs G. told the Probation Officer that she had lost her temper again and struck her neighbour and proceedings for assault were being brought against her. She had seen the Family Practitioner and told him of her losses of temper and her hitting out at the children and he had changed her tablets. He was alleged to have told her that if she wanted the children taken away they would have to go into care and there might be difficulty in getting them back. Mrs G. was therefore trying to arrange for them to have a holiday through the Railway Welfare Board and her husband was seeing about this. Mrs G. therefore withdrew her request for a recuperative holiday.

31. On the same day the Social Worker (later known to have been a trainee) informed the Probation Officer that she had been assigned to the case following a case conference. In the discussion about the family, the Probation Officer mentioned that Mrs G. was beginning to talk about her battering of the children. Reference was made to the holiday now being arranged for the family, to the problems with the neighbours and to the Probation Officer's view that rehousing would help the family. Apart from this, the Probation Officer did

not envisage any other social work. She reported that she was in contact weekly. In discussing the case the Probation Officer took the view that a significant stage had been reached and that the involvement of another worker might be unwise. She would nevertheless refer to the Social Services Directorate when there were any local authority matters to discuss. At this, the Trainee Social Worker said she would keep the file open but take no further action for the moment but, after discussion of the case with her Senior, it was decided to seek an appointment with the Probation Officer to discuss the matter. The Senior Social Worker telephoned the Probation Officer and in the course of a frank exchange, the latter took the view that she should be the worker to give casework support, but he felt nevertheless that his Directorate still had a clear responsibility as the child could be at risk and that a meeting should be arranged. The Senior Social Worker therefore, on the 12 February 1973, caused the Trainee Social Worker to write to the Probation Officer expressing concern about the family and suggesting this. Before the letter was sent, the Probation Officer herself telephoned to report a deterioration in the domestic situation and the two workers met that day to discuss the case.

32. The Probation Officer had been pressing the Housing Directorate regarding the request to be rehoused and, during this meeting, the Social Worker agreed to speak to her Senior about a case conference as requested by the Probation Officer. The Social Services record of this discussion is of considerable length, covering most aspects of the family's background and history as revealed by the Probation Officer, including her knowledge of the bruising of the children reported by the Health Visitor in the course of the Probation Officer's inquiry of the 16 January 1973, and Mrs G.'s mixed feelings about L.

33. On the following day, the 13 February, the Probation Officer understood from the Trainee Social Worker that a case conference could be arranged, but she was not sure that the Housing Directorate would be represented. The Probation Officer's reaction was that, if this were so, there could be no point in having the conference; but she agreed to discuss the case with the Senior Social Worker who, in the course of the subsequent conversation, said he would speak to the Housing Directorate himself and telephone her again.

34. On the 15 February the Senior Social Worker told the Probation Officer of his discussion with the Area Housing Officer, who had agreed that the family should be rehoused as soon as possible and had asked for copies of the relevant correspondence to be sent to her, which the Probation Officer sent on the following day.

35. On the 22 February the Trainee Social Worker recorded that apparently two offers of accommodation had been made to the family

which had been refused. The Senior Social Worker, having telephoned the Probation Officer, who was then thinking that no case conference would be necessary, wrote on the 23 February to her seeking her views in writing on the further involvement of the Social Services Directorate with the family as soon as possible, so that the future role of the Directorate with this family could be determined. During the period of February and March the Health Visitor recorded that Mrs G. was not a clinic attender and did not seek her support, but that Mrs G. always chatted freely to her. The Health Visitor felt that this mother was receiving regular social work support so her visits were of a routine nature.

36. On the 7 March the Probation Officer replied to the Senior Social Worker, thanking him for his efforts regarding rehousing, mentioning some improvement in the relations with neighbours and saying that she would continue to see Mrs G. frequently and regularly and that there was therefore no need for Social Services to be involved any further. No reference to this letter appears in the Probation Officer's records, neither is there any record of any prior consultation with the Senior Probation Officer about the significance of this step to the future relationship between the probation services and the social services. No reference is made in the Probation Officer's quarterly assessment to this or to the possibility of 'battering' taking place.

37. On the 14 March Mrs G. reported to the Probation Officer on difficulties with the Housing Department about the latest arrears of rent impeding their rehousing; and the Probation Officer agreed to help by taking the matter up with the Area Housing Officer, which she did over the following three weeks.

38. On the 19 March the Probation Officer visited and noticed bruising on L.'s face but recorded no explanation of it. On the 23 March the Playgroup Leader reported to the Health Visitor the bruising of L. seen on that day and she was referred to the Social Services Directorate: there is no information of any other action or response by the Health Visiting Service or any entry in their records. On the instructions of the Senior Social Worker, the Probation Officer was informed and said that she had noticed bruising on her last visit but that Mrs G. was not very forthcoming about it. The Probation Officer noted in her records the information from the Playgroup; her reaction was to contact the Housing Directorate that day. On the same day, when the Probation Officer was able to speak to the Area Housing Officer, she told her of the reports of the children being illtreated and the Area Housing Officer said she would try to rush things through.

39. On the 28 March Mrs G. reported to the Probation Officer to the

effect that things were improving but that she had lost her temper again and had swiped L. across the face. She said that the child bruised very easily and that she (the mother) was scared that somebody might find out.

40. In the first week of April the family were rehoused and Mrs G. informed the Probation Officer on the 10 April that things were going well. She reported to the same effect on the 25 April but also that L. had had a bad fall and had bumped her head again although she now seemed to be all right. Mrs G. asked about the prospects of full time nursery places for the children so that she could go out to work to help with the family finances as their rent had now increased. They were talking of going to a holiday camp and were looking forward to this.

41. On the 7 May Mrs G. reported that things were going very badly: the children were playing up, she doubted if she could cope any more and she wanted L. sent away. She said that L. seemed deliberately to provoke her and that she had taken to striking the child again. The Probation Officer responded to this by asking Mrs G. whether she thought the Child Guidance Clinic could help by finding out why L. behaved in this way and by helping her (the mother) to understand, so that she could cope with the child better. Mrs G. did not like the idea at first but gave a half-hearted assent. The Probation Officer called next day (the 8 May), intending to follow up the suggestion of the Child Guidance Clinic, but Mrs G.'s attitude had changed and she said, in front of the child, that she wanted L. sent away. The Probation Officer tried to advise her about the difficulties of this but Mrs G. did not respond and although the Probation Officer said she would call again next day, the atmosphere between them was cool.

42. Mrs G. saw her Family Practitioner in May and told him about her family history and deafness (see paragraph 6).

43. On the 9 May, when the Probation Officer called, Mrs G. told her with an air of triumph that the children were going to the Railway Children's Home at Woking. It transpired that L. and her oldest sister were going, the youngest staying at home with Mrs G. The Probation Officer again mentioned the Child Guidance Clinic but Mrs G. did not think it would help. On the 15 May the two older children were away at the Home. Mrs G. was enjoying the rest and thought she would take advantage of the time to go to hospital for some tests.

44. On the 30 May Mrs G. expressed concern at the possibility of having more children and the Probation Officer suggested attendance at the Family Planning Clinic, to which Mrs G. agreed.

45. On the 8 June, when the Probation Officer was on leave, there was a

285

request for an immediate visit, which the Probation Officer achieved by coming back from leave a day early. The three children were back at home, Mr and Mrs G. having collected them from the Children's Home because they could not afford the charge of nearly £20 a month. Mrs G. said she could no longer afford to stay at home because of increased costs, particularly of food and clothing, and she wanted the Probation Officer to get the children into a day nursery urgently. The Probation Officer asked Mrs G. whether she had herself approached any day nursery or raised the matter with the Health Visitor. She replied that she had made no inquiries and that the Health Visitor was not visiting. There was some discussion as to whether Mrs G. was really strong enough to go out to work, bearing in mind the three children; and although the Probation Officer said she would speak to the Health Visitor, her report expressed some doubt about Mrs G.'s genuineness and motives.

46.   On the 12 June the Trainee Social Worker recorded that it was three months since the Probation Officer's letter of the 7 March (stating that Social Services involvement was unnecessary) and that she had accordingly telephoned the Probation Officer, who told her that Mrs G. had been rehoused and that she still felt Social Services need not be involved. She concurred with the Trainee Social Worker's suggestion that the case be closed. On the 30 June the Senior Social Worker agreed and on the 14 July he transferred the case papers to the office serving the area into which the family had moved with a memorandum recommending the closure of the case; giving the brief facts, including the fact that the family was referred to Social Services because one of the children could be at risk as she appeared at one time to have had severe bruising; and referring to the feeling of the Probation Officer that it was no longer necessary for the Social Services Directorate to remain involved. There was no reference in the probation record to the closing of the case by Social Services, nor in either the Probation Officer's or Social Services' record, to any arrangement having been made for future contact between the two Services.

47.   In the meantime, on the 19 June the Probation Officer spoke to the Playgroup Organiser and then to the Health Visitor about a recommendation for free nursery places. As a result, the Health Visitor called on Mrs G. the same day and told the Probation Officer she had left application forms for nursery places for completion and would keep an eye on the situation and report back to her.

48.   On the 20 June Mrs G. took L. to an Infant Welfare Centre for a routine medical check when the Clinic Doctor is reported to have found the child to be friendly, normal and healthy. Unsteadiness on her feet was not observed nor was it mentioned by Mrs G. and

there is no record of any sign of previous injuries having been found. A statement from the Doctor recalls Mrs G.'s concern to get the child into a day nursery. When discussing this subsequently with the Health Visitor, the Doctor was informed of a 'family history of battering' but this was not pursued and it is not clear from the records whether this referred to the present family or to Mrs G.'s own family upbringing.

49. On the 20 June Mrs G. reported to the Probation Officer and renewed discussions about wanting to go out to work. She also said that the youngest child was now behaving like the other two. The Probation Officer again raised the question of consulting the Child Guidance Clinic which Mrs G. again refused.

50. On the 18 July Mrs G. reported that all the children were playing up and sometimes she did not know what to do with herself—L. was again wetting herself. She asked the Probation Officer if she could arrange for the Health Visitor to visit and the Probation Officer left a message for the Health Visitor at the Infant Welfare Centre. In July the Health Visitor was pressing for admission of the children to the day nursery and places were offered from the 10 September.

51. In August Mrs G. visited the Family Practitioner with L. who had severe bruising and a black eye, said by Mrs G. to have occurred when the child fell down some stone steps two days previously. He had offered Mrs G. the opportunity of having L. x-rayed and he telephoned a hospital for this purpose.

52. On the 1 and the 8 August Mrs G. failed to see the Probation Officer, neither did she attend on the 15 August notwithstanding a letter having been sent to her. On the 21 August she told the Probation Officer of the unbearable relations at home and of her proposed visit to Ireland; that she was pregnant and of her husband's negative attitude to abortion; that he was drinking and illtreating her; that there were rent arrears of £100 and that she felt she must get work to reduce them.

53. On the 4 September Mrs G. failed to keep an appointment and the Probation Officer visited the home on the 5 September. Relations between husband and wife were bad and Mrs G. was talking about going to hospital to see about abortion and sterilisation before going to Ireland and leaving the two younger children there.

54. On the 6 September Mrs G. went to see the Matron of the Day Nursery, vacancies having been offered for the children from the 10 September. Mrs G. explained to the Matron that she needed nursery places for L. and her younger sister so that she could go out to work to clear the rent arrears; and about her intended termination of pregnancy. No background information had been given about L. but,

when the children were admitted on the 17 September, L. was seen to be badly injured and bruised and Mrs G. explained that L. had fallen down the stone steps outside the flats and that, in trying to save her, Mrs G. had accidentally hurt the child's arm. She said the Family Practitioner had seen the child and had said that the shoulder might be 'put out'. The Matron asked Mrs G. to take the child back to the Family Practitioner for a note as to the fitness of L. to attend the Nursery. Instead of going back to the Family Practitioner, Mrs G. took L. that day to a hospital's Accident and Emergency Department where a diagnosis was made of a swollen upper left arm and a healing greenstick fracture of the upper end of the right humerus was noted and the child was referred to the next orthopaedic clinic. The Family Practitioner received a report from the hospital of this visit and the diagnosis.

55. On the 18 September Mrs G. brought L. and her younger sister to the Day Nursery and told the Matron that she had taken L. to the hospital where she had been advised to keep L. at home for a few days. The arm was not dislocated but bruised and had been put in a collar and cuff sling. Mrs G. was expecting the Matron to take the youngest daughter into the Day Nursery but the Matron refused to take in a child so young without her sister as she would be unhappy. L. was wearing the collar and cuff sling. Matron informed the Health Visitor about the visit to the Day Nursery and about the injury; and that L. had been x-rayed at the hospital. The Health Visitor paid a visit to the home but received no reply.

56. On the 19 September L. was seen at the same hospital's Orthopaedic Clinic. No special treatment was prescribed and the child was to be seen again in one week. There is some doubt as to whether this appointment was kept.

57. On the 21 September the Probation Officer paid a home visit and L. was seen to have her arm in a sling and her face bruised around the eyes: the explanation given by Mrs G. and supported by L. was that she had fallen down outside. As to the arm injury, Mrs G. explained to the Probation Officer how she had pulled the child because she had not responded promptly when told to go out of the kitchen, and how L., having complained of pain the next morning, Mrs G. had taken her to the Family Practitioner, who arranged for an x-ray, from which it had been found that the child's arm had been badly sprained. She also said that as a result the Nursery Service had not taken L. because of her bad arm and that they would not take the other child either; so the mother for the time being was having to look after both the younger children.

58. Mrs G. told the Probation Officer about her recent visit to the Gynaecologist, who had confirmed the pregnancy but did not

support her request for termination. The Family Practitioner disagreed and thought she could not stand the strain of another child. The Probation Officer mentioned the possibility of psychiatric advice, which Mrs G. refused, saying she was considering sterilisation. She was beginning to accept the idea of a new baby and the relationship with her husband had improved. Her husband was very busy doing overtime and they were clearing the rent arrears, although there were other debts, and she would appreciate help with baby clothes, etc.

59. On the 25 September both L. and her younger sister returned to the Day Nursery. At the request of the Matron, L.'s injured arm was examined by the Medical Officer (Child Health), who was carrying out routine duties as Session Clinic Doctor. Her examination showed multiple heavy bruising of at least three different ages. The Doctor asked the Matron to telephone the hospital and they confirmed that Mrs G. had attended the Accident and Emergency Department with L. on the 17 September.

60. On the 26 September L. again attended the Day Nursery and was not wearing the sling. Mrs G. was angry because this had been replaced by the Clinic Doctor the previous day, and insisted on demonstrating to the Matron how easily L. could move her arm. The children ceased to attend the Day Nursery after this and the Matron had no further contact with Mrs G.

61. On the 2 October the Health Visitor, having been informed about the non-attendance of the children at the Day Nursery, inquired the position from the Probation Officer, who explained that they could not attend until L.'s arm was better. She also told the Health Visitor about Mrs G.'s pregnancy and the Health Visitor said she would keep an eye on the situation.

62. On the 4 October the Health Visitor called at the house but there was no reply. When the Health Visitor called again on the 8 October Mrs G. was out but Mr G. was at home and asked the Health Visitor in. He told her that Mrs G. was at work and that an aunt was looking after the children during the day. He said that the children had been refused admission to the Day Nursery as L.'s arm was in a sling and the youngest child had eczema of the hand.

63. Mrs G. did not keep her appointment with the Probation Officer on the 3 October but reported on the 10th. She was feeling sick from her pregnancy and had the children at home because of the row she had had with the Matron of the Day Nursery over L.'s arm and the misunderstanding over her attendance at the hospital. The rent arrears were being paid off and she was working while the children were being looked after by her sister. The Probation Officer arranged to see Mrs G. next on the 31 October and said that she was going on

289

L

leave and that, if Mrs G. wished to get in touch before, she could telephone the office.

64. There is no record of any further official contact with the family after the 10 October until the 18 October, the day when L. was finally admitted to hospital; but from the statements made by Mrs G., the husband, and the lodger on Monday 15 October, Mrs G. had lost her temper with L. because she had wetted the bed twice, and Mrs G. had assaulted her severely. When the husband came home from work that evening L. was lying in an armchair with a purple mark at the back of her left ear, and Mrs G. admitted that she had hit her. The husband was not anxious for Mrs G. to take the child to the hospital because the hospital would report the injury to the local authority. The child seemed dazed and half asleep. L. was vomiting on Tuesday the 16 October and Mrs. G. said that she must have influenza. The lodger noticed a red mark on the left side of the child's face and her mother admitted to him that she had hit L. the day before. On the evening of Wednesday the 17 October, according to the lodger, L. seemed better and was playing about and seemed full of life.

65. On the morning of Thursday, the 18 October, Mrs G. collected a neighbour's child to take with one of her own to school, but she did not come back to the neighbour for coffee as was usual. Later the neighbour saw Mrs G. again and noticed that she was crying; Mrs G. said that L. was inside the flat and unconscious, explaining that she had fallen down the stairs on the previous Monday.

66. The explanation eventually given by Mrs G. to the Police (having first stated that Monday, the 15 October, was the last day on which she had injured L.) was that on the Thursday morning, the 18 October (presumably after Mrs G. had returned from taking the two children to school) she had found L. standing in the room and wetting the carpet. The mother had lost her temper and committed such violence to the child as to render her unconscious.

67. At 10.30 that morning Mrs G. telephoned the Family Practitioner, saying that L. was unconscious arising from a fall down the stairs, and asking him to call. He immediately arranged for an ambulance which took L. to the Accident and Emergency Department of a London hospital, where she was found to have

Bruises all over body, including face. Right black eye. Heavy bruises over both buttocks. Bruises all over both arms. Paralysis left side.

X-ray—Chest
Epiphyseal dislocation of both humeri, with marked periosteal reaction down both upper humeral shafts, compatible with previous repeated injury.

No evidence of fractured ribs.

X-ray—Skull

Large fractures involving most of the right side, parietal and occipital regions. Some diastasis of the sutures. Suspected that X-rays of pelvis and other limbs would reveal evidence of other trauma as seen in the humeri.

68. None of these events involving the injuries to L. were known to the Probation Officer or to the Social Services Directorate until the next day the 19 October and the Health Visitor was not aware that L. was in hospital until informed by the CID on the 22 October. During the 18 October the Health Visitor spoke to the Probation Officer about the unused day nursery places; her visit to the home on the 8 October; and her talk with Mr G. when Mrs G. had been out. The Health Visitor mentioned the good condition of the home and thought there might be some improvement in Mrs G., but both the Health Visitor and the Probation Officer agreed that the situation needed watching closely, particularly in view of the new pregnancy. The Probation Officer told the Health Visitor that the children would not return to the Day Nursery and that Mrs G.'s sister would look after them until Christmas. On the 19 October the Health Visitor spoke with the Area Nursing Officer regarding the non-completion of the 'handicapped form' (i.e. registering the child as 'at risk').

69. On the 19 October the Consultant Physician at the Accident and Emergency Unit of the hospital left a message at the Social Services Directorate about L.'s admission to the hospital as a suspected battered baby and about her serious injuries and asking for information about the home situation. The message was passed to the appropriate Senior Social Worker who took a number of steps, including notifying the Police (who commenced their inquiries) and informing the Probation Officer with a request for her to call at the G.'s home to check the position of the other two children. This she did on the afternoon of the 19 October.

70. During the evening of the same day, the Probation Officer received a telephone call from a Police Inspector asking for details of the case and requesting her to call at the Police Station to assist them. She replied that she would need to discuss the matter with her Senior who would accompany her and this was agreed by the Police Inspector. Following a telephone call from the Police on the 20 October, an appointment was made and the Senior Probation Officer and the Probation Officer attended at the Police Station.

71. On the 22 October the Health Visitor was notified by the CID that L. was in hospital. On the 23 October 1973, the child died there.

V The communications problem

[This chart demonstrates some of the organizations and individuals who may be concerned with child abuse. The diagram does not show links for communication but organizational links. Communication links to cover all possible cases would probably involve a link between each unit and every other group of units. The diagram is an over-simplification and there are omissions, for example, the consultant psychiatrist, child minders and hospital nurses.]

EAST SUSSEX COUNTY COUNCIL (1975) Chart from *Children at Risk. A study into the problems revealed by the Report of the Inquiry into the Case of Maria Colwell,* between pp. 15 and 19.

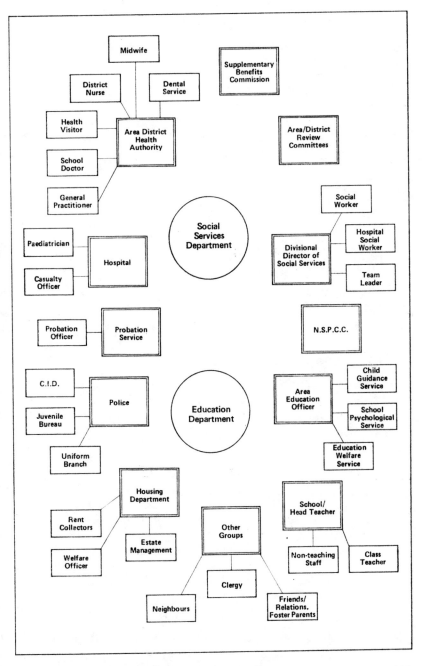

33 The normal child

[Growth and development are not identical. Growth is increase in size and is mainly structural; development is increase in complexity and involves both structure and function. Normally growth and development of body, intellect and personality progress harmoniously.

Weight and length

The normal baby gains steadily in weight and length, the rate of weight gain is a better indication of satisfactory progress than actual weight (charts iv and vi). Allowance must be made where necessary for prematurity and for low birth weight (charts i and ii).

The average baby will double his birth weight by six months and treble it by one year. During the second year the rate of growth is slower. At the end of one year about 7–8 inches (18–20 cm) will have been added to the length and by two years another 5 inches (12–13 cm) (charts iii–v).

Head circumference

The maximum head circumference is an essential part of the routine examination of the baby. The tape measure is passed round the forehead above the eyes and round the occiput, the measurement should be taken twice for accuracy. The size of the skull reflects the growth and size of the cranial contents (charts ix and x). In certain cases of mental subnormality the brain is small and this is reflected in a small skull circumference. If the skull is larger than normal it may be due to hydrocephalous from blockage of fluid pathways in the brain. There are several other conditions which also increase skull circumference, all these need immediate medical attention.

The head circumference at birth in the normal full term infant is about 13¾ inches (35 cm). The rate of gain in the early months is ½ inch per month for 5–6 months, then slows to ¼ inch a month for the rest of the first year. The head size is related to the size of the baby as well as to his age. The premature baby has a relatively large head for his size.

Any unusual appearance of head or face should be compared with the parents for a possible hereditary reason before assuming that it is abnormal.]

i Centile chart: girls 0–5

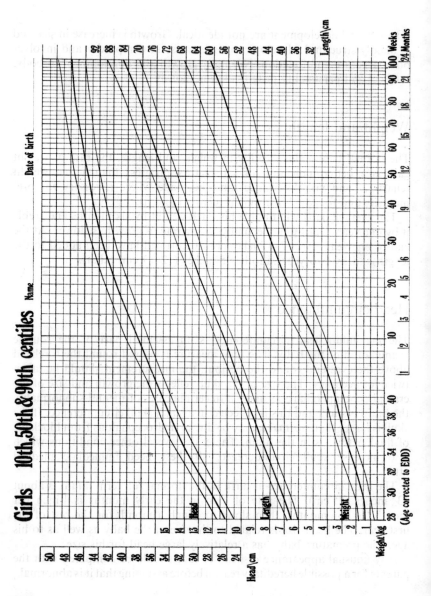

ii   Centile chart: boys 0–5

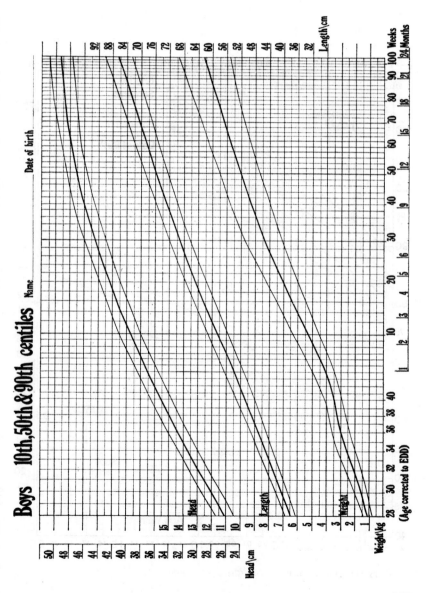

iii   Length/height: girls 0–5

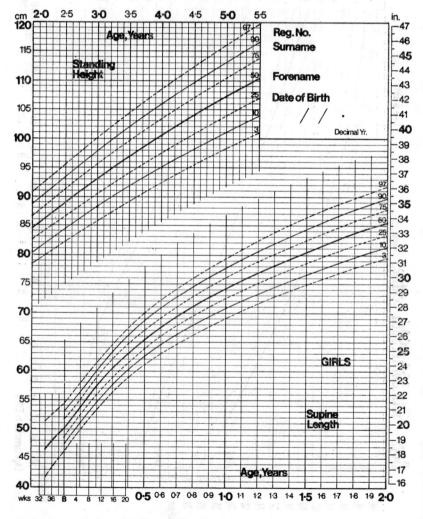

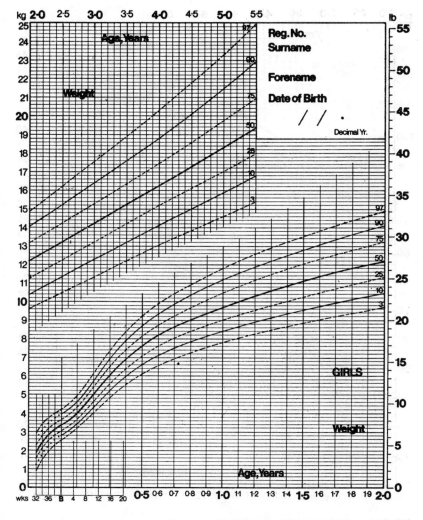

v   Length/height: boys 0–5

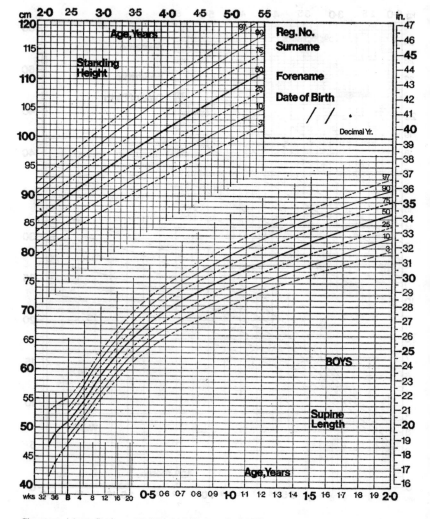

Chart copyright © Castlemead Publications (Creaseys Ltd) 1970

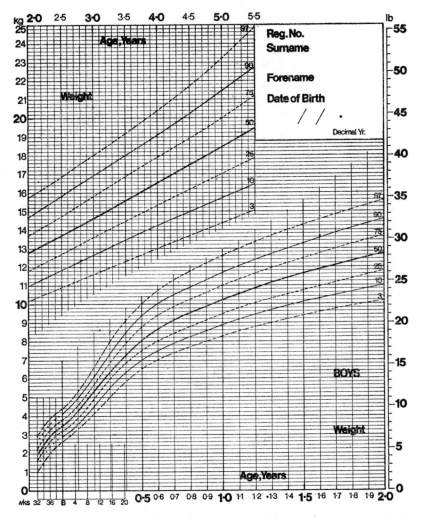

Standards for height and weight for boys and girls from birth to five years: (British children), 1970

J. M. Tanner and R. H. Whitehouse

1 *Weight* is preferably taken in the nude; otherwise the estimated weight of clothing is subtracted before plotting.

2 When a child is born earlier than at 40 weeks' gestation ('pre-term') the birthweight is plotted at the appropriate number of weeks on the chart. Subsequent weights are plotted in relation to this 'conception age'; thus for a child born at 32 weeks the 8 week-after-birth weight is plotted at B on the scale, the 12-week weight at 4 weeks after B and so on. Length is plotted in the same manner.

3 The main age scales are in decimal years (see page 305).

4 *Supine length* (up to age 2.0 years) should be taken with the infant lying on a measuring table constructed for this purpose. One person holds the infant's head so that he looks straight upward (the lower borders of the eye sockets and the external auditory meati should be in the same vertical plane), and pulls very gently to bring the top of the head into contact with the fixed measuring board. A second person, the measurer, presses the infant's knees down into contact with the board, and, also pulling gently to stretch the infant out, holds the infant's feet, with the toes pointing directly upward. He brings the moveable footboard to rest firmly against the infant's heels and reads the measurement, to the last completed 0.1 cm.

5 *Standing height* should be taken without shoes, the child standing with heels and back in contact with an upright wall, or preferably a stadio-meter made for this purpose. His head is held so that he looks straight forward, with the lower borders of the eye sockets in the same horizontal plane as the external auditory meati (i.e, head not with nose tipped upwards). A right-angled block (preferably counter-weighted) is then slid down the wall until its bottom surface touches the child's head, and a scale fixed to the wall is read. During the measurement the child should be told to stretch his neck to be as tall as possible, though care must be taken to prevent his heels coming off the ground. Gentle but firm pressure upwards should be applied by the measurer under the mastoid processes to help the child stretch. In this way the variation in height from morning to evening is minimised. Standing height should be recorded to the last completed 0.1 cm.

6 The sources of the standards are:
   a. weight from 32 to 40 weeks gestation, Tanner-Thomson standards (published by Creaseys 1970 and in *Archives of Diseases of Childhood 45*, 566, 1970) from Aberdeen data
   b. length from 32–40 weeks estimated from West European and North American data, not available for U.K.
   c. weight and length after 40-week birth, same sources as Tanner-Whitehouse 0-18 year old standards (published by Creaseys 1966 and detailed in *Archives of Diseases of Childhood, 41*, 454, 613, 1966.)

7 Charts (iii-vi) obtainable from Creaseys of Hertford Ltd., quote reference SHWB28 (boys), and reference SHWG29 (girls). [Editorial edition.]

DECIMAL AGE

The system of decimal age has been used. Thus the year is divided into 10, not 12. Each date in the calendar is marked (from the table below) in terms of thousandths of the year. Thus January 7th 1962 is 62.016. The Child's birth date is similarly recorded, e.g. a child born on June 23rd 1959 has the birth day 59.474. Age at examination is then obtained by simple subtraction, e.g. 62.016—59.474=2.542, and the last figure is rounded off. This system greatly facilitates the computing of velocities, since the proportion of the year between two examinations is easily calculated.

TABLE OF DECIMALS FOR YEAR

	1 JAN.	2 FEB.	3 MAR.	4 APR.	5 MAY	6 JUNE	7 JULY	8 AUG.	9 SEPT.	10 OCT.	11 NOV.	12 DEC.
1	000	085	162	247	329	414	496	581	666	748	833	915
2	003	088	164	249	332	416	499	584	668	751	836	918
3	005	090	167	252	334	419	501	586	671	753	838	921
4	008	093	170	255	337	422	504	589	674	756	841	923
5	011	096	173	258	340	425	507	592	677	759	844	926
6	014	099	175	260	342	427	510	595	679	762	847	929
7	016	101	178	263	345	430	512	597	682	764	849	932
8	019	104	181	266	348	433	515	600	685	767	852	934
9	022	107	184	268	351	436	518	603	688	770	855	937
10	025	110	186	271	353	438	521	605	690	773	858	940
11	027	112	189	274	356	441	523	608	693	775	860	942
12	030	115	192	277	359	444	526	611	696	778	863	945
13	033	118	195	279	362	447	529	614	699	781	866	948
14	036	121	197	282	364	449	532	616	701	784	868	951
15	038	123	200	285	367	452	534	619	704	786	871	953
16	041	126	203	288	370	455	537	622	707	789	874	956
17	044	129	205	290	373	458	540	625	710	792	877	959
18	047	132	208	293	375	460	542	627	712	795	879	962
19	049	134	211	296	378	463	545	630	715	797	882	964
20	052	137	214	299	381	466	548	633	718	800	885	967
21	055	140	216	301	384	468	551	636	721	803	888	970
22	058	142	219	304	386	471	553	638	723	805	890	973
23	060	145	222	307	389	474	556	641	726	808	893	975
24	063	148	225	310	392	477	559	644	729	811	896	978
25	066	151	227	312	395	479	562	647	731	814	899	981
26	068	153	230	315	397	482	564	649	734	816	901	984
27	071	156	233	318	400	485	567	652	737	819	904	986
28	074	159	236	321	403	488	570	655	740	822	907	989
29	077		238	323	405	490	573	658	742	825	910	992
30	079		241	326	408	493	575	660	745	827	912	995
31	082		244		411		578	663		830		997
	JAN. 1	FEB. 2	MAR. 3	APR. 4	MAY 5	JUNE 6	JULY 7	AUG. 8	SEPT. 9	OCT. 10	NOV. 11	DEC. 12

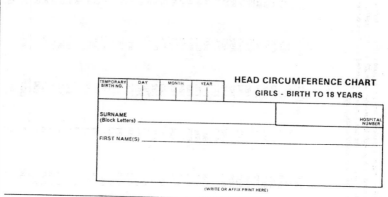

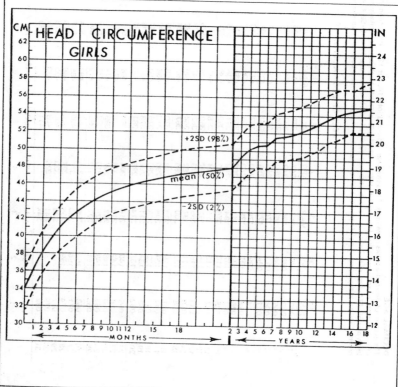

x Head circumference: boys 0–18

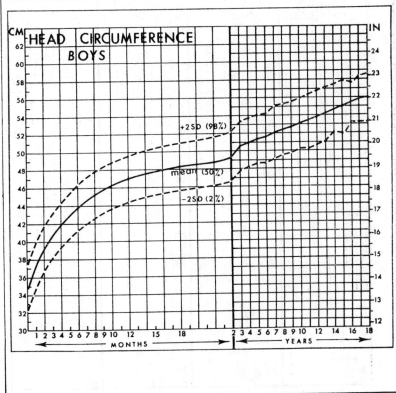

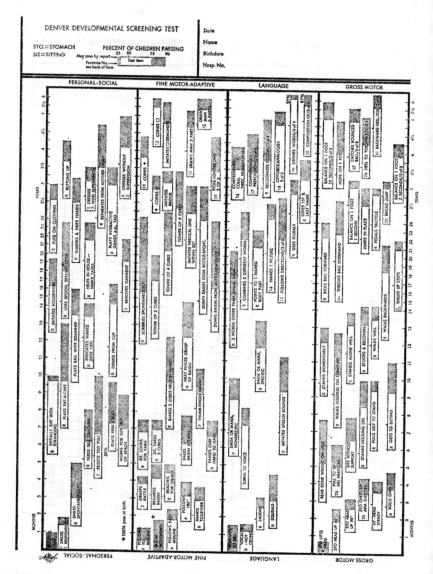

308

1. Try to get child to smile by smiling, talking or waving to him. Do not touch him.
2. When child is playing with toy, pull it away from him. Pass if he resists.
3. Child does not have to be able to tie shoes or button in the back.
4. Move yarn slowly in an arc from one side to the other, about 6" above child's face. Pass if eyes follow 90° to midline. (Past midline; 180°)
5. Pass if child grasps rattle when it is touched to the backs or tips of fingers.
6. Pass if child continues to look where yarn disappeared or tries to see where it went. Yarn should be dropped quickly from sight from tester's hand without arm movement.
7. Pass if child picks up raisin with any part of thumb and a finger.
8. Pass if child picks up raisin with the ends of thumb and index finger using an over hand approach.

 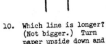

9. Pass any enclosed form. Fail continuous round motions.
10. Which line is longer? (Not bigger.) Turn paper upside down and repeat. (3/3 or 5/6)
11. Pass any crossing lines.
12. Have child copy first. If failed, demonstrate

When giving items 9, 11 and 12, do not name the forms. Do not demonstrate 9 and 11.

13. When scoring, each pair (2 arms, 2 legs, etc.) counts as one part.
14. Point to picture and have child name it. (No credit is given for sounds only.)

15. Tell child to: Give block to Mommie; put block on table; put block on floor. Pass 2 of 3. (Do not help child by pointing, moving head or eyes.)
16. Ask child: What do you do when you are cold? ..hungry? ..tired? Pass 2 of 3.
17. Tell child to: Put block on table; under table; in front of chair, behind chair. Pass 3 of 4. (Do not help child by pointing, moving head or eyes.)
18. Ask child: If fire is hot, ice is ?; Mother is a woman, Dad is a ?; a horse is big, a mouse is ?. Pass 2 of 3.
19. Ask child: What is a ball? ..lake? ..desk? ..house? ..banana? ..curtain? ..ceiling? ..hedge? ..pavement? Pass if defined in terms of use, shape, what it is made of or general category (such as banana is fruit, not just yellow). Pass 6 of 9.
20. Ask child: What is a spoon made of? ..a shoe made of? ..a door made of? (No other objects may be substituted.) Pass 3 of 3.
21. When placed on stomach, child lifts chest off table with support of forearms and/or hands.
22. When child is on back, grasp his hands and pull him to sitting. Pass if head does not hang back.
23. Child may use wall or rail only, not person. May not crawl.
24. Child must throw ball overhand 3 feet to within arm's reach of tester.
25. Child must perform standing broad jump over width of test sheet. (8-1/2 inches)
26. Tell child to walk forward, ⊂○⊃⊂○⊃⊂○⊃ heel within 1 inch of toe. Tester may demonstrate. Child must walk 4 consecutive steps, 2 out of 3 trials.
27. Bounce ball to child who should stand 3 feet away from tester. Child must catch ball with hands, not arms, 2 out of 3 trials.
28. Tell child to walk backward, ⊂○⊃⊂○⊃⊂○⊃ toe within 1 inch of heel. Tester may demonstrate. Child must walk 4 consecutive steps, 2 out of 3 trials.

DATE AND BEHAVIORAL OBSERVATIONS (how child feels at time of test, relation to tester, attention span, verbal behavior, self-confidence, etc,):

309

Recommended for further reading

ANTHONY, E. JAMES and BENEDEK, THERESE (eds) (1970) *Parenthood: its Psychology and Psychopathology*, New York, Little, Brown and Company Inc. 600 pages.

BORLAND, MARIE (ed.) (1976) *Violence in the Family*, Manchester, Manchester University Press. 145 pages.

CASTLE, RAYMOND L. (1977) *Case Conferences: a Cause for Concern?*, London, NSPCC. 15 pages.

CAVENAGH, W. (1976) *The Juvenile Court*, London, Barry Rose Publishers Limited.

EGAN, D. F., ILLINGWORTH, R. S. and MACKEITH, R. C. (eds) (1969) *Developmental Screening 0–5 years*, London, Spastics International Medical Publications in Association with William Heinemann Medical Books Ltd. 65 pages.

HELFER, RAY E. and KEMPE, C. HENRY (eds) (1976) *Child Abuse and Neglect. The family and the community*, Cambridge (Mass.), Ballinger Publishing Company. 438 pages.

MARTIN, HAROLD P. (1976) *The Abused Child. A multidisciplinary approach to developmental issues and treatment.* Cambridge (Mass.), Ballinger Publishing Company. 300 pages.

MAYALL, BERRY and PETRIE, PAT (1977) *Minder, Mother and Child* (Studies in Education 5), London, University of London Institute of Education, distributed by NFER Publishing Company Ltd. 96 pages.

SHERIDAN, MARY D. (New illustrated edition 1973) *Children's Developmental Progress from Birth to Five Years: the Stycar Sequences*, London, NFER Publishing Company Ltd. 70 pages.

First Report from the Select Committee on Violence in the Family: Violence to Children, HC 329 (1976–77), London, HMSO.

Acknowledgements

Grateful acknowledgement is made to the following sources for permission to reproduce material used in this Reader:

Plates
Plates between pp. viii and 1 courtesy of *The Police Surgeon*.

Text
Kennell, J. *et al.* (1976) 'Parent-infant bonding' in Helfer, R. E. and Kempe, C. H. (eds.) *Child Abuse and Neglect*, copyright © 1976 Ballinger; Erikson, E. H. (1967) 'Growth and crises of the healthy personality' in Lazarus, R. S. and Opton, E. M., Jr. (eds.) *Personality, Selected Reading*, Penguin, first published in (1959) *Psychological Issues*, Vol. 1 copyright © 1959 W. W. Norton; Pringle, M. K. (1974) *The Needs of Children*, Hutchinson/Schocken Books Inc., copyright © 1974 National Children's Bureau; Brim, Orville G., Jr., (1959) *Education for Child Rearing*, The Free Press © 1959 Russell Sage Foundation; White Franklin, A. (ed.) (1975) 'The nature of the task' in *Concerning Child Abuse*, Churchill Livingstone; Peckham, C. (1974) 'The dimensions of child abuse' in Carter, J. (ed.) *The Maltreated Child*, Priory Press; Gil, D. G. (1973) 'Violence against children' in Dreitzel, H. P. (ed.) *Childhood and Socialisation*, Macmillan/Harvard University Press, first published in (1971) *Journal of Marriage and the Family*, November, National Council on Family Relations; Lynch, M. A. (1976) 'Child abuse: the critical path' in *Journal of Maternal and Child Health*, Vol. 1 Barker Publications; Hull, D. (1974) 'Medical diagnosis' in Carter, J. (ed.) *The Maltreated Child*, Priory Press; Hall, M. H. (1974) 'The diagnosis and early management of non-accidental injury in children' in *The Police Surgeon*, October, Association of Police Surgeons of Great Britain; Baher, E. *et al.* (eds.) (1976) *At Risk: An Account of the Work of the Battered Child Research Department*, Routledge and Kegan Paul/NSPCC; Kempe, C. H. (1971) 'Paediatric implications of the battered baby syndrome' in *Archives of Disease in Childhood*, Vol. 46 British Medical Association; Bentovim, A. (1974) 'Treatment: a medical perspective' in Carter, J. (ed.) *The Maltreated Child*, Priory Press; Jones, R. and Jones, C. (1974) 'Treatment: a social perspective' in Carter, J. (ed.) *The Maltreated Child*, Priory Press; Jones, C. O. (1977) revised version of 'The predicament of abused children' in White Franklin, A. (ed.) *The Challenge of Child Abuse*, Academic Press; Anon. (1976) 'Consumer's Viewpoint' in *Social Work Today*, Vol. 7, British Association of Social Workers; Steele, B. F. and Pollock, C. B. (1968) 'A psychiatric study of parents who abuse infants and small children' in Helfer, R. E. and Kempe, C. H. (eds.) *The Battered Child*, 2nd edn. 1974 University of Chicago Press; Smith, S. M. (1975) *The Battered Child Syndrome*, Butterworths; Ounsted, C. *et al.* (1974) 'Aspects of bonding failure' in *Developmental Medicine and Child Neurology*, Vol. 16 Spastics International Medical Publications; Reavley, W. and M. and Gilbert, M.-T. (1976) 'The behavioural treatment approach to potential child abuse' in *Social Work Today*, Vol. 7 British Association of Social Workers; Cavenagh, W. (1975) 'A view from the courts' in *Royal Society of Health Journal*, Vol. 95 Royal Society for the Promotion of Health; Jackson, A. (1975) 'Court procedures in child abuse' in *Midwife, Health Visitor and Community Nurse*, Vol. 11 Recorder Press; Renvoize, J. (1974) *Children in Danger*, Routledge and Kegan Paul; MacKeith, R. (1975) 'Speculations on some possible long-term effects' in White Franklin, A. (ed.) *Concerning Child Abuse*, Churchill Livingstone; Friedman, S. B. and Morse, C. W. (1974) 'Child abuse' in *Pediatrics*, Vol. 54 American Academy of Pediatrics; Kempe, C. H. and Helfer, R. E. (1972) 'Innovative therapeutic approaches' in Kempe, C. H. and Helfer, R. E. (eds.) *Helping the Battered Child and his Family*, Lippincott; Koluchová, J. (1972) 'Severe deprivation

313

in twins' in *Journal of Child Psychology and Psychiatry*, Vol. 13 Pergamon; Koluchová, J. (1976) 'A report on the further development of twins after severe and prolonged deprivation' in Clarke, A. M. and A. D. B. (eds.) *Early Experience: Myth and Evidence*, Open Books; Anon. (1975) 'The battered. . .' in *The Lancet*, May 31; D.H.S.S. (1974) *Government Circular LASSL (74) 13CMO (74) 8*, reproduced by permission of the Controller of HMSO; D.H.S.S. (1976) *Government Circular LASSL (76) 2CMO (73) 2 CNO (76) 3* reproduced by permission of the Controller of HMSO; Coventry Area Health Authority (1976) *Child Abuse: A Professional Guide on the Detection and Treatment*, City of Coventry Social Services Dept.; D.H.S.S. (1974) *Report of the Committee of Inquiry into the Care and Supervision Provided in Relation to Maria Colwell*, reproduced by permission of the Controller of HMSO; D.H.S.S. (1975) *Report of the Committee of Inquiry into the Provision and Co-ordination of Services to the Family of John George Auckland*, reproduced by permission of the Controller of HMSO; Lambeth, Southwark and Lewisham Area Health Authority (Teaching) (1975) 'Case history of the Godfrey family and Lisa' in *Report of the Joint Committee of Inquiry into Non-Accidental Injury to Children*, reproduced by permission of the Authority.

Charts

Organisational Chart East Sussex County Council (1975) *Children at Risk: A Study into the Problems Revealed by the Report of the Inquiry into the Case of Maria Colwell*, by courtesy of the Council; *Charts (i)-(ii)* Gairdner, D. and Pearson, J. (1971) *Archives of Disease in Childhood*, British Medical Association; *Charts (iii)-(viii)* Tanner, J. M. and Whitehouse, R. H. (1973) *Archives of Disease in Childhood*, Vol. 48 British Medical Association, by permission of Castlemead Publications; *Charts (ix)-(x)* courtesy of the American Academy of Pediatrics; *Charts (xi)-(xii)* courtesy of University of Colorado Medical Center.

Index

315